Linking with Nature in the Digital Age

Communication, Environment, Science and Society Set

coordinated by
Andrea Catellani and
Céline Pascual Espuny

Volume 1

Linking with Nature in the Digital Age

Edited by

Émilie Kohlmann

ISTE

WILEY

First published 2024 in Great Britain and the United States by ISTE Ltd and John Wiley & Sons, Inc.

ISTE Ltd
27-37 St George's Road
London SW19 4EU
UK

www.iste.co.uk

John Wiley & Sons, Inc.
111 River Street
Hoboken, NJ 07030
USA

www.wiley.com

Library of Congress Control Number: 2023949931

British Library Cataloguing-in-Publication Data
A CIP record for this book is available from the British Library
ISBN 978-1-78630-858-0

Contents

Acknowledgments

The creation of this book would simply not have been possible without the support of the entire Muséum interface de médiation pour l'environnement et les sciences en Isère (MIMESIS)[1] research team: Camille Bernard, Marie Cambone, Catherine Gauthier and François Munoz. Many thanks to them for their constant presence and motivation, and for the relevance of their scientific contributions. This two-year collaboration has been extremely enriching. I would also like to thank our master's research intern, Dieynaba Kouyate, whose work has contributed to the progress of the project.

Thanks to the chapter authors in this book for their interest in this theme, and for their ability to respect all editorial constraints and build a coherent dialogue between their research, across the pages and the different sections.

Our thanks also go to Marie Arthuis for her excellent editorial support, which has enabled us to meet deadlines and harmonize all contributions as closely as possible.

Thanks to Julie Polge for the sketches she drew during the *Penser le(s) lien(s)* study day, and who gave us permission to publish them to accompany the various chapters of this book.

Finally, we would like to thank the coordinators of this set of books, Andrea Catellani and Céline Pascual-Espuny, who are also in charge of the "Communication, environnement, sciences et société" research group, for the trust they placed in us and for organizing the final proofreading. We would also like to thank all reviewers of the chapters in this book.

1 Available at: https://mimesisere.hypotheses.org/ [Accessed on November 22, 2022].

Introduction

Choosing the notion of linking to talk about nature and digital technology

The reflections presented in this book, reformulated a posteriori around "linking with nature in the digital age", emerged from a multidisciplinary research project in which researchers in information and communication sciences, computer science and ecology had to learn to articulate their disciplinary thinking with others[1]. The notion of a link seemed to be particularly well-suited to this exchange, as it was sufficiently mobilized by all concerned and sufficiently ambiguous to be malleable and questioned from different angles. Indeed, the notion of a link seems to be something that can be approached from an angle and not head-on. The term "link" cannot be qualified as a firm concept and, if it is mobilized more precisely, it is often by being associated with an adjective that qualifies it: the "social link" (Durkheim and Paugam 2013), the "weak link" (Granovetter 1973), etc. However, the word and metaphor of link are regularly used in scientific texts, but without really being thought of as a concept, and sometimes without any real reflection on the choice of this term in place of another.

Another advantage of a link as a way of thinking about the nature and influence of digital technology is that the word evokes something and makes sense in several disciplines. In computer science, we speak of "linked data", "hypertext links" or even links in man–machine interfaces or networks. In ecology, we talk about "interspecies links", "links to the environment", etc. Two terms are possible in

---

Introduction written by Émilie KOHLMANN.

1 The Muséum interface de médiation pour l'environnement et les sciences en Isère (MIMESIS) project received government funding managed by the Agence nationale de la recherche under the "Investissement d'avenir" program, reference ANR-15-IDEX-02. Available at: https://mimesisere.hypotheses.org [Accessed on 24 November 2022].

ecology: *relationship* and *link*, the latter being stronger and associated with close interactions, as in the case of symbiosis, which highlights the gradation in the strength of links. In the humanities and social sciences, the link is mobilized in all of its forms: the link is therefore "social", "weak", as well as "affective", "symbolic", "interindividual", etc. However, this ease of presence can also be a flaw in the term. This begs multiple questions: how does the link relate to closely related notions such as networks (Latour 1999), communities (Kaufmann 2022a, 2022b), connections (Klein and Proulx 2012), interactions (Goffman 1998), or mediations (Deschamps 2019)? In an attempt to answer these questions, we began with the linguistic meaning of the word "link".

The peculiarities of the "link": semantic duality

The Centre national de ressources textuelles et lexicales (CNRTL, the French National Center for Textual and Lexical Resources) offers several definitions of the term "*lien*", French for "link", at different times and in different contexts of use[2]. Here, the term is defined *materially* as "a flexible, elongated object used to enclose a thing to hold its various parts together, or to attach two or more things together" and more *figuratively* as "that which joins, attaches two or more things together". The link is first considered in its physical dimension – it is the object that attaches – before being extended by analogy to an immaterial dimension – that which ensures the relationship, of a more symbolic order. The imaginary then comes into play as a means of maintaining ties, particularly for the societies and communities that result from them (Anderson 1983).

A double movement is also present in the different definitions of the word link. It can have a *positive connotation*, creating solidarity – "that which unites two or more people (or groups of people) and establishes social, moral or emotional relationships between them" – or a *negative connotation* – "that which restrains an animal, chains or binds a prisoner or a slave". The link thus oscillates between positive stability and negative limitation, dependence of the individual on a third party or on society. This is reminiscent of the work of Elias (2004), who described individual interdependencies as "the fabric of the social". Individuals, the "I", are seen as a form of modern society, different from traditional forms of society, the social "we".

Finally, the link can be considered as *innate* – the family bond, the kinship bond – or as *requiring a construction*, sometimes of a legal nature – the marriage bond as contractualization. This distinction is also found in the work of Dumont (1983), for example, when he highlights two ways of relating to others during the French Revolution: the traditionalist ties of interdependence between the constituted social

2 Available at: www.cnrtl.fr/definition/lien [Accessed 12 July 2022].

bodies of the monarchist community, and the contractual ties of revolutionary society (Kaufmann 2022a).

Thinking in terms of links means looking not at objects in terms of their *identification*, but rather at their *relationships* (Descola 2005), what links them together, what holds a heterogeneous set of elements together, and ensures cohesion, even if only fleetingly (Latour 1999). Yet beyond these etymological and semantic elements, in the scientific literature, the link is often an implicit order or a metaphor used to illustrate a point, rather than a firm concept.

Why choose to question the link?

While Klein and Proulx (2012), in the introduction to their book devoted to the strong presence of digital technologies in human communication, raise the question of "the nature and forms of the link that is established between individuals, groups, organizations, communities [...] in and outside the digital universe?" (Klein and Proulx 2012, p. 5, author's translation), they nevertheless fail to define the term link, quickly preferring "connection", which refers to the idea of a society technically connected by digital technology. The authors postulate the existence of "connected individuals", whose online activity reinforces their individuality. However, this multiplication of digital connections would weaken the significant symbolic links between people, or at least transform them. We can therefore postulate that the term connection has been retained here in a digital context, whereas link has a broader meaning.

In the same work, Heaton et al. (2012) study the naturalist communities created around the Tela Botanica collaborative network. The term "link" disappears in favor of the idea of a networked device that "connects its members, and [circulates] anything that can circulate: information, reflection, resources, people [...]" (Heaton et al. 2012, p. 255, author's translation). The term community, itself imprecise and polemical (Kaufmann 2022a), is then preferred to emphasize the idea of cooperation, of coordinating contributions, of the collective.

It is perhaps then by comparing the notion of link and that of community that we can better understand the epistemological difference between the works that mobilize them. In sociology, the nature of the link, its temporality, its strength, its intensity, its permanent or ephemeral character, are used to understand the difference between society and community, and the place of individuals in the different models (Tönnies 1944).

> Political in nature, the opposition between society and community is also *ontological*. Whereas the bond of society is a contingent and a

> posteriori bond, which can only unite beings superficially and from which it is always possible to withdraw, the bond of community is an a priori bond that immerses its members in a totality that shapes them through and through [Kaufmann 2010] (Kaufmann 2022a, paragraph 1).

Thinking in terms of link(s) rather than network(s) or community(-ies) could then enable a complex approach to articulations between actors, as well as between objects, and reveal the richness of the worlds that can be built up according to the possibilities they are offered of attaching themselves to one another (Hennion 2004). The focus would no longer be on an overall, finalistic view of the worlds, societies or communities created, but rather on the choices, imaginaries, techniques, etc. that support them and bring them into being. For the elements that interest us in this book, this level seems rich in potential: nature and the digital enable – oblige? – the inclusion in our reflections of those on objects and techniques and on what they do to the possibilities of links, to the imaginaries they mobilize (Cardon 2010). However, nature and the digital also lead us to question the introduction of "non-human" actors[3] into these possibilities of connection: animals, plants, as well as, more broadly, "nature" in its entirety. In this way, we are approaching the project outlined by Gefen and Laugier in *Le pouvoir des liens faibles* (2020):

> [...] to extend [...] Granovetter's concept [i.e. the weak link] to describe forms of tenuous attachments to beings and the world, non-utilitarian solidarities, complex and non-deterministic relationships, not only of humans to humans, but also of humans to things, natural beings, fictional and virtual beings (Gefen and Laugier 2020, pp. 17–18, author's translation).

In the following chapters, however, we will take a broader and more circumscribed approach to these aspects. We shall limit ourselves to thinking about the link when it involves the triptych nature, digital and human actors, whilst opening onto questions of intensity and quality of links without restricting ourselves to postulating their initial weakness. Moreover, the links studied and presented here do not only concern the links between humans and things, but may also concern the links between the things themselves. Finally, the various chapters have been written by researchers from a variety of disciplines, but with a common aim: to reflect on the meaning of the link to nature and the influence of the digital on it. To answer these questions, we have structured this book in three parts.

---

3 We have chosen here to use the vocabulary of actor–network theory (Latour 1999), although this seems to us to preserve a potentially dichotomous vision of the world between humans and others.

Extension; materiality and structure; gain or loss: questioning links to nature in the digital age

In the first part of this book, entitled "Extending Links through Digital Devices", Chapter 1 presents the work carried out by the MIMESIS team. We have drawn up a periodization of the major temporalities around biodiversity observation, digital technology and issues of citizen participation (participatory science) when these issues are mediated by technological devices. The aim of this chapter is to provide a frame of reference that enables us to keep abreast of legislative and social developments, as well as technological, scientific and ideological ones.

Following on from this, we examine the impact that digital technology has had on the possibilities for creating links with nature, as well as social ties. We question the massive growth in the use of digital technology as a link facilitator and the assumption that digital technology makes it possible to extend links and connect more and more things and more and more beings with each other.

With this in mind, Lisa Chupin (Chapter 2) examines the communicative stakes of documentary links in digitized herbarium collections. The arrival of digital technology is studied both as a new way of linking documents and specimens together and as a transformation of the communicative relationships mediated by collections for the people who produce or consult these documents. The author also discusses the forms of attachment to nature and to the species studied by naturalist communities, and reflects on the possibilities for breaking down or renewing forms of naturalist sociability linked to collections.

Marie-Caroline Heïd and Catherine De Lavergne, in Chapter 3, leave the world of naturalist databases to focus on digital social networks with a study of the mobilization of links to nature by winegrowers on their Facebook pages. They study a form of sensitive attachment to species and territory that can be seen in the diversity of the forms and content of publications, despite a highly standardizing socio-technical device. Their analysis leads to a proposed typology of five values attributed to nature by the actors: the domains of "inspired nature", "domestic nature", "civic nature", "industrial nature" and "nature of renown".

To close this first part, Émilie Kohlmann (Chapter 4) presents the results of an analysis of a digital platform intended to become a space for exchanging and sharing nature observations and practices in Isère: Nature-Isère. In this chapter, she demonstrates that, while digital technology may have generated new links and collaborations between previously separate players, it has also frozen the links and possibilities for change within a socio-technical framework that is hardly conducive to change. The participation set, as the objective and desired outcome at the outset of the project, was thus limited and restricted by the digital device and had to be supported by human links and various forms of mediation.

This chapter makes the transition to the content of the second part of this book, which focuses on the materiality and structure of links enabled by digital devices for observing and collecting naturalistic data.

Ikram Chraibi Kaadoud presents in Chapter 5 the implications of explainable artificial intelligence (XAI for eXplainable AI) in the field of naturalistic data. By illustrating through concrete examples of mobilization of the XAI in this sector, it aims to highlight its impact on the production of scientific knowledge, as well as on the links that are built between individuals and societies through these different models. According to the author, by helping to make the behavioral mechanisms of an AI model less opaque, by demystifying it and the reasons for the choices made, the retained factors, XAI can serve as a mediation tool to preserve nature and allow for a rise in the power to act of the various stakeholders.

Following this demonstration, Camille Bernard (Chapter 6) discusses the challenges of sharing biodiversity observation databases. After describing the evolution of nature observation platforms and biodiversity databases over the last 20 years, the author examines the question of sharing standards and formats, in order to demonstrate how this impacts the possibilities for links between the various players. In this chapter, she examines the emergence of new communities stemming from the technological innovations of the Semantic Web (crowdsourcing, linked open data, etc.), as well as the limits to sharing, whether technical or symbolic. For example, the question of data ownership can be an obstacle to sharing, even for players who are already committed.

In Chapter 7, Daniel Thonon shares his views on the development of the Ligue pour la protection des oiseaux's (LPO) naturalist information system (NIS) in Auvergne-Rhône-Alpes. As an IT specialist and volunteer with the naturalist association, he has followed and participated in the development of the NIS for several years. His feedback enables us to understand the issues involved in setting up this type of system, seen from the inside, as well as the reasons for the evolution of the various functionalities, particularly around the conditions of contribution and communication between partners.

Finally, in the third and final part of the book, the various authors address the question of the gains or losses of the link to nature thanks to digital technology.

The various technological evolutions mentioned in the previous section, and in particular the development of big data and artificial intelligence, are also changing the way in which citizens can participate in biodiversity data collection and naturalistic observation. Such is the case with the Pl@ntNet application presented by Pierre Bonnet, Alexis Joly and François Munoz in Chapter 8. Digital tools are used to remove obstacles to species identification, in this case through image recognition based on photographs taken from a smartphone or recorded online on a computer. The authors turn to an analysis of the app's user "groups", to highlight the wide variety of practices and contributions it authorizes and which are facilitated by digital technology, thus helping to strengthen the links between nature and amateurs.

In Chapter 9, François Munoz and Pierre Bonnet examine the contribution and interest of Pl@ntNet for communities of botanists and nature professionals. Through interviews with professionals (mountain guides and park scientists) and a study of Facebook discussion threads, the authors highlight the tool's expectations, criticisms and development prospects. A central aspect is the understanding and management of the uncertainty inherent in analyzing the limited and imperfect content of a photographic medium. The application provides not one, but several answers to the user's query, with a certain confidence score reflecting the level of uncertainty of the identification. This score is little taken into account and little understood by users, and a major challenge will be to better understand and take into account uncertainty via this score.

Minh-Xuan Truong (Chapter 10) examines forms of experiencing nature mediated by technology. In so doing, he highlights the variety of possibilities for experiencing nature, encompassing in his reflection direct experiences – immersion in a natural environment – or indirect, through different media such as books, cinema, digital social networks or video games. He then seeks to present these alternatives to direct experiences as legitimate and equally part of environmental education and raising awareness of natural environments. By not separating these two forms of experiences, but creating links between them, the author sees them as a lever for a new techno-mediated way of life.

Conversely, to close this book, in Chapter 11, Amélie Coulbaut-Lazzarini exclusively analyzes embodied experiences of nature in a mountainous territory. In a natural environment, she observes the ways in which we relate to ourselves, to others and to the world as three interconnected axes. While corporeality plays an important role – through the place of the human body in nature, physical and sensory immersion and sensory immersion in natural environments – the author proposes to question the role of the imaginary in representations of nature and in the possibilities of connecting with it, and to open up to the influence of narratives and art.

References

Anderson, B. (1983). *L'Imaginaire national. Réflexions sur l'origine et l'essor du nationalisme*. La Découverte, Paris.

Cardon, D. (2010). *La Démocratie internet. Promesses et limites*. Le Seuil, Paris.

Deschamps, J. (2019). *Mediation: A Concept for Information and Communication Sciences*. ISTE Ltd, London, and John Wiley & Sons, New York.

Descola, P. (2005). *Par-delà nature et culture*. Gallimard, Paris.

Dumont, L. (1983). *Essais sur l'individualisme. Une perspective anthropologique sur l'idéologie moderne*. Le Seuil, Paris.

Durkheim, É. and Paugam, S. (2013). *De la division du travail social*. Presses universitaires de France, Paris.

Elias, N. (2004). *La société des individus*. Pocket, Paris.

Gefen, A. and Laugier, S. (2020). *Le pouvoir des liens faibles*. CNRS, Paris.

Granovetter, M.S. (1973). The strength of weak ties. *American Journal of Sociology*, 78(6), 1360–1380.

Heaton, L., Millerand, F., Proulx, S. (2012). Émergence d'une communauté épistémique : création et partage du savoir botanique en réseau. In *Connexions : communication numérique et lien social*, Klein, A. and Proulx, S. (eds). Presses Universitaires de Namur, Namur.

Heaton, L., Millerand, F., Dias da Silva, P., Proulx, S. (2018). *La reconfiguration du travail scientifique en biodiversité : pratiques amateurs et technologies numériques*. Les Presses de l'Université de Montréal, Montreal.

Hennion, A. (2004). Une sociologie des attachements. D'une sociologie de la culture à une pragmatique de l'amateur. *Sociétés*, 85(3), 9–24.

Kaufmann, L. (2022a). Communauté 1. Du concept au "Peuple-Un" Publictionnaire. Dictionnaire encyclopédique et critique des publics [Online]. Available at: http://publictionnaire.huma-num.fr/notice/communaute-1 [Accessed 5 June 2022].

Kaufmann, L. (2022b). Communauté 2. Du communautarisme aux collectifs. Publictionnaire. Dictionnaire encyclopédique et critique des publics [Online]. Available at: http://publictionnaire.huma-num.fr/notice/communaute-2-du-communau-tarisme-aux-collectifs [Accessed 5 March 2022].

Klein, A. and Proulx, S. (2012). *Connexions : communication numérique et lien social*. Presses Universitaires de Namur, Namur.

Latour, B. (1999). *Politiques de la nature : comment faire entrer les sciences en démocratie*. La Découverte, Paris.

Roux, J., Charvolin, F., Dumain, A. (2009). Les "passions cognitives" ou la dimension rebelle du connaître en régime de passion. Premiers résultats d'un programme en cours. *Revue d'anthropologie des connaissances*, 3(3), 369–385.

Tönnies, F. (1944). *Communauté et société. Catégories fondamentales de la sociologie pure*. Presses universitaires de France, Paris.

Part 1

Extending Links through Digital Devices

1

Benchmarks: Biodiversity, Participation and Digital Technology

Figure 1.1. *Natural science: the long journey of the amateur. Émilie Kohlmann (2022). For a color version of this figure, see www.iste.co.uk/kohlmann/linking.zip*

This first chapter has a rather special status in the project for this book. It answers the desire that the Muséum interface de médiation pour l'environnement et les sciences en Isère (MIMESIS)[1] project team had to work together on the major temporalities associated with the themes studied and to think about these stages in a multidisciplinary way.

Chapter written by Émilie KOHLMANN and Catherine GAUTHIER.

1 https://mimesisere.hypotheses.org. Multidisciplinary, exploratory research project on nature and digital technology. The project brought together researchers in information and communication sciences, ecology and computer science.

Different phases of reflection have led to the definition of four main periods, described by the major developments in the various disciplines (ecology, information technology, information and communication sciences), as well as in practices and in administrative and legislative standardization, whether at national or international level.

Thus, this proposal for a time frame for issues relating to biodiversity, to contributors and to digitization has been drawn up in a collegial manner based on the aggregation and synthesis of various scientific readings[2] and on the emergence of a number of biodiversity observation, monitoring and counting systems, as well as the testimonies of the stakeholders involved.

This effort to pool knowledge that is sometimes embedded in – and circumscribed by – specific disciplines has led to the identification of strong currents that we feel are important for contextualizing and understanding the "linking with nature in the digital age"[3] discussed in this book.

We therefore propose to share them here as a starting point for the texts that follow.

We develop each of the peculiarities of the periods identified using the proposed Figure 1.2 as a guide:

1) the first trials of participatory biodiversity inventories;

2) opening up of digitally mediated observations to the "general public";

3) the process of standardizing data for interoperability and technological acceleration, with analyses opened up to deep learning and artificial intelligence;

4) the exploitation of big data and the hijacking of systems by practices.

1.1. 20th century: the pioneers

Although naturalistic observation is an older practice, we have chosen to focus on biodiversity observation[4] organized on a large scale and designed for a wide audience.

---

2 See reference list.

3 This result was one of the expectations of the MIMESIS project when it was launched, thanks to its multidisciplinary framework.

4 We understand "biodiversity" here in the very broad sense of observing and counting living things. The term "biodiversity" itself appeared in the 1980s (Takacs 1996; Mauz and Granjou 2010).

20th century: the pioneers. First participatory biodiversity inventories	• *Early leisure initiatives:* 1900 *Christmas Bird Count* in the United States • *The beginning of participatory sciences*: 1989 in France, launch of *suivi temporel des oiseaux communs* (STOC, monitoring of common birds over time)
2000–2009: opening mediated observations, open data and data reliability for the "general public"	• *Beginnings of Web 2.0 and crowdsourcing*: 2001 Wikipedia and 2004 OpenStreetMap • *Standardization of data*: 2002–2006 deployment of TAXREF • *Opening of online observatories*: 2006 Opération Papillons and Vigie-Nature in France and 2008 launch of iNaturalist as an interface with the "general public"
2010–2014: global interoperability and technological acceleration	• *Technical advances:* 2009–2013 launch of Pl@ntNet, Web version then smartphone application • *Coordination:* 2012 creation of the National Participatory Biodiversity Science Collective to coordinate the growth of initiatives • *Data standardization:* 2013 GBIF International Data Portal
2015–2022: big data processed by AI and deep learning; diversion of devices	• *Evolution in Deep Learning*: 2015 Pl@ntNet moves from machine learning to deep learning and 2017 iNaturalist integrates artificial intelligence • *Large-scale exploitation*: 2017 creation of the biodiversity information system (BIS) and 2018 creation of the OPEN portal which lists 130,000 biodiversity programs

Figure 1.2. *Summary of data collected to establish four main periods*

We therefore take the *Christmas Bird Count in the USA in December 1900* as the starting point for mass citizen involvement in this type of program: "You can add to a century of community science by joining a count near you".[5] In these programs, the naturalistic observation of specific species is presented to the public – and not just to birdwatchers – as part of nature *leisure activities*:

> […] You have to go to the United States at the turn of the 20th century to see the beginning of leisure activities and the widespread use of the car in excursions outside the city to observe animals, birds and insects. This massification of the interest in nature was to determine a quantum leap in the number of species recognized worldwide by outdoor enthusiasts on their weekend outings. (Charvolin 2019, p. 22)

From the Christmas Bird Count until the 2000s, various programs emerged with varying degrees of openness. The launch of *suivi temporel des oiseaux communs (STOC, monitoring of common birds over time)*[6] *in France in 1989*, now run by the Muséum national d'histoire naturelle (French Natural History Museum) in association with the Ligue de protection des oiseaux (French League for the Protection of Birds) and the Office français de biodiversité (French Biodiversity Office), united amateur biologists and ornithologists around a common scientific protocol, just as *Tela Botanica*[7] *in 1999* brought together professional and amateur botanists: "Le réseau Tela Botanica, c'est vous !" (The Tela Botanica network is you!)[8]

In the humanities and social sciences, the practice was then studied and linked to the question of *participatory sciences*, citizen science*s* (Irwin 1995), and much less to the question of leisure activities, particularly outdoor activities. In a context where big data collection is becoming increasingly important, the "citizen" is called upon to help researchers collect these data:

> The discovery of the importance of the citizen and their contribution to the definition of knowledge goes beyond the strictly institutional framework; it has also developed in other, more informal sectors, leading to the formation of what has been called the scientific third sector […]. (Severo 2021, author's translation)

In the model of biodiversity-related participatory observation programs, the citizen is considered less as a partner in this research, as in the "participatory action

5 The observing program still exists and celebrated its 122nd anniversary in 2022. Available at: www.audubon.org/conservation/join-christmas-bird-count [Accessed 14 June 2022].

6 Available at: https://crbpo.mnhn.fr/spip.php?article41 [Accessed 14 June 2022].

7 Available at: www.tela-botanica.org [Accessed 14 June 2022].

8 Verbatim extract from the Tela Botanica website, "About us" section.

research" of 1940–1970, and more as a producer of data, a "*petit main*" [helper] (Fages 2021), as in older models, notably in astronomical observation (Fages 2018).

These first observatories were not systematically computerized and organized into large databases, as is currently the case. Biodiversity data collection and processing, and possible exchanges between databases, were still in their infancy. It was from the 2000s onwards that the movement gained momentum in France, and recourse to the participatory science model became systematic, being included in the general French public agenda in 2016 with the Houllier report (Houllier and Merilhou-Goudard 2016).

1.2. 2000–2009: obtaining reliable data accessible to all

This second period was characterized by the convergence of three major trends that led to the proliferation of digital biodiversity observation systems open to all:

– the standardization of naturalistic data;

– the development of Web 2.0, which enables online contribution;

– open access to public data for all stakeholders.

The first issue to consider for this period is that of *data "consolidation", i.e. verifying their reliability, whether in terms of determining the species observed, its geolocation or the fact that it may have been saved two or three times in the databases at different aggregation times*. The Global Biodiversity Information Facility (GBIF)[9], created in 2001 and strengthened following the Nagoya Protocol in 2010, assigns a standardized international number to data producers. This makes it possible to eliminate duplication, which creates observation bias, while verifying the scientific quality of the observer (if a determination needs to be revalidated). Automated processing of batches of data is becoming essential to produce legitimate data in the eyes of the scientific community, for example, in entomology, where dissection of certain species is essential for identification. Consolidation spreadsheets were therefore created from 2013 onwards as part of the coordination of insect data standardization carried out by the Muséum national d'histoire naturelle, a coordination commonly referred to as the "Insect project"[10]. This was followed by online training programs. Data standardization, i.e. the pooling of fields from compatible databases, became a necessity in order to automate exchanges, but paradoxically led to a loss of data through smoothing in the recipient aggregation

9 Available at: www.gbif.org/fr [Accessed 14 June 2022].

10 Bilan d'activités 2013. Available at: http://spn.mnhn.fr/spn_rapports/archivage_reports/2014/SPN%202014%20-%2029%20-%20SPN-bilan-2013-LD.pdf [Accessed 14 June 2022].

database. At the same time, the TAXREF systematics repository was gaining ground in France for standardizing naturalistic data and "the knowledge that is the foundation of nomenclature and taxonomy"[11].

The second advance of broadening contributions to obtain mass data was made possible by the emergence of Web 2.0, its democratization and the practice of *crowdsourcing*. From 2001, Wikipedia[12] was emblematic of this movement, as was OpenStreetMap[13] from 2004. While the former is a participatory encyclopedia and the latter a participatory cartography project, both aim to share and co-produce knowledge on a global scale: "OpenStreetMap is the open, collaborative map of the world. It is improved every day by over a million contributors" (extract from the site's homepage). This movement coincided with European directives requiring access to data produced by member state bodies, such as the new Public Sector Information (PSI) directive of 2003, which aimed to free up information produced by the public sector in a context of concern over the monetization of data. It was also the start of the ideal of co-production of content with citizens, facilitated by new IT developments (Flichy 2019), as well as "science and society" action programs (Las Vergnas 2016).

These data were supported by a legal framework that guaranteed free access to the public. In 2007, the French government launched the Observatoire national de la biodiversité (National Biodiversity Observatory), linked with an Internet portal[14]. This initiative followed Directive 2003/4/EC on public access to environmental information, which states that:

> (1) Increased public access to environmental information and the dissemination of such information contribute to a greater awareness of environmental matters, a free exchange of views, more effective participation by the public in environmental decision-making and, eventually, to a better environment. (OJEU L41, 14 March 2003)

In the same year, the INSPIRE directive[15] was translated into France's environmental code, requiring public authorities to make environmental data easily, if not freely, accessible on the Internet. The système d'information sur la nature et les

---

11 Available at: https://inpn.mnhn.fr/programme/referentiel-taxonomique-taxref [Accessed 14 June 2022].

12 Available at: https://fr.wikipedia.org/ [Accessed 14 June 2022].

13 Available at: www.openstreetmap.fr [Accessed 14 June 2022].

14 https://naturefrance.fr.

15 See the presentation on the Ministry's website: www.ecologie.gouv.fr/directive-europeenne-inspire [Accessed on 14 June 2022].

paysages (SINP, Nature and Landscape Information System) was launched as a result of this[16].

At the same time, and by bringing these movements together, the *new data collection systems, increasingly accessible to the "general public"*, were multiplying and being deployed on the Internet.

In 2002, Tela Botanica "set up a collaborative project space for experienced and novice botanists, to enable the exchange and co-construction of projects"[17]. In 2006, the Observatoire de la biodiversité des jardins (French Garden Biodiversity Observatory) launched Opération Papillons (Operation Butterfly), one of the first participatory science projects open to all in France[18]. The same year, the Vigie-Nature program was launched, offering two levels of entry: the general public and naturalists (Julliard 2017). In 2008, iNaturalist, a US-based biodiversity observation system, launched a Web interface for the "general public" to contribute data to the GBIF[19].

Finally, in 2009, the Pl@ntNet application was created by computer scientists, botanists, a large consortium of institutions (IRD, ICAD, INRA, INRIA, etc.), private players such as the Agropolis foundation and Tela Botanica amateurs. Pl@ntnet is emblematic of the arrival of a new period in the deployment of applications that enable observer mobility (live data capture in the field) and the amplification of data standardization issues associated with accelerating technological developments (Bonnet et al. 2020).

1.3. 2010–2014: technological acceleration and international expansion via global observation programs

Biodiversity took center stage in 2010. UNESCO was supporting the theme and helping to publicize it in the media by declaring the "International Year of Biodiversity"[20]. The question of highlighting the "erosion of biodiversity" – a slogan of the time – had been topical since the National Forum on Biodiversity in 1986, and scientists were wondering about the reasons for its lower media profile, particularly in comparison with climate issues (Legagneux et al. 2018).

16 Available at: https://sinp.naturefrance.fr/ [Accessed 14 June 2022].

17 Verbatim extract from the Tela Botanica home page.

18 Available at: www.vigienature.fr/fr/operation-papillons [Accessed 14 June 2022].

19 Available at: www.inaturalist.org [Accessed 14 June 2022].

20 Available at: www.cbd.int/2011-2020/ [Accessed 14 June 2022].

The responses that would be provided over the next five years were twofold:

– First of all, there was a need to continue consolidating the biodiversity data already held, always at a larger scale, by reinforcing standardization, coordination and the opening up of data for all on an international scale. Thus, in 2013, the GBIF international data portal was launched. Operating as a network, GBIF "provides data-holding institutions worldwide with common standards[21] and open-source tools to share information on when and where species have been observed"[22]. The aim was to provide scientists and policy-makers with the information they needed to understand the various geopolitical issues associated with biodiversity (zoonoses, agriculture and invasive species, as well as ecosystem conservation through the increased creation of protected areas, etc.).

– Secondly, citizen participation was greatly enhanced by its technological facilitation. To take the example of Pl@ntNet, the Web version was launched in 2011, and by 2013, an application for smartphones/tablets[23] was proposed for potentially even more novice and mobile users. The temporality of observation, as well as the associated protocols, was evolving (Heaton et al. 2018, p. 242).

Over the next five years, the challenge would be to enable mass data management (big data), freely accessible (open data) to as many users as possible, at different scales, in different organizations, for different purposes. Coordinating initiatives and projects, making them interoperable and keeping a grip on the proliferation of initiatives became central.

In 2012, in France, the Collectif national sciences participatives biodiversité (CNSPB, French National Participatory Science Biodiversity Collective) was created to structure the players involved in participatory science into a national network[24]. The aim was to federate and bring biodiversity-related participatory science initiatives to the public arena in a structured way, with a general institutionalization of the tools. This movement would continue and intensify in the last period identified, but would also be "poached" by unanticipated individual uses and by initiatives that moved away from an accounting and managerial approach to living things.

21 Here, the Darwin Core standard.

22 Available at: www.gbif.org/fr/what-is-gbif [Accessed 30 June 2022].

23 In the same year, Naturalist also launched a mobile application.

24 Available at: www.open-sciences-participatives.org/sciences-participatives/collectif/2/collectif-national-des-sciences-participatives-biodiversite [Accessed 30 June 2022].

1.4. 2015–2022: optimized exploitation of big data by the scientific community versus hijacking of observation devices by the "general public"

We have grouped the last few years around a double characteristic that opposed elements of standardization and authority linked to devices (Lafleur 2015) to elements linked to the agency of actors and to tactics for avoiding the framework.

Following on from the previous period, the Houllier report was drawn up in 2016 at the request of the Minister of Higher Education and Research. It took stock of the state of participatory science at the time and a framework of best practices for the future. Two years later, the OPEN portal[25] inventoried over 130,000 participants in a participatory program dedicated to biodiversity to "gain a better understanding of biodiversity in our territory and, in fine, contribute to its preservation". Meanwhile, in 2017, the système d'information biodiversité (SIB, biodiversity information system) was set up. This is a "system that aims to *federate* all data from *31 public policies related to biodiversity issues*"[26]. Its aim "is to organize and *offer free, open, public access to these data,* to simplify and promote their use. Ultimately, this facilitated access to knowledge will make it possible to better preserve biodiversity"[27]. As we can see, the issue of biodiversity is being taken on by the State within a normative framework in which the mass collection of data is a priority for knowledge and protection and must also be made available as part of participatory science. Moreover, this succession of systems and their growing sophistication is reminiscent of the increase in the number of public action instruments from the 2000s onwards (Lascoumes and Le Galès 2005).

However, the contemporary period has seen the emergence of new forms of knowledge production on the periphery of institutions, developing new ways and means of producing knowledge (Volny 2022). A critique of expertise, and of the dichotomy long maintained in the field of participatory science between lay people and experts, is emerging. In this sense, we agree with the conclusion of Heaton et al.:

> The proliferation of participatory science initiatives in the field of biodiversity has helped to focus the spotlight on amateurs who were, until now, almost invisible [...]. The new tools made available to them, notably cell phones and specialized mobile applications, are now

25 Available at: www.open-sciences-participatives.org/home/ [Accessed 30 June 2022].

26 Available at: https://naturefrance.fr/systeme-information-biodiversite [Accessed 30 June 2022].

27 Available at: https://naturefrance.fr/systeme-information-biodiversite [Accessed 30 June 2022].

> helping them to get involved by facilitating the collection and the rapid, automated restitution of data. (Heaton et al. 2018)

We are however going a step further, taking applications out of the expected framework of participatory science and noting that in recent years they have given rise to unanticipated and unframed practices. Pl@ntNet can be used to identify wild edible species, to manage pastures or to have fun photographing cannabis plants[28]. Although photographs become data and feed the biodiversity database, this is not necessarily where the commitment of individual players lies. The proliferation of mobile applications and the increasing use of artificial intelligence should be questioned.

In 2015, Pl@ntNet moved from machine learning to deep learning, enabling a greater complexity in rule production and deeper learning from data. In 2017, iNaturalist integrated artificial intelligence. Applications such as BirdNET no longer require human intervention other than triggering a sound recording from a cell phone. What are the conditions for inputting data into these applications? What are the motivations of "amateur" contributors who participate on a voluntary basis? What visibility is there regarding the future of the data produced?

1.5. Conclusion

We hope that this inventory and the resulting synthesis will open up avenues for enrichment and reflection for other researchers and professionals and even be debated and contradicted, because with the limited historical perspective on this object, we had no ambition to embrace its totality or freeze its landscape; quite the contrary, outlining its contours convinced us of the need to deepen our questioning of the periodization of biodiversity data collection systems open to the public, within more complex processes. It was also an opportunity to cross-fertilize our disciplines.

Nonetheless, in our opinion, this result bears witness to a number of flagrant factors, and in particular to the fact that the issue of biodiversity is becoming increasingly embroiled in and dominated by the question of data, through an increasingly strong technological, digital and legal apparatus. In addition, the issue of digital technology and public participation in the observation of nature also raises the question of public empowerment and a potential increase in knowledge (autonomization) and the power to act (empowerment). The detours of use that we observe are part of this latter trend, and remobilize the work of de Certeau (de Certeau and Giard (2010)) through the study of the "poaching" of devices.

---

28 *Penser le(s) lien(s)* study day, 30 September 2021, Grenoble Alpes University.

1.6. References

Bonnet, P., Joly, A., Faton, J., Brown, S., Kimiti, D., Deneu, B., Servajean, M., Affouard, A., Lombardo, J., Mary, L. et al. (2020). How citizen scientists contribute to monitor protected areas thanks to automatic plant identification tools. *Ecological Solutions and Evidence*, 1(2) [Online]. Available at: https://onlinelibrary.wiley.com/doi/10.1002/2688-8319.12023 [Accessed 24 January 2022].

de Certeau, M. and Giard, L. (2010). *Arts de faire*. Gallimard, Paris.

Charvolin, F. (2019). *Les sciences participatives au secours de la biodiversité : une approche sociologique*. Éditions Rue d'Ulm, Paris.

Fages, V. (2018). *Savantes nébuleuses : L'origine du monde entre marginalité et autorité scientifiques, 1860-1920*. Éditions EHESS, Paris.

Fages, V. (2021). Participer à la science : l'enjeu de la production de connaissances du XVIIe siècle à nos jours. *NOV'AE*.

Fages, V. (2022). Participations aux sciences : institutions, périphéries, braconnages. Enjeux et perspectives de la culture scientifique, seminar, Grenoble Alpes University, Maison des Sciences de l'Homme.

Flichy, P. (2019). Le travail sur plateforme. Une activité ambivalente. *Réseaux*, 213(1), 173–209.

Frénot, S. and Grumbach, S. (2014). Les données sociales, objets de toutes les convoitises. *Hérodote*, 152(153), 43–66 [Online]. Available at: https://doi.org/10.3917/her.152.0043 [Accessed 30 June 2022].

Heaton, L.D., Millerand, F., Dias da Silva, P., Proulx, S. (2018). *La reconfiguration du travail scientifique en biodiversité : pratiques amateurs et technologies numériques*. Les Presses de l'Université de Montréal, Montreal.

Houllier, F. and Merilhou-Goudard, J.B. (2016). Les sciences participatives en France. Report [Online]. Available at: https://hal.inrae.fr/hal-02801940 [Accessed 14 June 2022].

Irwin, A. (1995). *Citizen Science: A Study of People, Expertise, and Sustainable Development*. Routledge, London.

Julliard, R. (2017). Science participative et suivi de la biodiversité : l'expérience Vigie-Nature. *Natures Sciences Sociétés*, 25(4), 412–417.

Lafleur, S. (2015). Foucault, la communication et les dispositifs. Information médias théories pratiques. *Communication*, 33(2) [Online]. Available at: https://journals.openedition.org/communication/5727?lang=en [Accessed 30 June 2022].

Lascoumes, P. and Le Galès, P. (2005). *Gouverner par les instruments*. Presses de Sciences Po, Paris [Online]. Available at: https://doi.org/10.3917/scpo.lasco.2005.01 [Accessed 30 June 2022].

Las Vergnas, O. (2016). De la médiation scientifique aux sciences dans la société, 30 ans d'ambiguïtés de l'action culturelle scientifique. In *La médiation culturelle : cinquième roue du carrosse*, Serain, F., Vaysse, F., Chazottes, P., Caillet, E. (eds). L'Harmattan, Paris, 177–187.

Legagneux, P., Casajus, N., Cazelles, K., Chevallier, C., Chevrinais, M., Guéry, L., Jacquet, C., Jaffré, M., Naud, M.-J., Noisette, F. et al. (2018). Our house is burning: discrepancy in climate change vs. biodiversity coverage in the media as compared to scientific literature. *Frontiers in Ecology and Evolution*, 5, 175.

Mauz, I. and Granjou, C. (2010). La construction de la biodiversité comme problème politique et scientifique, premiers résultats d'une enquête en cours. *Sciences Eaux & Territoires*, 3, 10–13.

Prévot, A.C., Dozières, A., Turpin, S., Julliard, R. (2016). Les réseaux volontaires d'observateurs de la biodiversité (Vigie-Nature) : quelles opportunités d'apprentissage ? *Cahiers de l'action*, 47(1), 35–40.

Severo, M. (2021). Sciences et recherches participatives. *Publictionnaire. Dictionnaire encyclopédique et critique des publics* [Online]. Available at: http://publictionnaire.huma-num.fr/notice/sciences-et-recherches-participatives [Accessed 14 June 2022].

Takacs, D. (1996). *The Idea of Biodiversity: Philosophies of Paradise*. Johns Hopkins University Press, Baltimore.

2

The Documentary Links of Herbarium Collections and Their Communicative Stakes

Figure 2.1. *Updating herbarium plate labels to link collections. Julie Polge (2021). For a color version of this figure, see www.iste.co.uk/kohlmann/linking.zip*

Chapter written by Lisa CHUPIN.

2.1. Introduction

Herbarium collections, herbaria or dried plant collections, are made up of different types of links that enable the fragments that make them up to be attached and the documents in the same category to be grouped together. We analyze the role of these attachment and classification methods in the production, conservation and communication of scientific information on biodiversity, taking into account the hybridization of media collections (paper and digital): the largest of these – according to the number of specimens held – are now digitized, described in databases and consultable via an online catalog.

We introduce this chapter by outlining the communicative approach we adopt for understanding herbaria. Natural history collections make it possible to exploit or reinterpret observations without having to go to the field where they were made, thanks to the centralized conservation of specimens that have been collected and notes taken about them, guaranteeing the possibility of resituating them in the area where they were collected (Latour 2001). The specimen, transported to the place where the collection is kept (laboratory, museum, library, etc.), enables the user to appropriate the observations made in the field, by reinterpreting the traces kept in the collections. A communication relationship is thus established, made possible by the document in the collection and characterized by discontinuity: there is no direct link with the field, since the user remains at a distance from the document's authors; specimens are transported from the field (Latour 2001), but their meaning is reconstructed on the spot as they are read (Jeanneret 2009) – the information itself is not disseminated, but only its formats, and the communication presupposes the reinterpretation of the specimens each time. This form of communication, known as "mediatized", is conditional on bringing together in space, and thus materially linking, the documentary formats brought back from the field. Collections enable users to find the specimens they are looking for, and to integrate the results of new analyses to make them available to other researchers. They are an integral part of the knowledge production process. They constitute a mechanism for mediatizing knowledge concerning species from the regions represented in the collections – the term mediatization underlines the role of the device in a social and symbolic construction, as opposed to a neutral intermediary ensuring the mere circulation of a message already constituted upstream.

We investigate the new possibilities for linking and reconciling digitized specimens, once they are stored in databases, and how this is transforming the communication relationships mediatized by the collections. We also use the term communication "link" to qualify these relationships, since this term allows us to characterize both the material level of the assembly in the space of documentary formats and the social relationships envisaged as forms of dependence and solidarity, which are created between the people who produce, maintain or consult the herbaria and/or associated databases. Finally, we examine the way in which these links are expressed at a symbolic level, through the study of the construction of new knowledge and forms of attachment relating to nature.

Our question is whether the digitization of herbaria can be analyzed with the same assumptions as naturalist inventories that take the form of databases, studied by Arpin, Charvolin and Fortier as a "banking" of inventories (2015). Databases have been analyzed as vectors for the circulation of objectified data, detached from their social context of production, whereas naturalist inventories are approaches anchored in the field, based on a sensitive relationship with the latter. However, natural history collections have also been built up by people motivated by an emotional attachment to certain species, and grouped together by learned societies whose members come together to share knowledge. Does the creation of specimen image databases represent a break with, or a renewal of, the forms of communication inherent to the naturalist sociability associated with the creation and management of collections?

To answer these questions, this chapter remobilizes a survey on the uses of collections, whether digitized or not, carried out for the French network of naturalist collections Recolnat[1]. A research infrastructure created in 2013 to promote natural history collections, Recolnat has digitized the collections of partner museums and universities. The network became a *Groupement d'intérêt scientifique* (GIS, scientific interest group) in 2020 and is also responsible for promoting digitized collections. To this end, it has enabled the development of websites and applications for the consultation and scientific exploitation of digitized images as well as for the participation in their documentation. Our investigation contributed to the design of interfaces best-suited to these objectives.

In the first part of this chapter, we begin by analyzing the documentary links and social relationships that make up herbaria, before considering their transformations in the context of the digitizing of collections.

2.2. The constructive documentary and social links of herbaria

2.2.1. *Intra-documentary and inter-documentary links between collections*

Notes on the context of the collection (date, locality, state of the surrounding environment, specified in greater or lesser detail) are an essential condition for referring to the field from a distance, situating as precisely as possible the observations made in the territory explored at a given date (Latour 2001). Reference to field observations

1 Available at: www.recolnat.org [Accessed 14 June 2022].

is achieved through the herbarium's ability to form a documentary unit by linking a multiplicity of fragments of different materials (paper and dried plant parts, especially leaves, flowers and seeds): for example, in the plate shown in Figure 2.2, we can see the collage of the specimen's harvest label, an extract from Jean-Baptiste Lamarck's *Encyclopédie de la botanique* mentioning the species concerned and the two labels associated with an additional expert assessment in 2011. Preserving the information derived from naturalistic observation means keeping together, using specific fastening techniques (such as pins, stitching or glue), the notes taken about the context of the observation, the samples taken on site and their interpretations.

Holding these elements together requires a variety of binding techniques to ensure the document's solidity and preservation. Binding may not be carried out until long after the harvest, in which case the labels are reconstituted from a copy of the information in a harvest notebook written at the time of collection. In this case, two distinct media coexist – the numbered specimens and the harvest notebook, symbolically linked by the numbering of specimens cited in the notebook[2]. Reading them together is essential for reconstructing information from the field – the loss of the notebook means the loss of much of the herbarium's value.

Insofar as it holds together several heterogeneous media of inscription and observation, each herbarium document organizes intra-documentary links, i.e. relating to the fragments of the document or to the zones that make it up, according to the terminology developed for navigation in the digital document (Laignelet 2006). The dichotomy between intra-documentary and inter-documentary links makes it possible to distinguish between those that unite fragments of the same document and those that link different documents, as Bardiot (2017) proposes when contrasting annotations relating to the content of video vignettes and those that establish links with other films. Bardiot proposes to think of the links between fragments making up the document on the annotation model, which is also appropriate for the herbarium: all labels and notes can be considered as annotations of the specimen, which itself relates to the plant observed on site. Bardiot points out that certain annotations can be considered as intra-documentary as well as inter-documentary; in the case of the herbarium, inter-documentary links are built up from certain fragments associated with the specimen at the intra-documentary level: the determination label that pre-specifies the species of a specimen enables it to be linked with others that also belong to it. Inter-documentary relationships between specimens arise from their many points in common: the fact that they come from the same harvest, the same collection, etc. Researchers use these commonalities to select a set of specimens in support of a study. Bardiot describes the operations involved in establishing inter-documentary links, as relayed by Briet (1951): "Juxtaposition, selection and

2 The Geoffroy Saint-Hilaire digital herbarium provides free access to the botanist's collection notebooks (Pignal et al. 2013).

comparison of documents and production of auxiliary documents". These steps correspond well to the operations that lead to highlighting inter-documentary links between specimens as part of studies aimed at describing a species, distinguishing it from another or characterizing morphological specificities peculiar to a geographical area.

2.2.2. *Inter-documentary links at the heart of knowledge production*

The objective of describing and arranging species (specific to systematics) translates into the establishment of links between documents in collections in their storage space. It is on the classification of species that the documentary classification of herbaria is based; this is a taxonomic classification that consists of matching specimens on the basis of their common relationship to the same entity, in this case the species or genus to which they belong. Some collections, however, are still arranged according to other logics, particularly when they are of great historical value.

This classification presupposes the use of suitable materials to preserve the classification established following expert appraisals: folders or boxes hold together bundles of specimens grouped in the same category – researchers use multiple bundles to build up documentary sets suited to their studies. Once the specimens to be studied have been selected, their analysis involves examining them side by side and comparing them. The unbound nature of most herbaria facilitates these reclassification operations.

The classification adopted in a collection depends on the scientific objectives for which it was conceived: research into systematics (which includes work on the description and classification of species) or work focused on a particular region (which involves drawing up an inventory of its flora), for example. However, specimens can also be grouped together according to multiple criteria, such as belonging to the same historical collection, a common harvest or an institution in which they have been conserved. The choice of a classification for a collection leads to the loss of certain links between specimens: this is the case when a taxonomic classification has been favored over the historical conservation of the collection, as in the case for the Vaillant herbarium (Lamy and Pelletier 2010).

By preserving the labels attesting to the species attributed to a specimen or the institutions where it was kept, the collections keep track of the different classifications, and therefore the interpretations, to which they have been subjected. By reading the document, the user of the collections is also put in the presence of a state of historical knowledge, on which they can base their critical analysis. Through the labels attesting to its place in an institutional collection, it is also possible to understand the exchanges that have taken place between collectors and institutions.

Figure 2.2. *Herbarium plate from the Lyon Botanical Garden*[3]

2.2.3. *Documentary links as traces of social ties between botanists*

Herbarium labels enable us to understand certain relationships between specimens (e.g. between those from the same harvest, locality or geographical area), as well as between people or institutions involved in the harvests. These links are not always apparent, since they have to be located in the collections held by different

3 The collections of the Lyon Botanical Garden can be viewed on the Flickr site: www.flickr.com/photos/jardin_botanique_lyon/10572480014 [Accessed on 17 November 2022].

institutions (to which specimens from the same harvest may have been sent). Search operations in different collections are necessary to reconstitute these inter-documentary links: they consist, for example, of finding specimens from the same harvests as those cited in support of a scientific publication – these particularly valuable specimens, comparable to those cited in a publication devoted to the description of a species, are called "type specimens".

The distribution of specimens from the same collections between different establishments is the result of consignments of specimens following agreements between institutions, the purchase of specimens to complete a collection or, more occasionally, a request to a specialist for help with identification (Lamy 2005). It attests to the multiplicity of social and institutional links at the origin of herbaria. Established to preserve observations and communicate them to others across time and space, the herbarium is itself the product of existing social relationships between naturalist institutions. These relationships are particularly valuable, since they enable us to increase the number of specimens available for consultation, especially "type" specimens. The metaphor of a social bond between collection users is justified by the fact that the discoveries of some depend on the solidarity of others, in particular through this system of exchanges. These social links are partly documented in the labels of the collections they have enriched. The digitization of collections raises the question of how to reconstitute and valorize, in digitized corpora, the intra- and inter-documentary links of herbaria and the social links that are intrinsically associated with them.

2.3. Databases as vectors of new documentary, social and symbolic links

Herbarium digitization operations (in the Recolnat infrastructure, as well as in the many institutions involved) have gone hand in hand with a campaign to computerize label elements. This latter work is essential to reconstituting the specimen's symbolic link to its collecting ground (its ability to refer to it) and to use digital devices that enhance the inter-documentary links between collections.

2.3.1. *Creation of a new reference system between image, field and specimen*

The digitized specimen is all the less directly linked to the field in that it has lost the plant material that came from it. Despite this, it retains the power to overcome its absence by conserving an image that preserves the morphological characters observable on the surface, and the possibility of reading harvest notes and determinations. Researchers who use the digitized specimen as a substitute for consulting the physical specimen, or as a complement, need to ensure that the image on the screen reflects the observation made in the field, without error or distortion. At the intra-documentary level, this translates into systems for controlling the quality of digitization and in particular to the attachment of new fragments to the herbarium plate before it is digitized according to metric and colorimetric standards. In addition to the addition of these new elements to the fragments making up the herbarium document, digitization may be preceded by the attachment of fragments to specimens or the restoration of plates, sometimes carried out by volunteers, as was the case at the herbarium of the Muséum national d'histoire naturelle (MNHN, French National Museum of Natural History)). The aim is to prevent any alteration of the documents during digitization operations (particularly when these are not carried out in-house, and involve moving the collections to the digitization site and returning them to their place of preservation).

At the same time, new habits are emerging among users of digital collections, as the scientific use of images becomes more widespread and goes beyond the use of the online catalog as a tool for previewing non-digitized collections. In the first place, the scientific use of images requires the researcher to critically interrogate the data provided about the specimen (in order to detect any data entry or label reading errors) – this is already the kind of examination of information that researchers carry out when studying a non-digitized specimen, in order to guard against identification errors. In the case of digitized specimens, greater attention is paid to ensuring that the image is not distorted. This is why, in order to measure morphological characteristics directly on digitized specimens, we have developed the habit of checking the consistency of distances measured from the image with control standards, initially with generalist digital photo processing software. A calibration function was integrated into the scientific image processing software developed for the Recolnat network, Annotat[4] (see Figure 2.4 for a screenshot of the prototyped calibration function).

In addition to the faithfulness of digitization to the original specimen, the computerization of donated labels concerning the place of collection, essential for keeping intact the way in which they can refer to the field, facilitates the enhancement of the collections' inter-documentary links.

2.3.2. *Hypertextual enhancement of inter-documentary links in collections*

Recording the information contained in the collections in the structured form of a database makes it possible to sort specimens according to their common features; this is the prerequisite for developing interfaces to visualize links between specimens

4 Available at: www.recolnat.org/fr/annotate [Accessed on 17 November 2022].

in the collections. The database records and stores the data describing each specimen, structured according to a model chosen in advance – specific to the institution or network involved in the digitization program. This computerization requires time-consuming label analysis, which has led various institutions to seek solutions for opening up this documentary work to amateurs. In the Recolnat network catalog, not all images are described with the same level of precision: only those that have been computerized by collection staff, or by online contributors, present collection geolocation information.

The data resulting from the computerization of labels lend themselves to various exploitations facilitating knowledge of the collections. They can be used to build up the corpus of work by means of multi-criteria queries in the database, replacing searching through bundles of specimens arranged according to the classification principles retained for the collection. The compilation of geolocation data associated with a species provides a visualization of its distribution – this draft distribution map presupposes a critical study of the biases associated with the representation of the species in the database consulted.

Web browsing makes it possible to preserve the categories linking certain specimens together in accordance with the classification of the historical herbarium's author, without preventing the corresponding images from being made available for user search results – an example of this is the site dedicated to Lamarck's herbarium[5].

Some online databases also make it possible to enhance the value of complementary research carried out in parallel with digitization by providing a hypertext link between a specimen and the publications that cite it. This is the case with the JSTOR Global Plants bibliographic database[6], a program that financed the research and digitization of type specimens in several major international collections. Other links between the databases of one or more institutions can also be established, as was the aim of the DataPOCMNHN project[7], which proposed methods for aligning data concerning botanists mentioned in the multiple databases managed by the MNHN. The resulting proof of concept provides records enriched with data from the various MNHN databases and the partner Biodiversity Heritage Library, an open-access bibliographic database of biodiversity studies.

5 Available at: https://redi.imss.fi.it/lamarck/ [Accessed on 17 November 2022].

6 Available at: https://plants.jstor.org [Accessed on 17 November 2022].

7 Available at: https://datapoc.mnhn.fr/about [Accessed on 17 November 2022].

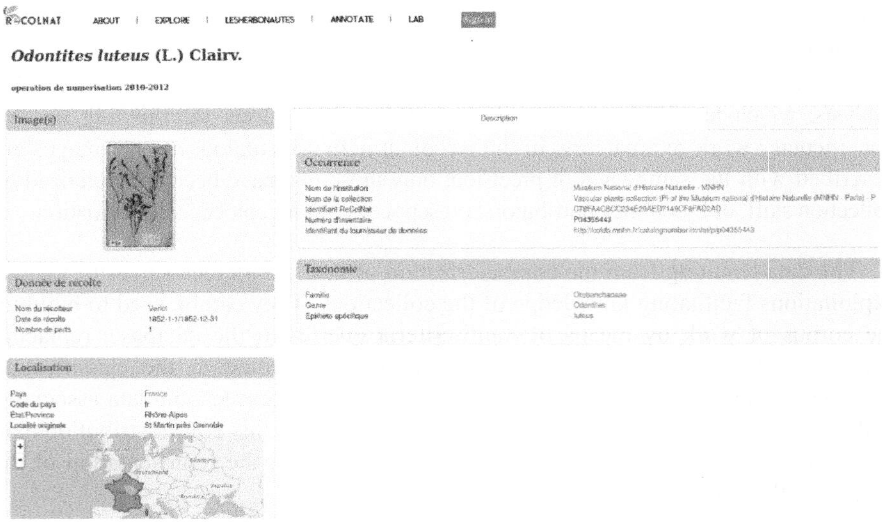

a) Description tab

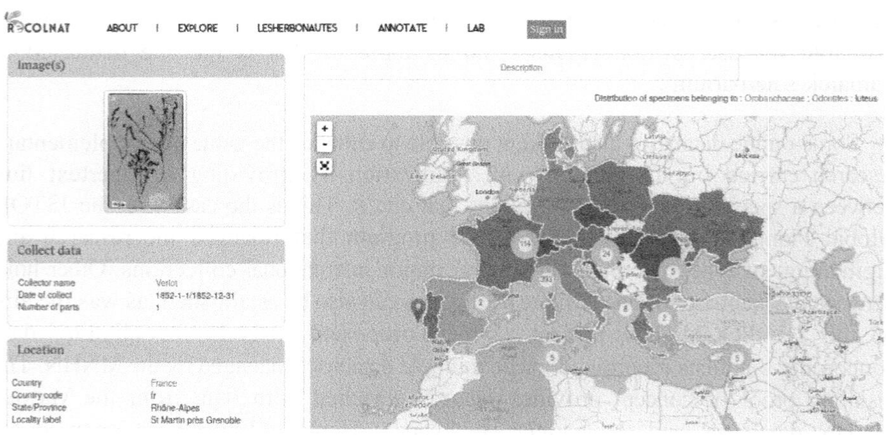

b) Allocation tab

Figure 2.3. *Interface for consulting a digitized specimen stored in the Recolnat database[8]. For a color version of this figure, see www.iste.co.uk/kohlmann/linking.zip*

8 Available at: https://explore.recolnat.org/occurrence/C78FA4CBCC234E29AED7149CF8FAD2AD [Accessed on 17 November 2022].

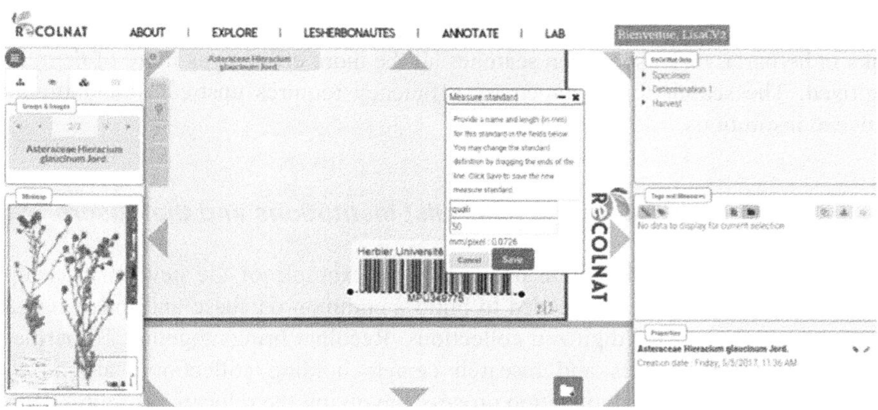

Figure 2.4. *Screenshot of the online laboratory prototype behind the Annotate application – calibration tool*

In addition, within the Recolnat infrastructure, functions have been developed for free categorization by the user as they observe and measure digitized specimens: this involves reproducing the possibility of building up stacks of specimens as we observe and discover commonalities between them or storing in the botanist's office useful material for different ongoing studies. In the Annotate software, tags – labels made up of terms freely chosen by the user or taken from a data model created beforehand – can be associated with measurements or specimens, bringing them together in the same category as their common characteristics are discovered. These tags and annotations highlight the inter-documentary links revealed by a study.

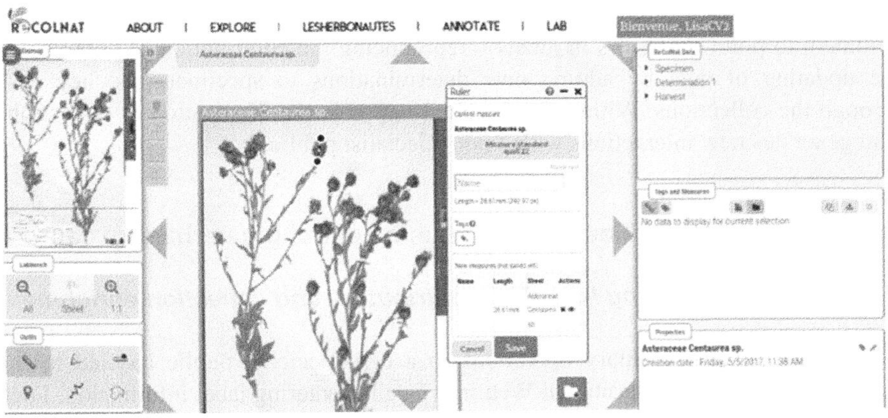

Figure 2.5. *Screenshot of the online laboratory prototype behind the Annotate application – tagging measurements taken from the image*

All these browsing possibilities, highlighting different kinds of inter-documentary links in herbaria, make specimen searches all the more efficient as more of them are digitized. The search for documentary efficiency requires upstream collaboration between institutions.

2.3.3. *Stronger links between naturalist institutions and their users*

The creation of the Recolnat network is an example of the new relationships between institutions that are needed to build a common database and to harmonize management choices for digitized collections. Recolnat brings together 18 partners (universities, metropolises and research centers holding collections) around the acceptance of a common digitization process (involving the relocation of most of the collections concerned) and to enhance the value of digitized collections (the network's constitutive agreement specifies, in particular, elements concerning image distribution rights and the management of photographic credits to be integrated into images consulted on the portal). The same type of organization is being set up in other regions, with national organizations integrated into regional programs. Recolnat is the French nodal point of the European Distributed Systems of Scientific Collections (DiSSCo) research infrastructure. The centralization of biodiversity data is the mission of the Global Biodiversity Information Facility (GBIF), an international network maintaining an infrastructure of biodiversity data of all kinds (inventory occurrences and specimen collections in particular).

The constitution of a common catalog also modifies the relationships of users with institutions, since it becomes the first intermediary making it possible to identify specimens that the user will ask to consult on site. New relationships are also established with users when online catalogs offer the possibility of adding a comment to point out errors in labels – reproducing the contribution of botanists to the updating of data by adding new determinations to specimens as they pass through the collections. Within the Recolnat network, the digitization of collections also generates new interactions with a non-specialist public.

2.4. The new sociabilities of Internet users enriching herbarium data

2.4.1. *Hyperlinks linking herbaria, contributors and collection enrichment*

Opening up documentary operations to a non-specialist public has led to the development of a fun, educational Web interface for entering label information. Each specimen is placed in the middle of a new network of hypertext links which renews the inter-documentary links highlighted by classification in the physical space of the collections. Categorization by species and geographical zone takes a back seat, as the images are presented within sets of specimens chosen in relation to a theme determined by the needs of a scientific study or for the interest it may spark in the public. Each of these sets of documents constitutes a "mission" proposed to Internet users. For example, this may involve mobilizing contributors who are particularly familiar with a geographical area, as in the Flora of Canada missions, or contextualizing the transcription of specimens of a given species, as in one of the missions underway in 2022: "Take to the water for the *Nymphaeaceae*!".

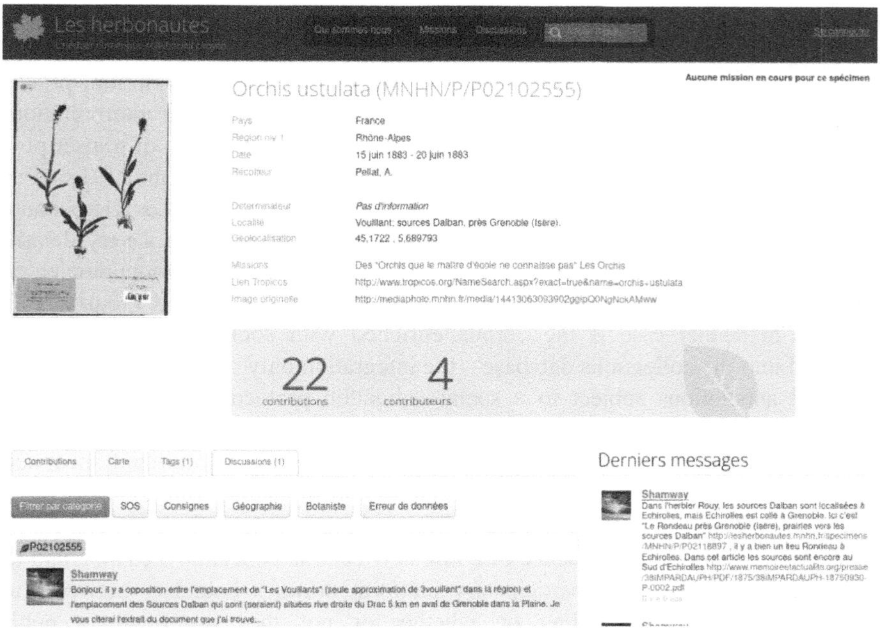

Figure 2.6. *Web page devoted to a specimen on the Les Herbonautes site, summarizing the associated information and contributions (screenshot)*[9]

As the transcriptions and discussions between contributors progress, each specimen of the missions created in this way is associated with data of a new kind: a Web page summarizes the contributions of the relevant labels, specifying the contributors, the mission concerned, as well as the specific discussion space and possibly the associated tags, chosen by the contributors (Figure 2.5). This Web page is generated using various tables in the platform database (table of missions, specimens, contributions and comments associated with each of them, and contributors). The Web page for each contributor provides a summary of the operations they have carried out; the

9 Available at: http://herbonautes.mnhn.fr/specimens/MNHN/P/P02102555 [Accessed on 17 November 2022].

hypertext links on the Web page dedicated to each specimen allow us to navigate from an image to the profiles of the people involved in documenting it or to view all the specimens in the mission or the associated discussions.

The corpus of annotations produced on the platform further enhances the already contributory nature of the paper herbarium document, and correlatively its intra-documentary complexity: in addition to the labels affixed to specimens as they are redetermined or reclassified within a new institution, the platform also includes notes on observations made by Web users.

These annotations are increasingly numerous as the transcription process brings together the contributors involved in the event of conflicting interpretations: Internet users are then invited to modify, confirm or justify their choice of transcription by sending a message. This confrontation stage leads them to quote the URLs of the Web pages that were useful in finding certain information. The Les Herbonautes platform documents the exchanges required for computerization in a very detailed way, reminiscent of the notes taken in the registers of the teams computerizing the images – a wiki, in the case observed in Montpellier by Heaton and Proulx (2012). However, in neither case is the corpus enriched with social contributions fully integrated into the collections database – the integration only concerns the part of the structured annotations subject to a social validation protocol. While participatory information platforms aim to specify as much as possible the collection context from which the photographed specimen originates, the banking of digitized specimens involves, as in other cases studied (Arpin et al. 2015), an erasure of the social context of data production – constituted in the platform we are studying by the transcription interpretation context. This absence of a link between the collection's catalog and the corresponding pages of the participatory platform draws a boundary between two documentary spaces, depending on whether or not they are open to public participation. The digital herbarium reproduces the boundary that separates signed annotation, considered as the result of expertise, and the many anonymous participations that take place in the maintenance of collections (with attachment operations).

2.4.2. *The quest for quality in participatory data at the origin of the creation of new social ties*

Data quality is essential to the use of a specimen: an error in the data can render it invisible in searches. The coherence of the corpus is maintained by new documentary boundaries and by the platform's specific framing and animation. The platform operates on the basis of its own database, which is fed images from the Recolnat network database, into which data from the transcription process are integrated. The independence of the databases means that only results validated by a majority of

Internet users can be included in the institutional corpus. Non-protocol enrichments, freely added as comments or tags, are therefore only accessible to people who are aware of the participatory documentation process, and who may wish to consult the specimen in the context of the platform.

The consistency of transcriptions is ensured by a strong framework of input fields, each with a help section. In addition to tutorials and quizzes, which renew the form of transcription, the integration of transcription rules by members is achieved through community animation by MNHN staff, assisted by researchers recruited through calls for projects. They can also act as intermediaries with the collection areas (when a document is illegible due to faulty digitization, as in the case of a label folded in on itself). Exchanges between members, even if these are few in number relative to the volume of specimens transcribed, are essential to the integration of new participants and the learning of instructions. A symbolic reward in the form of a specific badge added to the contributor's profile enhances the value of answering questions posed by others.

Internet users' participation in the documentary work of enhancing a scientific corpus is based on pre-configured tasks, with different roles corresponding to the level of contribution and status (researcher, mission leader or layperson). These roles (facilitators, contributors) and contribution levels reproduce the boundaries of a scientific community – with the nuance, however, that professionals also contribute to transcription tasks on the platform, alongside the initially uninformed public. Furthermore, the transcription task is only configured by the device in its final stage, at the moment of entry, leaving the way open to the initiative of the contributor, in the way they search for information, without any proposed methodology. Exchanges between contributors testify to the variety of approaches used and the questions they raise. A number of contributors' initiatives were recognized and framed a posteriori in a second version of the site developed in 2016: in addition to features developed in response to needs expressed by contributors (such as a full-text search of all contributions and messages), additional badges were created, including one for contributors involved in helping novices. The platform's ability to take into account users' suggestions arising from their involvement and the innovation they demonstrate is essential if contributors are not to be locked into a role pre-set by the system. Indeed, this is an inherent risk of contribution mediatized by digital tools, as highlighted by Kohlmann in Chapter 4, based on the Nature-Isère study.

The exchanges between contributors and moderators generated by the platform, particularly with a view to the integration of instructions by new members and the correction of transcriptions, lead them to get to know each other without actually meeting. We sought to compare the profiles of the members of this new collective with those of other naturalist collectives and clarify the motivations of the contributors behind the documentary enrichment of the collections.

2.4.3. *Herbonauts' links with naturalist sociabilities and motivations*

A survey carried out in collaboration with the Tela Botanica online botanical network in 2014 on the platform's audience sought to situate contributors in relation to existing botanical collectives. A study of the 120 responses tallied showed that communication by members of the Recolnat infrastructure, and in particular the Tela Botanica network, with its newsletter sent to 18,000 subscribers, corresponded to 40% of the sources of information that helped raise awareness of the platform. The majority of contributors who took part in at least one proposed mission were also recruited thanks to communication from Recolnat's partners. However, there were also newcomers to the field of naturalist collections who had no previous knowledge of them: they were mobilized following high-profile press articles or radio broadcasts on the occasion of the renovation of the Paris herbarium. The questionnaires distributed to regular contributors show that even if a naturalist interest already existed, the field of collections was unknown to many. However, it is worth noting that certain professions close to biology (notably life and earth sciences teaching), already well represented among the volunteers involved in maintaining the collections, each bring in around a quarter of the participants.

In terms of motivations, the reasons for liking the site "a lot or particularly" were: "to help facilitate the work of scientists" (almost 90% of responses), "to solve difficult puzzles" and "to acquire knowledge" (80%), "to discover a heritage" (75%) and "to relax" (70%). Testimonials from regular users collected in a more detailed questionnaire show that access to the documents in the collections plays an important role for them: "Today, I can compare, in a few minutes, plates from the four corners of the world, made by the most famous botanists of all time. It's simply fantastic", writes one of them. The interest aroused by the specimen stems from the link it maintains with the territories and their past, which it is up to the Web user to consolidate by entering information about the collection. For example, a very committed contributor writes:

> I really enjoy coming across (or searching on the mission's global geolocation map) places I know well […]. I like to (re)learn French geography, of a France that often no longer exists, locating a wood, a small forest in a commercial zone, reading about the ruins of Pierrefonds castle because the harvest was made before its 'renovation', about 'maritime meadows' where there are now residential quarters, buildings. I also like to read the notes or copies of letters that appear on the plates.

The study of titles, freely chosen by Internet users to tag certain specimens, also testifies to the type of interest contributors have in the collections: the most frequently used words relate to specimen provenance regions, and historical collectors or collections scattered across current classifications. The recontextualization of specimens leads contributors to develop a view of collections that is in line with the approach of curators involved in the reconstitution of historical documentary sets – it does not correspond to a botanical learning approach to collections – which is the primary reason for amateur herbarium-building (Lamy 2005).

2.5. Conclusion

For each specimen, digitization increases the number of fragments that need to be matched to reconstruct a usable record of observations made in the field (in particular with new annotations, and standards used to check the fidelity of digitization). Recording information about the specimen in structured form in a database is a new way of ensuring the intra-documentary link between these constituent fragments of the document. It makes it possible to formalize and enhance the value of the common features that unite certain specimens, transversal to the classification of collection consultation areas. This opens up the possibility of new ways of enhancing the inter-documentary links between collections, automatically produced on the basis of similarities in the descriptive data of certain images. Input interfaces open to participation offer users the possibility of creating inter-documentary links in herbaria based on the transcription of labels or free annotations common to different specimens.

Our study within the Recolnat infrastructure highlighted the dependence between the establishment of documentary links necessary for the scientific interpretation of digitized specimens and the new relationships and forms of communication they imply between collection staff and users and with new enthusiasts. By documenting not only field observations but also the conclusions of specimen identifications, their citation in publications or their holding in an institution, collections weave links that are at once social, symbolic and material. The term "link" encompasses them all, thanks to its proper meaning rooted in a material dimension, and to its derived meanings that qualify social and symbolic relationships (notably reference links), always materialized by hypertextual links between digital documents.

Social links between players involved in the conservation or scientific exploitation of collections are affected by the creation of databases. This applies not only to relations between curators and users but also to relationships between institutions holding collections that form research infrastructures and mobilize new amateur collectives.

The development of new documentary links to contextualize images or link them to publications presupposes new forms of communication between professional and amateur contributors to the computerization process – who are the first to use the first resources already put online. For curators and researchers involved in the platform, mobilizing contributors implies developing a new kind of scientific mediatization to accompany non-specialist Internet users through the computerization process.

The sources of interest for the site mentioned by the participants suggest that the herbarium document, recontextualized in the transcription missions, fascinates because of the traces it preserves of the context in which it was produced. The document is interesting not because it produces a direct immersion in nature, but because it preserves the trace of a representation of the knowledge of an ancient state of flora and landscapes.

The sensitive attachment to certain species that characterizes naturalist collectives is transformed into an attachment to territories. Contributors are also mobilized by the opportunity to interact with scientists using the collections. Missions give contributors the opportunity to become involved in scientific work in the sense of showing solidarity with it and becoming a stakeholder in their own modest way.

2.6. References

Arpin, I., Charvolin, F., Fortier, A. (2015). Les inventaires naturalistes : des pratiques aux modes de gouvernement. *Études rurales*, 195 [Online]. Available at: http://journals.openedition.org.erproxy.u-paris.fr/etudesrurales/10232 [Accessed 10 May 2022].

Bardiot, C. (2017). Organiser et conserver la mémoire de l'éphémère : Les capsules de MémoRekall. *Culture & Musées*, 30 [Online]. Available at: http://journals.openedition.org.ezproxy.u-paris.fr/culturemusees/1261 [Accessed 17 August 2022].

Briet, S. (1951). *Qu'est-ce que la documentation*. Edit, Paris.

Chupin, L. (2015). Enjeux de la numérisation des herbiers pour l'information et la communication scientifiques : de la transformation des matières documentaires à l'évolution des pratiques. *Les Enjeux de l'Information et de la Communication*, 16(2), 69–82 [Online]. Available at: https://lesenjeux.univ-grenoble-alpes.fr/2015/dossier/05-enjeux-de-numerisation-herbiers-linformation-communication-scientifiques-de-transformation-matieres-documentaires-a-levolution-pratiques/ [Accessed 15 May 2022].

Chupin, L. (2017). Enjeux communicationnels de la conception de dispositifs de médiation documentaire augmentée pour les herbiers numérisés. PhD thesis, Conservatoire national des arts et métiers, Paris.

Heaton, L. and Proulx, S. (2012). La construction locale d'une base transnationale de données en botanique. *Revue d'anthropologie des connaissances*, 6(1), 141–162.

Jeanneret, Y. (2009). Faire avec le faire communicationnel. *Actes Sémiotiques* [Online]. Available at: https://www.unilim.fr/actes-semiotiques/3336 [Accessed 14 June 2022].

Laignelet, M. (2006). Les titres et les introductions de cadres comme indices pour le repérage de segments d'information évolutive. *Schedae*, 7(1), 51–56. Available at: http://marion.laignelet.free.fr/articles/laignelet_isdd.pdf [Accessed 14 June 2022].

Lamy, D. (2005). Le savoir botanique par les herbiers. *Voyages en Botanique*, 16–17 June, Besançon [Online]. Available at: https://fdocuments.fr/document/denis-lamy-le-savoir-botanique-par-les-herbiers.html?page=13 [Accessed 14 June 2022].

Lamy, D. and Pelletier, A. (2010). La conservation et la valorisation de l'Herbier de Tournefort au Muséum national d'Histoire naturelle. *La Lettre de l'OCIM*, 130 [Online]. Available at: http://journals.openedition.org.ezproxy.u-paris.fr/ocim/132 [Accessed 16 May 2022].

Latour, B. (2001). *L'Espoir de Pandore*. La Découverte, Paris, 33–82.

Pignal, M., Romaniuc-Neto, S., De Souza, S., Chagnoux, S., Lange Canhos, D.A. (2013). Saint-Hilaire virtual herbarium, a new upgradeable tool to study Brazilian botany. *Adansonia*, 35(1), 7–18.

3

Investigating the Relationship with Nature in the Animation of Wineries' Facebook Pages

Figure 3.1. *Pic Saint-Loup winegrowers create their winery's Facebook page. © Julie Polge (2021). For a color version of this figure, see www.iste.co.uk/kohlmann/linking.zip*

Chapter written by Marie-Caroline HEÏD and Catherine DE LAVERGNE.

From vine cultivation to bottling and marketing, today's winegrower is a multitasker. To promote their wines, winegrowers are also encouraged to take part in numerous trade shows, which means they have to know how to talk about their products, their work and their winery, in order to forge special links with the public. Events are also becoming increasingly popular: wine tours, concerts or guided tours of the estate, introductions to oenology and so on. Winegrowers[1] are increasingly organizing cultural and tourist activities that encourage customers to visit the winery directly.

In this chapter, we focus on a specific winegrowing terroir, the Appellation d'Origine Contrôlée and Appellation d'Origine Protégée (AOC-AOP) Pic Saint-Loup, which sends a significant and constantly increasing percentage for export. The need to reach customers calls for an online presence. Digital communication for winegrowers often boils down to the creation of a commercial website, the management of which is costly and left to professionals. In addition, Pic Saint-Loup winegrowers have been developing their presence on social networks for several years (Heïd and De Lavergne 2017). They often initiate the creation of these accounts, which they manage intuitively with the help of family members, without any previous training in community management. For them, this activity represents a way of reclaiming their estate's online communications free of charge and of highlighting the role played by each member of the family, for example by publishing photographs of a family member at a trade show or of workers harvesting grapes. Also, through their posts and the activity on these pages, winegrowers showcase the organizational identity of their estates, their values and specificities. They enroll[2] human actors (their team, partners, local tourism actors, etc.) as well as non-human actors (bottles of wine, vineyards, flowers, insects, etc.).

Like Lisa Chupin in the previous chapter, we are looking at a sensitive attachment to certain (animal and plant) species, linked to the valorization of a territory. However, our focus here is not on links within the digital community, but on invitations for immersion in nature from Pic Saint-Loup winegrowers, who testify intuitively to their daily experience on social networks. We have chosen to restrict our study to the analysis of these wineries' Facebook pages, as this is the network they primarily use. We are looking to answer the following questions in turn: what are the objects, living beings, humans and non-humans that winegrowers

1 All these farmers cultivate vines and produce their own wine. For ease of reading, we use the simplified term "winegrowers" in this chapter.

2 In actor–network theory (Callon 2006), the socio-technical network brings together human entities (actors) and non-human entities ("actants"). For sociologists of translation (Akrich et al. 2006), "enrolling" means "assigning network members a specific task that makes them essential actors in the network's future". In this chapter, we focus on the "actants" and actors enrolled by winegrowers to express and consolidate a relationship with nature.

will use to bear witness to their relationship with nature? How do they mobilize nature when describing the characteristics of their estate, their wines and their activity? Drawing on the contributions of pragmatic sociology, we are looking to understand the explicit or implicit resources of justification that they call upon. What principles of valorization and underlying values can be identified in their communications on these pages?

We note a process of standardization at work in the pages consulted, emanating from the pre-scriptions of the Facebook device, the incorporation of norms of use of socio-technical networks, as well as the common characteristics of these winegrowing territories. However, even if the actants and actors enlisted to bear witness to relationships with nature are often identical or similar from one estate to another, the ways in which they do so are diverse. The winegrowers' digital activity also enables them to singularize the links they regularly maintain with nature and the values they attribute to it.

3.1. Ethnographic analysis of the Facebook pages of the Pic Saint-Loup estates

To contextualize this research, we need to turn our attention to Pic Saint-Loup, one of the main touristic attractions in the Montpellier hinterland, as well as a renowned winegrowing area. In 2017, this production area was granted its own AOC and AOP, and was previously one of the 15 geographical denominations of the AOC Languedoc. In 2022, it covered 1,300 hectares and included three cooperative wineries and 68 individual wineries.

Of these 68 wineries, 47 have a Facebook page, and 25 of these are updated at least once a month. The others are rarely updated, if at all. We have observed the relationship to nature of these 25 Facebook pages over the course of a year. To guarantee their anonymity, we do not mention the names of these wineries. We can, however, point out that these wineries are very diverse in terms of vineyard area, reputation and product price ranges. One of them has been in existence for 200 years and enjoys a solid international reputation, while another is a small family estate of four hectares that was created in 2018.

Thirteen of these estates produce organically and five others are in the process of conversion and aiming for certification. Six of these estates also mention that they operate biodynamic vineyards certified by the Demeter label[3]. As well as complying with organic farming specifications, they apply specific tillage techniques and

3 Specifications and guide available at: www.demeter.fr/produits/vins-bieres-et-spiritueux [Accessed on 20 May 2022].

animal and plant preparations to the vines according to a lunar and planetary calendar. Finally, some of the seven non-organic estates have been awarded the Haute Valeur Environnementale (HVE, High Environmental Quality) label.

Before presenting our methodology in greater detail, we would like to make it clear that we consider the Facebook digital network as a socio-technical device (Peeters and Charlier 1999), an "actant" prescribing a set of actions to its users (Granjon 2012). The scripts inscribed in the device and the "pre-scriptions" (Akrich 1987) indicated in Facebook's help sections are designed to guide users new to community management towards "best practices" for promotional activity on professional pages. Users then adapt these scripts to their needs, starting by filling in the page profile (cover photo, profile, "About Us" section), or the declarative identity in the words of Georges (2008). We began by conducting in-depth observations of these declarative identity propositions, which represent an initial staging of the domain's organizational identity and its relationship to nature. We then observed and analyzed the publishing activities on each of these pages – the active identity in the words of Georges (2008) – between February 2021 and March 2022. These publications reveal relationship strategies aimed at developing the organization's image and bringing their declarative identity proposition to life. With regard to our research question, we focused our observations on the objects, the humans, the living beings mobilized, and compared the modes of enrollment (Akrich et al. 2006) for each estate. These analyses then enabled us to propose a typology of forms of mobilization of nature in relation to the underlying principles of valorization and values (Boltanski and Thévenot 1991; Boltanski and Chiapello 1999).

3.2. Standardization of publishing on Facebook

Since our last survey (Heïd and De Lavergne 2017), we have seen a trend towards standardization of publication methods in line with current standards of societal use of social networks: an increase in the number of photographs published, short text messages, the presence of hashtags and short videos. Similarly, the photographs follow the current trend towards the aestheticization of everyday life; they are processed and incorporate an "aesthetic–emotional dimension" (Lipovetsky and Serroy 2016). In the following section, we summarize the various forms of the relationship to nature presented by all this content.

While 23 of the 25 Facebook pages analyzed are run intuitively by the winegrowers themselves, two wineries entrust this activity to communications specialists, or more precisely to students on work/study courses. These two pages follow community management techniques and generate engagement. For the others, the standardization of publications is an incorporation of norms, a mimetic standardization (Cardon 2019), and not a professionalizing approach that respects the techniques of communicators.

The declarative identity proposals are, on the whole, fairly consistent. The "About Us" section is small, often limited to contact information, a link to the website and directions to the estate. The cover photos show fields of vines with Pic Saint-Loup or Hortus, the mountain facing it, in the background. The profile photos usually feature the estate's logo.

As for publishing activity, few winegrowers maintain regular activity (several posts on the same day, then none for three weeks). They do not comply with the pre-scriptions from the device, which encourage them to publish on a daily basis or to get the public involved through games, competitions and so on. In fact, overall engagement rates are very low, and comments and likes are rare.

Winegrowers use Facebook as a tool to promote their wines and their winery. In so doing, they also enhance their professional and personal identities by sharing their relationship with nature and their community.

Overall, the majority of their publications follow one or more of the following temporalities:

– *diary of cultural and professional events*: publications keep track of winegrowers' participation in trade shows, wine competitions and cultural and tourist events offering wine tastings. Some also organize their own events (wine walks, concerts, introductions to oenology, open days, etc.). In addition, the estates occasionally publish articles in the trade press, award prizes and medals and invite partners to visit their winery;

– *holiday calendar*: publications follow a different timeline, that of marketing "evergreens": Christmas, Easter, Valentine's Day, as well as Father's Day, Mother's Day and so on. This is an opportunity for winegrowers to propose promotional offers or remind people where to buy their products.

Two other temporalities, directly linked to nature, are more specifically related to the object of our analyses, and we develop them in the following sections:

– *the seasonality of vine-growing and the wine-production calendar*: from the start of the vegetative cycle in spring to pruning in winter, winegrowers present the different stages in the work of winegrowing, as the seasons change. Readers can also follow all the winemaking activities;

– *seasons, weather and inclement weather*: photographs of vines and the natural surroundings of Pic Saint-Loup (trees, shrubs, flowers) also punctuate the publications throughout the seasons. In particular, we note a standardization of photographs of frozen vines or vines in beautiful fall colors. In addition, the frequent publications on climatic hazards and bad weather (frost, flooding, hail) testify to the dependence of these winegrowers on the weather.

3.3. Cross-sectional analysis of actants related to nature

The standardization of content also applies to actants related to nature, which are called upon from one page to the next. However, they are enlisted in different ways. We begin with a cross-sectional analysis that compares the way in which non-human actants are mobilized on different pages. Note that labels (organic agriculture, biodynamic, HVE) are rarely used in winegrower ads, contrary to what appears on their websites. Only one winery uses the Agriculture Biologique (AB) logo in its cover photograph. All the winegrowers focus their publications more on their experiences and concrete actions, as evidence of their respect for biodiversity, their attention to the quality of their terroir and their products. We present the different ways they enroll territorial, plant and animal actants, followed by the resources and techniques used in vine-growing and winemaking.

3.3.1. *Pic Saint-Loup and Hortus: nature, terroir and territory*

Many aesthetic photographs feature Pic Saint-Loup or the Hortus cliffs in the background (at sunrise, sunset, in the fog, etc.). These mountains are featured in the majority of cover photos, as well as ritually in shots of various outdoor activities. Collections of photographs of Pic Saint-Loup are even posted as slideshows: “A few shots of our emblematic Pic Saint-Loup and the magnificent Hortus cliff”. These references are, however, oriented differently. In some cases, they are incentives to discover this tourist area, with posts featuring videos from the Grand Pic Saint-Loup tourist office, for example. In other cases, they are appropriations, with publications associating this mountain with the collective of local winegrowers, “cleaning the barrels under the watchful eye of our beautiful Pic Saint-Loup” or even with the estate itself or its wines through a metonymic effect. Take, for example, the photo of a glass of wine in front of Pic Saint-Loup, with the caption: “We’ve always told you that our wines are the best reflection of our fascinating terroir”. Pic Saint-Loup is thus enlisted to promote wine as a common good open to all, as a famous vineyard with an international reputation and also as an inspiring natural site.

3.3.2. *Vines: nature personified*

The vines are photographed from all angles (sky views, fields, vine stocks, shoots, zooms on the leaves, bunches of grapes, etc.). Allegorical formulations are used to illustrate the different phases of vine growth, the vine being seen as a human being. "Fall arrives, the vines fall asleep"; "when spring arrives, the vine cries". Winegrowers watch over this growth with the rhythm of the seasons. Note that frequent publications show grass growing between the rows and at the foot of the stumps. This emphasis on grass can be seen as attention to soil regulation and plant diversity. Photographs of poppies in vineyards can be seen as decorative.

3.3.3. *The heath and wild and cultivated flora: between admiration and use*

Four definitions of nature are used in publications on wild and cultivated flora:

– *an expression of admiration*: most estates post photos of budding trees and wildflowers to celebrate their beauty (photos of the hackberry in front of the farmhouse, arbutus trees, lavender plants, gauras or cistus in bloom). These mark seasonal changes: "The violets will be here soon";

– *a cause-and-effect relationship between the finished product, the wine and the wilderness*: "And of course, the hackberry, which is deliciously present in the aromas of our wines". Wild flora and fruit are also used for promotional purposes to describe the "cuvées": pomegranate, mulberry, arbutus berry, snapdragons;

– *taking into account the use value of natural resources*: the gustatory value of mushrooms, wild asparagus; a biodynamic domain emphasizes the medicinal value of plants used to treat the vines, such as valerian, horsetail and yarrow;

– *decorative operations are also retained*: bottles are presented in the center of twigs, flowers or dead wood or next to bouquets of wild or cultivated flowers. Some compositions are totally disconnected from their territory: lily of the valley for May Day, cactus or roses as decoration for bottle presentation, etc.

3.3.4. *Shrubs and olive trees: biodiversity and crop diversification*

There are many illustrations of the vegetation on or near the estates. On the cover photographs of 14 estates, trees can be seen in two distinct forms: either in the background of the vines or integrated into the vines, which are planted with olive trees or enclosed in small patches by hedges. This seems to show the importance given to trees, hedges and groves in maintaining healthy biodiversity on the estate.

Ten estates publish photographs of olive trees. The estates harvest olives and/or produce several varieties of olive oil. These productions are exploited for commercial purposes, as they are sold at the estate, and the public is encouraged to discover the production process, with, for example, an old-fashioned press demonstration. However, they also have an ecological objective: "We finally took the plunge and planted olive trees on the edge of the plots and around the farmhouse, with the aim of diversifying the cultivation."

3.3.5. *Farm and domestic animals: main characters or extras*

Some estates inscribe their identity in a domestic tradition of sharing resources between the animal and plant worlds. Take the example of a biodynamic domain for example, where the plough horse is the main character on the cover photo, followed by the man holding the plough, with the vines and mountains in the background. This estate features many photographs of farm animals: horses harnessed to carts for tours of the estate, a donkey, a sheepdog driving a flock of sheep grazing in the vineyards.

Sheep are the subject of strong communication in four areas. Kohlmann (2017) describes the role of these animals, which have a strong "sympathy capital" for the general public. They are used to represent a sensitive approach to nature that can sometimes deviate from the scientific objective, as is the case in the communication of the regional national park she studies. Similarly, the many photographs of grazing sheep drinking, of newborns in the vineyard, of moving to new pastures, seem to symbolize an emotional gateway for winegrowers, a lever to encourage the public to visit the estate. However, the use of photographs of sheep is also intended to testify to a symbiotic relationship between living elements and an eco-responsible approach. The winegrowers leave the vines during the "vegetative rest" for grazing of the ewes, which "fertilize the soil". These photographs and incentives are proof that the domain uses no pesticides, fertilizers or LPG-guzzling tractors to plough the vines, which remain grassed over and fertilized by the sheep. They also bear witness to the collaboration and sharing of resources between winegrowers and livestock farmers. The same cannot be said of another estate, which publishes a photograph of a stray sheep in front of its offices, as a surprise, a curiosity.

Other estates publish photographs of pets that move in step with daily activities and are considered to be full-fledged members of the team: Tangor the dog sitting at the foot of the stump, or the one that accompanies the winegrower on his quad bike through the vines; the cat in the middle of the vines: "Even the cat comes to help us with the pruning." Animals also play their part as extras in a composition that seems more specifically promotional, to attract curiosity or show a love of animals: the dog or cat lying at the foot of a glass of wine or a Christmas tree, the portrait of a rooster, "our beautiful Maurice all proud", the domestic rabbit at Easter, with a daisy behind its ear and a glass of wine in front of it.

3.3.6. *Wildlife (birds, frogs, insects): between wonder, beneficial cohabitation and respect for wild nature*

Illustrations and texts relating to wildlife have three dimensions that can be combined: a sense of wonder at the wildlife; an appreciation of the biodiversity of the estate and the sustainable management of this ecosystem; proof of an activity that pre-serves wild nature.

Photographs of a kestrel "paying a visit to the warehouse"; a bird's nest on a vine, described as a "little treasure of the day"; a frog in a winegrower's earth-covered hand; and a grasshopper with the words "spring is on its way" all bear witness to this delight.

Other publications emphasize the welcoming quality of the estate, which shares its resources with wildlife. The vines are appreciated by the birds and the bees: "The birds spent the summer sheltered by the vine leaves. They moved in just in time to be able to harvest"; or again: "We welcome to our vineyards five beehives from our friends", "the bees have a beautiful territory to forage".

Respectful cohabitation and the preservation of wild nature without human interference are also evoked: an insect on a flower, a butterfly gathering lavender, it is "nature reclaiming its rights", "everyone has their own job to do, the bees gather, the violets smell, and for us, it's pruning time".

Finally, three estates show photographs of ladybugs on grapes. Two of them make reference to biodiversity in the text attached to the photo: "Quality control validated by the local fauna"; "The 2021 harvest is over and, as always, that means biodiversity". The importance of ladybugs as vineyard helpers is not explicitly mentioned, however.

3.3.7. *Soil, earth: the matrix*

The importance given to the soil is present in several areas. The publications relate to visits organized to study the terroir, photographs of the crushing of stones, of vine shoots to reincorporate them into the soil, of manure spreading, of vegetable compost. Six estates show photographs of the soil being plowed in preparation for the establishment of a new vine, with close-ups of clods of earth. These publications testify to the importance attached to the relationship with the land, to this resource on which the estate's productions depend, which must "reveal the terroir", and to the need to maintain the mineral and biological fertility of the soil to produce "a unique interaction between mineral and plant".

3.3.8. *Materials and techniques: a behind-the-scenes look at the trade, between tradition and modernity*

Nature is associated with rural tradition and sustainable construction. Restored stone buildings, the enhancement of vaulted cellars, the repair of dry-stone walls and the renovation of a cellar roof with rice straw all bear witness to a respect for heritage, but also to a desire to promote the skills of local people, as close as possible to the material.

With the exception of three pages devoted to promotion and sales with no concrete relationship with nature, subscribers are invited to follow the various stages of the vineyard and winery's work. Some of them are very clearly traditional: "The estate's philosophy is to get as close as possible to the raw material and its terroir", "Here, everything is natural". "Here, it's all about nature"; for example, using horses to work the land. These estates promote the authenticity of their activities: building upkeep, tilling the soil, tending the vines, maturing the wine. Others combine to a greater or lesser extent the use and restoration of old materials, traditional techniques (agropastoralism) and modern technologies. A stone crusher is used to maintain the minerality of the soil. The grapes are harvested by hand, using plastic buckets. Videos and photographs of state-of-the-art bottling lines show the metal and glass of the bottles. For four other estates, on the other hand, modern technology is seen as an ally in lightening the hard work in the fields. They publish photographs of modern tractors in the middle of the vineyards, and one of them even expresses their dismay when they finds themselves obliged to revert to traditional techniques: "When you get up at 4 a.m. to pick the grapes and your press breaks down, and you have to press them the old-fashioned way, what a day!".

It is worth noting that sometimes, in the course of discovering the different stages of wine-making, the subscriber is led to consult content that seems to run counter to any promotional logic. Lacking any aesthetic appeal, these photographs and videos show the backstage workings of the trade, with, for example, the winegrower in boots or bare feet crushing grapes in a vat, or photographs of wine bottles with provisional, rough labels.

3.3.9. *The weather: nature's giver and taker*

Many estates publish a catalog or calendar of photographs of their estate in the rhythm of the four seasons. The weather is mentioned in numerous posts as a determinant of the day's activities. "The weather sets its own timing"; "Cevenol episode [an intense storm in the Mediterranean area] expected tomorrow: olives are being harvested today". The weather also determines the activities offered to the public: "Take advantage of this beautiful blue sky to come and stroll around our estate". Many of the cover illustrations show estates under blue skies, with the occasional cloud reinforcing the impression of fine weather. Others depict a sunset or sunrise over the vines and surrounding vegetation, or the effects of fog in the fields.

The year 2021 was marked by a number of widely cited bad weather events: floods, hail and, above all, a frost episode occurring on the night of April 7 to 8, 2021, which devastated a large part of the Languedoc vineyards. This event is recounted by almost all the winegrowers, with photographs of frozen vines. This calamity is commented on in a variety of ways:

– *an emotional reaction to this harsh blow from nature*: "Immense sadness… We've just lost 80% of the next vintage"; "Fate is relentless"; "curse, after Covid, here comes the frost";

– *an acknowledgment of failure, of dependence, a message of mutual aid and support*: "Nature is beautiful, but hard at the same time. Good luck to all farmers and winegrowers"; "thank you for your messages. The weather is our best ally and our worst enemy";

– *a message of trust in nature, of adaptation*: "The vine froze, the vine grows again. Long live the vine!"

However, when frost arrives at the right time, it is considered beneficial for vines, and appreciated for the beauty it lends to landscapes.

3.4. Diversity of relationships with nature, valuation principles and underlying values

The study of the various actors in the winegrowers' publications has enabled us to understand the richness of the links they maintain with nature. For the vast majority of estates concerned, these nature-related communications go far beyond simple promotion disconnected from the work and production environment. It is now important to characterize the principles of valorization and the underlying values present in the communications of these fields. These relationships between humans and nature also involve links with pruning and harvesting teams, fellow winegrowers and livestock breeders and on-site or remote visitors.

Sabourin (2013) studies the contribution of the principle of reciprocity to the socio-anthropology of rural organizations. He draws on the theory of reciprocity developed by Mauss, who asserts that relationships between people are not only based on "self-interested" exchange, but are also motivated by "the creation and maintenance of social ties", even if the exchange also concerns "economic services" in a logic of reciprocity (p. 150). On the Facebook pages studied, this is evidenced by the large number of photographs of rituals maintained by winegrowers, always in the open air: the end-of-harvest meal, a show put on by the grape-pickers, public participation in the moving the sheep to new pastures… "Our team celebrates the end of the harvest! Even if there's still a lot of work to be done at the winery, we always take the time to share good times." Some of the publications also illustrate the family's personal bond with nature: the couple in the vineyard, balancing in front of the barrels; the mother leaning over her child, teaching him how to hold the pruning shears.

We note that on the Facebook pages of three estates, nature is rarely mentioned. When it is mentioned, it is purely decorative. The winegrowers are thus intuitively constructing a narrative mode, in which they establish a disembodied link between nature and their activity. Take the example of a winery that makes no mention of the frost episode of April 8, 2021, but publishes an aesthetically pleasing photograph of ice sculptures on the ground, stating: "At the moment, temperatures are reaching −8 degrees. Enough to create beautiful ice sculptures." This aestheticization of nature, in the difficult context of the profession, gives it an artificial aspect.

As for the other 22 domains, reciprocal relationships with nature manifest themselves in different ways. Sabourin identifies three elementary structures of reciprocity in the farmer–nature relationship that are still manifest today:

> – a) the binary relationship of interdependence (face-to-face) between the farmer and the land-living environment;
>
> – b) the binary relationship of sharing parcels of this land and (limited) resources with other living beings: plants, animals and, of course, other human beings who produce, use or consume the land and its resources;
>
> – c) the ternary relationship of the transmission of natural heritage to future generations and the preservation or enhancement of this heritage (Sabourin 2013, p. 251).

A cross-sectional study of the various nature actants enrolled, coupled with an analysis of the publication activities of each page over the course of a year, confirms and refines this typology.

The binary relationship of interdependence between the viticultural team and nature is evoked on the vast majority of pages. This relationship can be emotional: disappointment, despair after the frost, joy at the regrowth of buds. It can also be aesthetic: admiration, wonder, a feeling of well-being, of ecstasy. Nature gives and takes: "Here, everything is nature".

The binary relationship of sharing the land and its resources with other living beings is also present in winegrowers' publications. The face-to-face relationship with nature manifests itself first and foremost in the importance attached to the production of what might be referred to as "agro-environmental services" (Sabourin 2013). This technical mediation of the winegrower is reflected in the search for ways to ensure a harmonious cohabitation between wild nature and the vine. The relationship with nature is also mediated by technical and even experimental know-how in the accompaniment and maintenance of nature, either by mobilizing natural resources as a priority (crushing stones, vine shoots, composts, herbal infusions for treatment) or by sharing resources with fauna (sheep, bees, birds, insects) and flora (grass, hedges, groves, olive trees) so as to maintain biodiversity on the estate and in the environment. This binary relationship then takes on a collective form, in the sharing and cooperation between farmers or breeders: beekeeper, sheep farmer.

Other forms of relationship with nature are part of a ternary reciprocity, as they appeal more directly to responsibility and a sense of justice. These are fully integrated into the final human–nature relationship highlighted in Sabourin's typology. For some estates, this unilateral ternary relationship takes the form of a moral duty to maintain a historical heritage in order to pass it on to future generations. For others, this heritage is intangible, and it is the awareness of the importance of a small farm and the richness of an artisanal know-how respectful of nature that must be safeguarded, passed on from one generation to the next, but also supported by the public at the time of lockdown: "Save your winemaker, order a box of wine and drink at home."

We have thus drawn up a typology of interactional relationships with nature: interdependence, sharing, ternary reciprocity, involving human and non-human actants.

We now continue the analysis to distinguish the explicit or underlying values expressed by these different domains. To do this, we refer to convention theory, derived from pragmatic sociology. Boltanski and Thévenot (1991) and then Boltanski and Chiapello (1999) established a typology of seven cities, or models of consensus. In each city, communications and explicit or implicit justifications for qualities or ways of doing things refer to a common value deemed superior, called a common superior principle, and to explicit or implicit rules. Each of these seven cities is therefore a model of consensus, each with its own specific reference values (domestic, civic, fame, market, inspiration, industrial and project). None of these "classic" cities sets up nature as a common superior principle. Hence, given societal evolution, the emergence of a new city, a new order of justification, sometimes called a "green city", sometimes an "ecological city", or a "city of sustainable development", is under debate (Lafaye and Thévenot 1993; Latour 1995; Godard 2004; Mermet 2006; Rougemont 2017). No scientific consensus has yet been established to characterize this potential new city.

However, according to these authors, nature has already crept in, gradually infiltrating existing cities. Lafaye and Thévenot (1993, p. 496), for example, envisage the possibility of "nature being shaped into different orders of legitimate justification that have already been tried and tested". Latour (1995) points out that empirical work validates the interpretation of a "solvable ecology in other cities". As for Godard (2004, p. 308), he points out that "the plurality of orders has an obvious consequence, which is to construct different concrete worlds. There is no longer a single, unambiguous way of describing nature and the environment. Each order has its own representation of nature". He summarizes the ways in which nature is inscribed in already constituted cities (pp. 308–311).

Drawing on the work of these four authors, we can now identify the different "natures" that dominate winegrowing estates, and which contribute to the uniqueness of their communication. It should be pointed out here that we have excluded from the following typology the three wineries that make little or no reference to nature in their publications. Five major representations of the values attributed to nature can thus be identified. There are also hybrid forms between the different instances of the models identified and briefly described below.

The wine estate of "inspired nature" exalts the beauty of landscapes, and the intimate aesthetic and emotional connection with nature. Nature is art, an Eden, a source of wonder whose beauty should be celebrated. It combines art and nature, offering art exhibitions and vineyard walks in which artistic sculptures sublimate the landscape.

The wine estate of "domestic nature" is part of a historical tradition, of the upkeep of heritage, all in one piece, both handed down and to be handed down. It distinguishes between wild and domestic nature in a hierarchy of proximity. For example, farm animals and domestic pets are the first to be valued. The stages of agricultural work are ritualized and open to the public (new pasture days, harvest immersion days, etc.).

For the *"civic nature" wine estate*, nature must be made accessible to as many people as possible. In addition to inviting subscribers to discover their territory, these winegrowers are also keen to share their knowledge of the natural world around them, sharing their "little secrets" so that everyone can enjoy it to the fullest (when and where to find wild asparagus, mushrooms, how to recycle vine shoots into decorative objects, etc.).

The "industrial nature" wine estate enhances the work process in one of two dimensions: either the valorization of nature through transformation, the stages of wine maturing, or the natural resource to be exploited and maintained, the working of the soil and vines, the experimentation of treatment by plants. However, some wine estates combine these two dimensions. The viticulturist becomes a scientist and sometimes a teacher, ensuring that subscribers gain knowledge of these technical processes.

The wine estate "famous for nature" boasts the renowned beauty of its landscapes, site and buildings, all of which contribute to its celebrity, with this natural splendor earning it national and even international renown.

3.5. Conclusion

To conclude, we note that on the majority of pages, winegrowers do not follow Facebook's "pre-scriptions". Their practice with the apparatus is far from conforming to professional standards in community management, yet their pages testify to their strong relationship with nature, inherent to their activity. The activity of the Facebook account of the domain allows them to promote a difficult professional activity, showing the different elements of nature with which they deal on a daily basis. A transversal analysis of the Facebook pages, coupled with the in-depth study of each of them, enabled us to identify, beyond standardized forms, a diversity of methods of expression of the relationship of winegrowers with nature, as well as the specific values carried by each of these wine estates. Thus, in our study, the digital tools allow the expression of the relationship with nature and the values that the winegrowers attribute to it. However, these communications, even if they can contribute to sensitizing the public by immersion in a sometimes raw, sometimes sublimated experience, are not conducive to informational links, and above all generate emotional reactions. These expressions cannot be dissociated from the digital device in which they are deployed. The importance of these socio-technical choices is discussed further by Kohlmann in the next chapter.

3.6. References

Akrich, M. (1987). Comment décrire les objets techniques ? *Techniques et Culture*, 9, 49–64.

Akrich, M., Callon, M., Latour, B. (2006). *Sociologie de la traduction : textes fondateurs*. Presses des Mines, Paris.

Boltanski, L. and Chiapello, E. (1999). *Le nouvel esprit du capitalisme*. Gallimard, Paris.

Boltanski, L. and Thévenot, L. (1991). *De la justification. Les économies de la grandeur*. Gallimard, Paris.

Callon, M. (2006). Sociologie de l'acteur réseau. In *Sociologie de la traduction : textes fondateurs*, Akrich, M., Callon, M., Latour, B. (eds). Presses des Mines, Paris, 267–276.

Cardon, D. (2019). *Culture numérique*. Presses de Sciences Po, Paris.

Georges, F. (2008). L'identité numérique dans le web 2.0. *Le mensuel de l'Université*, 27.

Godard, O. (2004). De la pluralité des ordres, les problèmes d'environnement et de développement durable à la lumière de la théorie de la justification. *Géographie, économie, société*, 3(6), 303–330.

Granjon, F. (2012). *Reconnaissance et usages d'internet : une sociologie critique des pratiques de l'informatique connectée*. Presses des Mines, Paris.

Heïd, M.C. and De Lavergne, C. (2017). Pratiques d'amateurs en animation de communautés sur Facebook dans le domaine de la vitiviniculture. *Communiquer*, 19 [Online]. Available at: http://journals.openedition.org/communiquer/2135 [Accessed 20 May 2022].

Kohlmann, É. (2017). Gérer/aimer : Communication et nature dans le parc naturel régional du Pilat. *Questions de communication*, 32, 51–74 [Online]. Available at: https://doi.org/10.4000/questionsdecommunication.11432 [Accessed 20 May 2022].

Lafaye, C. and Thévenot, L. (1993). Une justification écologique ? Conflits dans l'aménagement de la nature. *Revue française de sociologie*, 34(4), 495–524 [Online]. Available at: https://www.persee.fr/doc/rfsoc_0035-2969_1993_num_34_4_4283 [Accessed 20 May 2022].

Latour, B. (1995). Moderniser ou écologiser. A la recherche de la "septième" cité. *Écologie politique*, 13, 5–27.

Lipovetsky, G. and Serroy, J. (2016). *L'esthétisation du monde*. Gallimard, Paris.

Mermet, L. (2006). La cité écologique : droit de cité pour la nature et les environnementalistes. *ENGREF Conférence du cycle Recherche Environnementale sur la société*. Montpellier.

Peeters, H. and Charlier, P. (1999). Contributions à une théorie du dispositif. *La Revue Hermès*, 25, 15–23.

Rougemont, E. (2017). Un monde à (re)trouver ? Essai en faveur d'une cité verte. *Pensée plurielle*, 2(45), 31–46.

Sabourin, É. (2013). La réciprocité Homme-Nature et les dérives de son abandon. *Revue du MAUSS*, 42, 49–62.

4

Forms of Linking with Nature and with Others through a Digital Device: "Let Them Know and Participate"

Figure 4.1. *What does digital technology change for biodiversity observation and participation? Émilie Kohlmann (2022). For a color version of this figure, see www.iste.co.uk/kohlmann/linking.zip*

Chapter written by Émilie KOHLMANN.

In this chapter, we present the results of the research carried out as part of the Muséum interface de médiation pour l'environnement et les sciences en Isère (MIMESIS)[1] exploratory project. These results make the transition between Part 1 and the following chapters. Indeed, we propose to explore the various dimensions of the links created through the implementation of a digital device in a very specific area: the Nature-Isère platform[2]. Published online in 2016 and still active to this day, it covers the Isère department and disseminates, promotes and offers a space for sharing information on nature, in the broadest sense. The platform was conceived by the Isère department, the Ligue pour la protection des oiseaux de l'Isère (LPO, French League for the Protection of Birds) and the Museum of Grenoble as a virtual space for creating links with nature, as well as links between communities that are supposedly reluctant to exchange (hunters, naturalists, farmers, etc.). What does its analysis reveal several years after its launch?

To answer this question, we mobilize a methodology inspired by sociosemiotics (Jeanneret 2010; Bonaccorsi 2013): semi-structured interviews, semiotic analysis of the website and discourse analysis. We confronted these findings with knowledge from several disciplines, the MIMESIS project team being made up of researchers from information and communication sciences, ecology and computer science.

We consider the link as something that facilitates contact and enhances information sharing and communication, and also as something that freezes, limits and hinders the latter from a critical perspective[3]. This brings us to Parts 2 (the materiality of links) and 3 (gains and losses in the relationship with others and with nature), which follow on from this collective work.

We show that the links that were stated as the site's objectives at the time of its conception (links to nature and between the communities that use it) may, on the contrary, have been hampered by other underlying links and objectives (injunction to digitalize, institutional partnerships, etc.). We postulate that overly rigid links, while favorable to the realization of a project, can be detrimental to its ability to adapt when the context evolves. Digital technology itself is considered in terms of its technical materiality and is questioned: is the use of digital devices over the past few

1 MIMESIS has benefited from a French government grant managed by the Agence nationale de la recherche under the "Investissement d'avenir" program, reference ANR-15-IDEX-02. Available at: https://mimesisere.hypotheses.org [Accessed 13 July 2022].

2 Available at: www.nature-isere.fr [Accessed 7 March 2022].

3 Based on this definition of link, we draw on its linguistic duality, which highlights its dimensions of linking and constraint. "Définition de LIEN" [Online], available at: www.cnrtl.fr/definition/lien [Accessed 29 March 2022].

years a way to carry out participatory projects in order to raise awareness of nature a solution, or is it a form of unthinking?

We explore these different dimensions in three stages. First, we review the history of the Nature-Isère platform and the context in which it was set up, in order to shed light on the underlying presuppositions regarding digital technology as a link-facilitator. We then analyze the digital device[4] in the way it was initially conceived so as to see what links and modes of participation are actually offered to users and contributors. Finally, we discuss the situation of the platform five years after its launch, and question the choices made and their adaptability.

4.1. The presupposition of digital technology as a link-builder: the Nature-Isère project

The Nature-Isère platform is a project confined to the Isère department, within a relatively short timeframe (2016–present day). The information presented in this chapter is based on a series of semi-structured interviews conducted between 2020 and 2021 with project stakeholders (designers, organizers, partners, etc.), as well as a set of internal documents designed to frame the project from its conception phase (2013–2015)[5].

4.1.1. *The Nature-Isère project: a digital dynamic to create links*

Nature-Isère presents itself as a "participatory platform for all those curious about nature"[6]. Spurred on by a combination of interests for the various partners (Kohlmann and Cambone 2021), in the speeches accompanying its conception, it carries the idea of being a project for a "general public" for whom the biodiversity data of Isère could be popularized whilst providing a framework for their participation:

> We also wanted something that would be participatory, so that we could involve the people who come. And that's why we also imagined that there could be a "post your experiences, post your questions,

4 Here, we mean the device in its technical, pragmatic and discursive dimensions, a device that defines a framework for collective action and makes it possible to reveal power and normative stakes (Larroche 2019). It is interesting to note that the device, like the link, oscillates between freedoms (adaptation of devices) and constraints.

5 Documents consulted: calls for tender, specifications and agreements signed for this project.

6 Site editorial published on 08 February 2022 at: www.nature-isere.fr [Accessed 24 March 2022].

post […]" section. A space open to all those who wanted to post something. Comments or experiences[7].

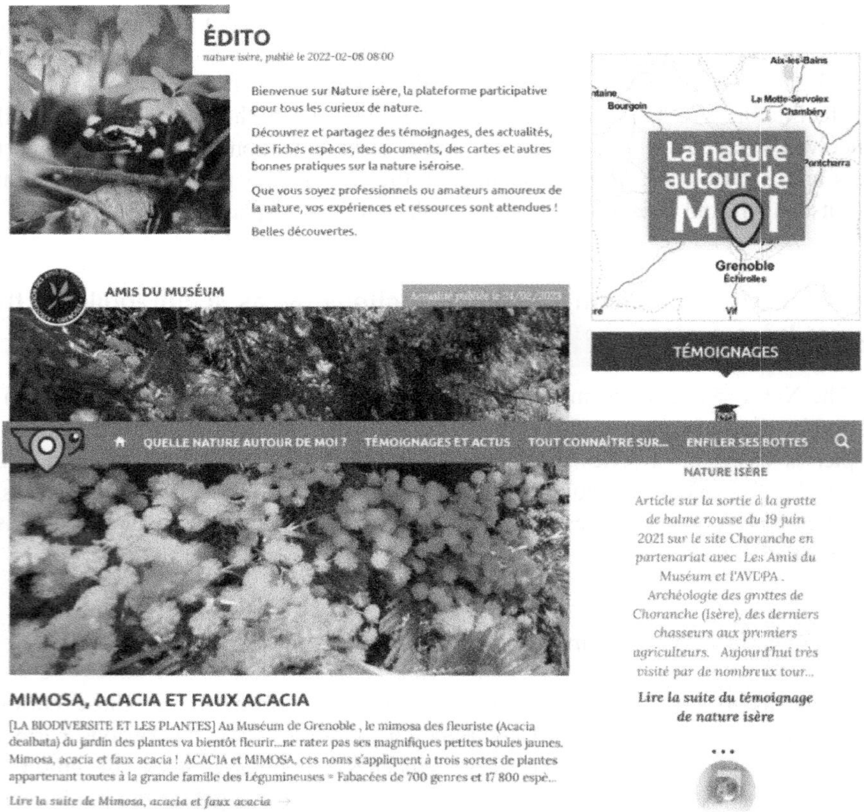

Figure 4.2. *Content of the Nature-Isère homepage and variety of conditions of enunciation: editorial, news, data visualization and testimonies*

The institutional actors involved insist on the convergence of interests for them at that time, around 2013–2014. The LPO Isère and the department were beginning to accumulate a significant amount of biodiversity data, both on sensitive species in Isère and on sensitive natural areas (SNAs). Furthermore, the city of Grenoble, through the Museum of Grenoble, was able to position itself as a mediator and strengthen its role in raising environmental awareness. A co-management agreement was signed in March 2015, an agreement whose preamble recalls the stakes for each of the actors:

---

7 Extract from an interview conducted with one of the partners of the Nature-Isère project during its conception (department).

– for the department, a policy linking SNAs and biodiversity protection in Isère;

– for the city of Grenoble, the use of the Museum of Grenoble as a naturalist awareness-raising tool;

– for the LPO, continuing to collect and valorize biodiversity data.

For stakeholders, these three challenges are reflected in the launch of a digital platform, Nature-Isère, presented as "a collaborative strategy for observing and sharing knowledge by all and for all"[8]. This synergy brought the project forward, and the platform was made available online in its current form in June 2016. A position dedicated to the management and communication of the tool was funded and attached to the museum, initially on a full-time basis until summer 2017, then on a 50% basis until the end of 2019, with the remaining 50% devoted to the museum's overall digital strategy. Initially, this position was dedicated[9] to communication, running the platform and encouraging contributions by, for example, inviting local nature-related organizations to publish content online or meeting "nature enthusiasts" during outings or events:

> She [the person in charge] used to go on outings. She took people out. They crossed paths. We had a birthday party with the elected representatives, everyone was there, and the mountain representative baked a big Nature-Isère cake. We invited anyone who wanted to come. There were about a hundred of us. We all ate the cake together. For me, it was really a human thing[10].

In its conception, Nature-Isère is already a part of a whole range of links at different levels, but always with the vocation of extending and multiplying these links: links between organizations of various statuses articulated around the same digital project, links between collectives led to meet and exchange within this framework and finally a link to territorialized nature, that of Isère:

> For me, it's a social space, symbolically. I believe in the power of tools like that in symbolism. In other words, at some point, a hunter can post, a guy from the LPO can post, a cook [...] That's it. And refer to

8 Nature-Isère co-management agreement, p. 9.

9 A Twitter account and a Nature-Isère Facebook page have been set up, with 244 and 279 subscribers respectively in 2019.

10 Extract from an interview with one of the partners in the Nature-Isère project during its conception (Museum of Grenoble).

> something else. That's what's missing in today's society for me. The silo is terrible.[11]

As for the choice of the digital, this is not questioned. There is an implicit reality, a leap in thinking, which reveals just how naturalized the use of digital technology is among the actors. It is presented as a natural solution to meet the needs and problems of data collection, mediation between communities in their relationship with nature and with each other, as well as in raising public awareness of environmental protection. The abandonment of support for the platform's animation, made official in 2020 with the nonrenewal of the position in favor of one for a communications officer, acknowledges this implicit fact: the digital device can stand on its own.

4.1.2. *The digital injunction for partners: linking data*

During the period that gave rise to the Nature-Isère project, a whole range of factors led the three partners to develop and systematize their use of digital technology, particularly the proliferation of biodiversity data in heterogeneous databases and a desire to modernize and open it up to the public.

In 2009, an audit of the Museum of Grenoble revealed that it was "lagging behind" when it came to digital technology. In 2012, the institution drew up a "digital strategy" document in line with national projects driven by the Conférence permanente des muséums de France (Permanent Conference of Museums in France). It was at this time that a real emulation was created around digital technology and museums. From 2010 to 2014, digital devices were deployed on a massive scale in museums, "testifying to a general movement to integrate digital strategies as a policy for cultural institutions" (Couillard 2017, p. 67). For the Museum of Grenoble, Nature-Isère is a way of responding to these new challenges (Gauthier 2016).

As for the city of Grenoble, digital technology is an important issue for town hall staff and the city has an open data representative, who contributed to Nature-Isère by commissioning a data-visualization project: "What Kind of Nature Is Around Me?". The following interactive map can be used to locate rare or emblematic species close to the user's location using a smartphone.

---

11 Extract from an interview with one of the partners in the Nature-Isère project during its conception (Museum of Grenoble).

Figure 4.3. *Nature-Isère's "What Kind of Nature Is Around Me?". Map: the circle indicates the location of the potential observer*

During this time, the LPO, for its part, was rethinking the operating methods of its naturalist data collections and sought to improve its transition to digital devices designed for the "general public". It has had a website (Faune-Isère[12]) since 2010, and the Naturalist app continued this trend in 2017:

> When the Nature-Isère project came along, Faune-Isère was just gaining momentum. And we were wondering how to make the most of all the knowledge that had been accumulated in this database, but which was of interest to those in the know, because you *already had to* know… Faune-Isère is a shared notebook, because you can share it with others. It's a little improved, because you can add sound and photographs, but in the end it's aimed at people with a certain level of competence.[13]

12 The www.faune-isere.org website is managed by Biolovision and data are uploaded internationally at: https://data.biolovision.net [Accessed 24 March 2022].

13 Extract from an interview with one of the partners in the Nature-Isère project during its conception (LPO).

Finally, at the departmental level, Nature-Isère was one of the first platforms dedicated to nature on this scale, but very quickly, platforms on a regional scale[14], then on a departmental[15] scale, emerged, demonstrating the extent to which digital technology was on people's minds between 2010 and 2015, but without any real coordination between projects:

> Basically, we thought we were the first in the Isère region to come up with this kind of media that would bring everything together, and since then others have sprung up [...].[16]

The Nature-Isère project was conceived in a particularly favorable context for the use of digital technology in the cultural, political and environmental fields. Whether it is the injunction to modernize museums through digital means, or the idea of democratizing naturalist practices with the development of digital tools (Julliard 2017), we can see how actors then see digital technology as a facilitator of links and exchanges between actors, and how little this link is questioned.

This creative context in favor of digital technology, which tends to see it as a natural solution for building links between communities and with nature, has not been limited to the creation of a digital tool, but has also influenced its form, navigation choices and contribution methods.

4.2. Analysis of the system: creating links through digital technology?

The Nature-Isère platform is examined here from two main angles. First, we look at the semiotization of the link to nature and to others on the platform. We look at the navigation offered on the site, as well as the elements that reveal the implicit link between digital and contribution, whether online or in the field (Bonaccorsi 2013). We mobilize the notion of "architext" (Jeanneret and Souchier 1999) as the way in which modalities of writing and ways of acting are delegated to inscription media. We then review the interviews conducted with the site's contributors to see the ways in which they understand this device and take their place within it.

---

14 For example, the Pôle d'information flore-habitats-fonge: www.biodiversite-auvergne-rhone-alpes.fr/pifh/ [Accessed 22 June 2022].

15 The Espaces Naturels Sensibles de l'Isère platform: https://biodiversite.isere.fr/ [Accessed 24 March 2022].

16 Extract from an interview with one of the partners in the Nature-Isère project during its conception (department).

4.2.1. *A platform that embodies the implicit link between digital devices and contributions in the field*

4.2.1.1. *Navigation from information transmission to contribution*

The design and organization of the platform's sections are conceived by the designers as a graduated way of bringing the "general public" to contribute. The main menu is designed so that "from left to right, you [move] more and more towards something expert"[17]. In this way, we imagine the audience of the various sections as becoming progressively more competent as they acquire the knowledge transmitted on this site.

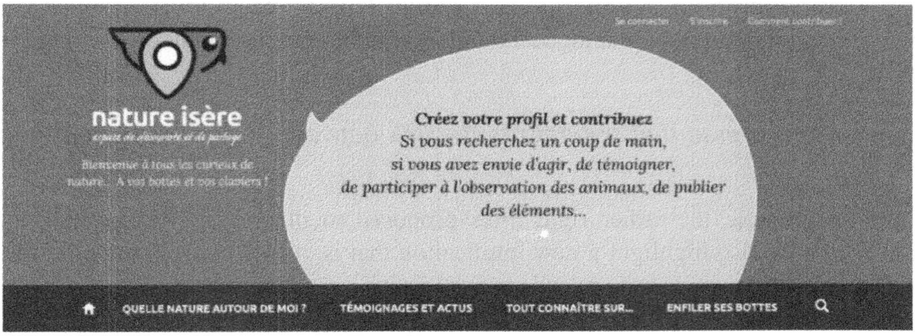

Figure 4.4. *From discovering "nature around me" to "putting on your boots" (nature-isere.fr home page [Accessed 14 February 2022])*

In this way, we find similarities with the place given to citizens in participatory science schemes, where their role is defined by science professionals and often limited to crowdsourcing tasks (Fages 2021). In the field of environmental awareness, this type of scheme is similar to those designed for the International Year of Biodiversity (Kohlmann 2016), in which public participation came only after a learning and skills-building stage, while remaining very marginal and individual. The injunction to citizen participation is regularly mobilized through various figures such as the drop of water or the legend of the hummingbird[18]: "I'm doing my bit".

As for the link between different communities of nature practices – this "digital agora" evoked by the actors during the interviews – it is severely limited by the

17 Extract from an interview with one of the partners in the Nature-Isère project during its conception (Museum of Grenoble).

18 For a critique of this apolitical use of this legend, see Lindgaard (2016).

choices that presided over the technical setup. While it is possible to post testimonials or news items, it is impossible to comment on posts or interact directly with other contributing members online, unless you are registered on the platform, which can be a hindrance, since less than 1% of users register. Like the transmission of naturalist knowledge, Nature-Isère remains a simple repository of testimonials, without really enabling the desired shift towards a "symbolic social space"[19]; in the words of the actors, "a pretty bric-a-brac where everyone could find what they wanted"[20].

In the platform's rubric, as in the technical settings chosen, the links to nature are highly framed and taken from a strongly naturalistic perspective: knowledge of species, places, observation protocols, etc., and the links to others are also limited to a precise framework: that of sharing testimonials without the possibility of exchange or debate[21].

4.2.1.2. *A discourse that naturalizes the link between digital technology and the field*

While we note the rather rigid links proposed to others and to nature in the device, we can also highlight a new implication that is very present in the platform: the fact that digital contribution leads to participation on the ground.

The heading "putting on your boots" is particularly representative of this leap, as we can read the following verbatim: "from keyboard to boots and back again: invite yourself into the field". With this slogan, we see a clear separation of the two forms of participation: digital and physical, as well as the reinforcement of an impression of fluidity in the transition from one to the other. The site's contribution, the "sharing of your discoveries", as well as the (digital) sharing of observations made in the field or concrete actions carried out to protect nature, actions which also combine the planting of pollarded trees in a park[22] or the fact of "transforming your terrace into a scientific laboratory" using the Bird Lab app[23]: they are all presented on the same level.

19 Extract from an interview with one of the partners in the Nature-Isère project during its conception (Museum of Grenoble).

20 Extract from an interview with one of the partners in the Nature-Isère project during its conception (department).

21 Here, we come back to one of the choices we made when designing the site, namely to create a "positive" space for nature, free from militancy and controversy. Comments are moderated.

22 Published on 12 October 2021 by Grenoble-Alpes Métropole.

23 Posted on 15 November 2019 by Siana.

Figure 4.5. *The "putting on your boots" section, creating an implicit link between digital contribution and engagement*

Thus, Nature-Isère was initially conceived as a space to foster links with nature, as well as exchanges between communities, and yet we observe a rigidity in the system in the forms of paths proposed, from the most profane to the most expert and, in the models of knowledge of nature, as well as a double implication regarding the participation of the citizens: they need to know this in order to contribute, and the use of digital technology facilitates their participation both online and in the field.

4.2.2. *A platform that creates links between contributors?*

To complete this semiological analysis, in the spring of 2021, we conducted eighteen 30 minute to 1 hour semi-directive interviews with the contributors of the Nature-Isère platform, in order to gain a better understanding of their view of the object, their reasons for contributing, as well as their obstacles. Getting in touch with the people registered on the platform was a complex task. Of the almost 370 people registered (2019 figures[24]), many had registered under a pseudonym, abandoned their account, changed their email address, etc. Furthermore, while an internal report from the Museum of Grenoble shows 48,000 users in 2019, we see that the proportion of registered users is very low, less than 0.8%.

24 The year 2019 can be taken as a benchmark, as it saw the most contributions posted in the "Testimonies" section: 73 contributions. The year 2020 saw this movement come to a halt, probably due to the health crisis, with just four contributions.

4.2.2.1. *Who contributes?*

The first observation is the limited contribution of this "general public", who are encouraged to also share their nature experiences. Only two people can be qualified as non-professionals, i.e. not working for a protected natural area or a local nature protection association (a very large minority). Furthermore, these two people cannot be considered as not acculturated to ecological issues, since they have all undergone some form of training in the scientific field. They all show a strong interest in the environment and natural sciences:

> I'm curious about nature, I want to discover and learn about everything that surrounds me in terms of flora and fauna, to follow their evolution and know how to act to respect and protect them.[25]

An appetite for knowledge is a common denominator for these contributors, whatever their status. The knowledge they wish to share is the driving force behind their long-term commitment, a form of "cognitive passion", as Roux et al. (2013) describe it:

> It's this thirst for knowledge that drives me forward, so that I can pass on this information at a naturalistic event. [...] It's this reciprocity that drives me to contribute: I want to learn more and I want to give more, that's the leitmotiv of my actions.[26]

There is another observation to be drawn from these interviews: how the site's participative dimension is downplayed compared to its transmissive dimension. The platform is mostly presented as a knowledge portal, a documentary space. Nature-Isère is described as a site providing access to knowledge about local nature, whether through the species sheets or the various news and testimonials published. In practice, users connect to find verified and reliable data, and value the fact that they can easily find this type of information for the "general public".

Finally, to conclude on the conditions of contribution, we note a difficulty among the most "lay" contributors – or those who consider themselves as such – in feeling legitimized to publish on the site. We find a strong differentiation between "knowers" and "non-knowers". The latter mentioned their apprehension about sharing content on the same digital space as seasoned experts, and have brought to light an aspect that had been completely erased by the site's designers: the symbolic obstacle of legitimacy. Some even admitted that they had never clicked on the "Contribute" tab, not believing they had the capacity to do so. The ergonomics of the site itself maintains this brake by moderating contributions, subjecting them to

25 Extract from an interview with a Nature-Isère contributor.

26 Extract from an interview with a Nature-Isère contributor.

"validation" and soliciting, in a jumbled but graded form of expertise, the "finest testimonials" from "the curious, teachers, hunters, students, artists, farmers, entrepreneurs, scientists, naturalists, enthusiasts, managers of sensitive natural areas, etc."[27]. Furthermore, unlike ordinary citizens, contributors attached to a nature conservation or awareness-raising organization are regularly approached by the Nature-Isère coordinator, who asks them to produce publications. They are therefore also more legitimate to publish.

4.2.2.2. *What type of link mobilizes?*

The latter contributors more readily identified the platform as a way of linking not between individuals but between organizations working to raise awareness and preserve nature in the Isère region:

> The idea was to create a link – we're more of a regional platform – we try to create a link with more local platforms for network animation, but also for information dissemination, we always try to find a synergy of actions with these local observatories or these platforms for information dissemination[28].

For them, Nature-Isère is a way of getting to know potential partners in a specific area and identifying them so that they can then make contact and set up joint projects. In this sense, the platform acts as a directory for identifying actors. The site has a dedicated page: "Find an actor".

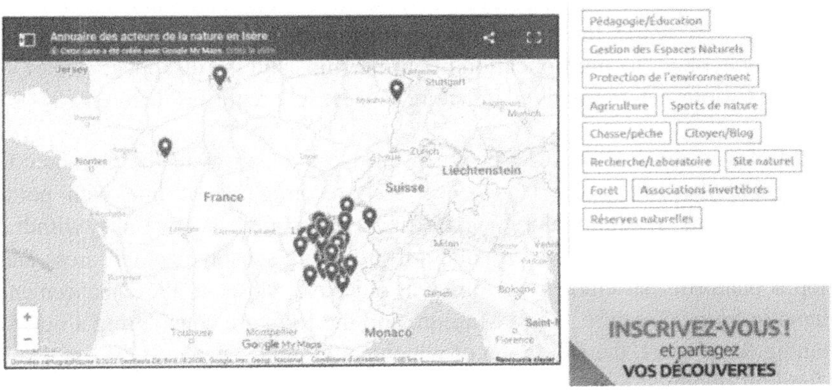

Figure 4.6. *Cartographic representation of nature stakeholders in Isère and filters to refine the search*

27 Extract from the "Testimonies" page. Available at: www.nature-isere.fr/temoignages-et-actus/testimonials [Accessed 25 March 2022].

28 Extract from an interview with a Nature-Isère contributor.

The links proposed here are rather succinct and basic. The digital possibilities are reduced to a directory and a means of communicating the activities of organizations. The mediations correspond to the archetypal database model: a few texts presenting the system, a great deal of work on documentary mediation, a scripted interface, no anticipated usage scenarios (Cambone 2019).

As for the contributors' feelings, many of them express a form of frustration in seeing their socialization severely limited online and little pursued in the field:

> It would be more about making a more human connection than through a site, finding each other again, making common places, listing things together, taking tours of existing places or that sort of thing. Being outside with lots of people, sharing our knowledge verbally rather than through a screen.[29]

Here again, as in the analysis of the system, we find the missing link between digital technology and the reality of face-to-face social interaction.

4.3. Institutions, representations and digital technology: the limiting link

4.3.1. *Partnership links and institutional expectations*

From a closer analysis of the platform and the various discourses that accompany it, we can see that while the initial project that presided over the conception of Nature-Isère evoked the multiplication of partnerships and the disappearance of silos among the various actors involved in nature in Isère, the reality is different.

The links established in 2013 between the Isère department, the Grenoble City Museum and the LPO Isère have since been reconfigured in line with political developments and institutional projects. The department has gradually withdrawn from the project to pursue its own policy of protecting sensitive natural areas and to develop a platform that embodies a different objective, closer to the enhancement of emblematic forms of nature[30]. The Museum and the LPO are considering a new way of running the project, the follow-up of which could be delegated to the association. The funding obtained to launch the site in 2016 has not been renewed. The initial alignment of objectives and the strong links which had anchored the site and created a dynamic around it have proven to be a burden in the long run, making it difficult for it to evolve over time.

29 Extract from an interview with a Nature-Isère contributor.

30 The site is available at: https://biodiversite.isere.fr/ [Accessed 28 March 2022].

In addition, the partners' desire for a common framework for the system led to an institutionalization of citizen participation, which turned out to be negative (Schiffino et al. 2013). The laymen or "general public" did not find the framework favorable to their participation.

Similarly, this digital requisitioning (Jeanneret 2014; Sandri 2016) seems to have been undertaken with little hindsight and little questioning when the platform was launched. It is often evoked as a solution, whether for biodiversity observation, for which it claims to shorten temporalities and facilitate data entry (Charvolin 2019), or for cultural and scientific mediation (Couillard 2017), where digital technology is seen as a facilitator of public understanding of these issues, as well as of its online participation.

However, as we have seen, this injunction to use digital technology must have a purpose, a reason, and be framed and thought through in the overall relationship with the objectives and the field. Otherwise, it can be a source of exclusion for certain forms of public participation and "marginalize those who don't use it" (Jeanneret 2014), and those whose uses have not been thought through, or too quickly, by institutions.

4.3.2. *The link between knowledge and participation*

This underestimation of the general public's participation can also be explained by the persistence of a representation of the general public as external to expertise, in this case, naturalist expertise. The "What type of nature is around me?" tab, which explicitly targets the general public, is designed for "the dad who rides his bike with his kids and wants to talk to them about nature"[31]. Instead of reading species sheets – that is the next step – the user can locate themself in the Isère region and see the "top 5 most-watched species" and the "top 5 most emblematic species"[32]. The user is then free to continue their discovery by consulting the corresponding species sheets.

Here we come back to the deficit model criticized by Irwin (1995), which presupposes that the public is ignorant to science, an ignorance that needs to be overcome to enable us to make reasoned choices and understand the scientific and technological challenges facing our societies. In the field of nature, and more particularly biodiversity, this vision of a public with little knowledge, but with an interest in science and the ability to participate once it has grasped the issues, is particularly marked (Fages 2021). In the same vein, it is considered to be natural that involvement in data observation systems, for example, should have the effect of raising public

31 This figure of the family man was echoed by several actors during the interviews.

32 On data processing issues, see Kohlmann and Cambone (2021).

awareness of nature conservation (Johnson et al. 2014), a major awareness-raising objective for scientists studying biodiversity (Takacs 1996).

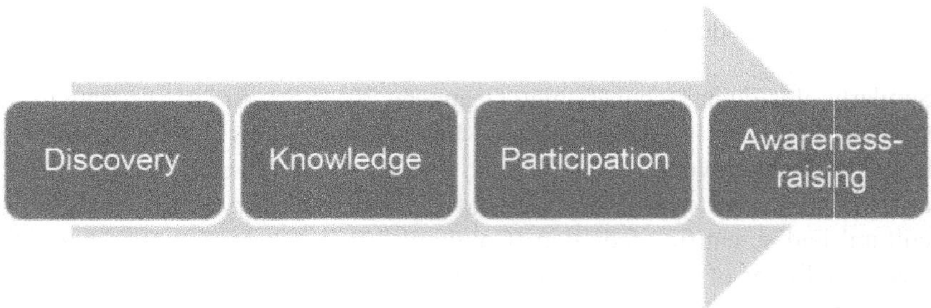

Figure 4.7. *Linear representation of the public's role in Nature-Isère*

Lastly, this representation of the public conceived in a particular relationship to science is also caught up in various representations linked to digital technology and an imaginary of contribution:

> The ubiquity of the Internet and digital technologies has given rise to the development of new practices of communication and exchange marked by the ideals of a participatory culture and oriented towards an imaginary of contribution (Heaton et al. 2018).

The digital world is supposed to encourage individual participation. However, talking about digital technology is meaningless in itself, since a technical dimension is necessarily present, made up of choices and evolutions, and the construction of a tool is also a way of freezing the modalities of participation and therefore the capacities of individuals to create links between themselves as well as with nature.

4.3.3. *The materiality of the digital link*

Finally, we look at the digital injunction by focusing on the materiality of a digital device, and its capacity to evolve. In the field of participation, procedures and devices tend to standardize the possibilities of action.

> In fact, the editorial logic put in place by the platforms, just as much as the "action" of the members of the community, does not necessarily lead to openness and cultural diversity (Rouzé 2015).

It would be absurd to think of online participation without observing the elements that structure it, and those which are part of prescribed uses: heading, registration, validation, comments, etc. However, beyond these ergonomic aspects, it would also be naïve to think of digital technology as a fluid space with the capacity to evolve. The Nature-Isère study is another example of this. Various partners have joined forces to set up this project, and companies have managed the IT dimension, whether for the Web platform or for the biodiversity data sharing modalities, their formatting, selection, input into international databases, etc. Although the need to develop the platform seems to be shared five years after it went online, the fact remains that it is complex:

> I think that since the platform was created in 2016, there have been a lot of evolutions both technologically and in the way we use these kinds of tools. I think that there's a lot of work to be done to review the architecture and perhaps be more on social networks. [...] On Facebook, there are ornithology groups, naturalist groups, etc. that exist and are very active. There are people who take a photo of something they've seen in their garden and ask what it is, or just say "I saw that and it's interesting", and that's something you don't find at all on Nature-Isère[33].

To switch a platform initiated in 2013–2014, conceived as a *responsive design website* but not as a mobile application – for reasons linked to the cost of the project – to a model inspired by social networks or the naturalist applications[34] that already existed at the time, using the Semantic Web or artificial intelligence seems extremely complex. Digital technology, conceived as an absolute, was proposed as a solution for creating links between nature stakeholders and nature itself, notably through biodiversity data. The digital system in place shows the limits of the choices made at the time. The links between the databases, the technical choices made, and the architectures put in place make it difficult to achieve the expected changes.

4.4. Conclusion

This chapter closes this first part on the possibility of extending links through digital devices.

Designed to foster links between the various nature communities in Isère, as well as the "general public's" link with nature, Nature-Isère reveals the darker side of strong ties. If they are favorable to the realization of a project, as here with the department–Museum–LPO partnership, they can also lack the fluidity to adapt.

33 Extract from an interview with one of the project's partners (Museum of Grenoble).

34 One example is the Pl@ntNet application, which launched a Web version in 2011 and a mobile app in 2013, while integrating deep learning in 2015.

The same observation that can be made about the links between actors can also be made about the technical choices made at the time and their ability to evolve without any funding.

Finally, despite the incentive to contribute, the proposed link to nature keeps it at a distance, reifying it as something observable and manageable. We are back to the classic paradigms surrounding the public in the sciences, and particularly in the environmental field. The public must learn to follow protocols, and its contribution is rather maintained on the side of the “little hands” of science: the ones who collect data on a massive scale for scientists, and who, in so doing, naturally become aware of the need to protect nature.

The extensive display of social links in the design of this project is in fact undermined by the choices made and limits the ability of certain elements to connect. In this case, it is interesting to see the double movement contained in the notion of link: the positive link that facilitates networking, and the link that hinders and limits.

At the end of this presentation, it therefore seems essential to go further into the role of digital technology in the production of data on nature, and to question the materiality of these links that are constructed by the various applications, which are the subject of the following chapter.

4.5. References

Bonaccorsi, J. (2013). Approches sémiologiques du web. In *Manuel d'analyse du web en sciences humaines et sociales*, Barats, C. (ed.). Armand Colin, Paris, 125–146 [Online]. Available at: http://www.cairn.info/manuel-d-analyse-du-web-en-sciences-humaines--9782200286279-page-125.htm [Accessed 17 February 2020].

Cambone, M. (2019). La médiation patrimoniale à l'épreuve du “numérique” : médiation patrimoniale, médiation documentaire et médiation expérientielle. *Revue française des sciences de l'information et de la communication* [Online]. Available at: http://journals.openedition.org/rfsic/5689 [Accessed 6 July 2019].

Charvolin, F. (2019). *Les sciences participatives au secours de la biodiversité : Une approche sociologique*. Éditions Rue d'Ulm, Paris.

Couillard, N. (2017). Les community managers des musées français : identité professionnelle, stratégies numériques et politique des publics. PhD thesis, Avignon University and Université du Québec à Montréal, Avignogn and Quebec [Online]. Available at: https://tel.archives-ouvertes.fr/tel-01715055 [Accessed 24 March 2022].

Fages, V. (2021). Participer à la science : l'enjeu de la production de connaissances du XVIIe siècle à nos jours. *NOV'AE* [Online]. Available at: https://hal.archives-ouvertes.fr/hal-03511884 [Accessed 25 March 2022].

Gauthier, C. (2016). Quel rôle pour les muséums dans la production et la diffusion de la connaissance naturaliste à l'époque d'Internet ? *La Lettre de l'OCIM. Musées, Patrimoine et Culture scientifiques et techniques*, 166, 5–12.

Heaton, L.D., Millerand, F., Dias da Silva, P., Proulx, S. (2018). *La reconfiguration du travail scientifique en biodiversité : pratiques amateurs et technologies numériques*. Les Presses de l'Université de Montréal, Montreal.

Irwin, A. (1995). *Citizen Science : A Study of People, Expertise, and Sustainable Development. Environment and Society*. Routledge, London.

Jeanneret, Y. (2010). L'optique du sustainable : Territoires médiatisés et savoirs visibles. *Questions de communication*, 17(1), 59-80.

Jeanneret, Y. (2014). *Critique de la trivialité : les médiations de la communication, enjeu de pouvoir*. Éditions Non Standard, Paris.

Jeanneret, Y. and Souchier, E. (1999). Pour une poétique de l'écrit d'écran. *Xoana*, 6, 97–107.

Johnson, M.F., Hannah, C., Acton, L., Popovici, R., Karanth, K.K., Weinthal, E. (2014). Network environmentalism: Citizen scientists as agents for environmental advocacy. *Global Environmental Change*, 29, 235–245.

Julliard, R. (2017). Science participative et suivi de la biodiversité : l'expérience Vigie-Nature. *Natures Sciences Sociétés*, 25(4), 412–417.

Kohlmann, É. (2016). Communication environnementale et biodiversité dans le Parc naturel régional du Pilat. PhD thesis, University of Reunion Island, Saint-Denis [Online]. Available at: https://tel.archives-ouvertes.fr/tel-01391443 [Accessed 4 March 2022].

Kohlmann, É. and Cambone, M. (2021). Plateforme Nature-Isère. In *Humains et Données : Création, Médiation, Décision, Narration. Actes Du Colloque "Document Numérique et Société", Nancy, 2020*, Simonnot, B., Broudoux, E., Chartron, G. (eds). De Boeck Supérieur, Brussels [Online]. Available at: https://hal.archives-ouvertes.fr/hal-03242713 [Accessed 4 March 2022].

Larroche, V. (2019). *The Dispositif: A Concept for Information and Communication Sciences*. ISTE Ltd, London, and John Wiley & Sons, New York.

Lindgaard, J. (2016). Pierre Rabhi, chantre d'une écologie inoffensive ? Dans la galaxie de la "sobriété heureuse". *Revue du Crieur*, 5(3), 104–119.

Roux, J., Charvolin, F., Dumain, A. (2013). *Passions cognitives : l'objectivité à l'épreuve du sensible*. Archives contemporaines, Paris.

Rouzé, V. (2015). Participatif. Publictionnaire. Dictionnaire encyclopédique et critique des publics [Online]. Available at: http://publictionnaire.huma-num.fr/notice/participatif [Accessed 4 March 2022].

Sandri, É. (2016). Les ajustements des professionnels de la médiation au musée face aux enjeux de la culture numérique. *Études de communication. languages, information, médiations*, 46, 71–86.

Schiffino, N., Garon, F., Cantelli, F. (2013). Visages de la participation et capacités critiques des citoyens. *Politique et Sociétés*, 32(1), 129–142.

Takacs, D. (1996). *The Idea of Biodiversity: Philosophies of Paradise.* Johns Hopkins University Press, Baltimore.

PART 2

Link Materiality and Structure: Generating Data on Nature

5

Explainable Artificial Intelligence for a Better Understanding of Naturalist Data

Figure 5.1. *Explainable artificial intelligence to better understand naturalist data. Source: Julie Polge (2022). For a color version of this figure, see www.iste.co.uk/kohlmann/linking.zip*

Chapter written by Ikram CHRAIBI KAADOUD.

5.1. The need for explainable artificial intelligence for naturalist data

Naturalist data provide a set of information concerning flora, fauna or a natural habitat, such as the location and conditions in which an animal or plant species has been observed. Once analyzed, these data can be used to improve knowledge and protect biodiversity, for example, by studying the distribution of species and their dynamics, drawing up red lists[1] or lists of protected species or drawing up species conservation plans. These invaluable data can be used on a more global scale, i.e. beyond a given habitat that is necessarily local, to work towards the preservation of flora and fauna throughout the world.

As in many fields where data, and by extension the information they carry, are precious, the scientific and technical communities working in artificial intelligence (AI) have taken up the issue of preserving biodiversity, asking themselves how they can contribute to solving the problem: on the one hand, by moving from information to knowledge, and on the other hand, by enlightening the parties normally involved (citizens, associations, politicians, etc.) to better understand and, hopefully, make better decisions regarding the actions to be taken.

AI is a field of computer science that deals with the construction of computer programs inspired by human cognitive abilities so that they can perform tasks such as understanding language, recognizing images, solving problems, making decisions and learning. Such programs, which we refer to as AI systems, are powerful, high-performance tools that have already proven their worth in the field of biodiversity: without being exhaustive, we can here identify AI systems for detecting and identifying animal or plant species from images (Benet et al. 2020), tracking and monitoring the development of marine or terrestrial animal or plant species (Sanchez-Pi et al. 2021; Goëau et al. 2022) and selecting plantation sites for large-scale reforestation automation based on plant health and the presence or absence of weeds (Rollnick et al. 2019). AI systems can also help us to understand changes in a particular ecosystem by monitoring the development of invasive exotic species (Bonnet et al. 2020) or by studying the impact of climate change on forest dynamics by studying the phenology of vegetation (Goëau et al. 2022). They can therefore be means of helping to adapt to these changes and even preventing them (Sanchez-Pi et al. 2020, 2021; Goëau et al. 2022).

AI systems can also be used to raise public awareness on biodiversity issues by generating simulations involving the risks associated with climate change: generating images of flooded neighborhoods or urban areas to raise awareness among residents of such a high-risk zone (Luccioni et al. 2021), modeling a complete meteorological system for the purposes of a video game based on real data, etc.

---

1 A red list is an inventory of plant and animal species that assesses their conservation status.

As a result, AI has been recognized by researchers, companies and civil society as a powerful tool for technological progress and environmental protection. From the issues surrounding smart farming (the use of information and communication technologies in the farm management cycle) to the fight against climate change, AI systems are becoming increasingly important tools for scientists working on these issues (Rollnick et al. 2019; Chukkapalli et al. 2020; Moysiadis et al. 2021).

However, the underlying reasons for the predictions and behaviors of these systems remain largely obscure. “What are the attributes that allow us to classify an animal species in one category rather than another?”, “why does an animal or plant species behave as predicted by an AI system?” or “why is a harvest better or worse than expected?” are all questions that can only be answered by experts in different fields (biology, agriculture or viticulture, for example). Yet, often faced with complex computational models known as “black boxes”, even these may find themselves unable to answer these questions, for a variety of reasons that we detail later in this chapter.

EXplainable AI (XAI[2]) aims to make AI systems, their behavior and predictions understandable for citizens, experts and institutions. Although the questions that XAI seeks to answer have been around for a long time (Shortliffe 1977; Chraibi Kaadoud et al. 2021), the field has become more structured in recent years and is currently continuing in this, particularly with the adoption in 2018 of the General Data Protection Regulation (GDPR) at the European level. This regulation has given rise to a “right to explanation”[3] requiring designers of AI systems to explain their system to any individual or organization who requests it. The term “explaining” refers here to providing information to an audience (e.g. a government agency) in a format that is intelligible and accessible to them about the AI systems used in a specific setting. This may relate to the system’s mechanics (its inner workings), a particular result (the reasons for a recommendation) or the overall behavior of the AI system. Explainable AI can be a tool for understanding naturalistic data and AI systems, but above all, it can be a tool for empowering the target audience.

A better understanding of the repercussions of the actions of each stakeholder (individuals, government bodies, associations, etc.) on the environment, thanks to XAI methods, can lead, for example, to greater awareness of ecological issues and thus better preservation of biodiversity. These XAI tools can therefore be used by experts in naturalist data and related fields, and also contribute to mediation awareness-raising, by linking these data with the general public.

2 The acronym XAI is widely accepted and used by the international scientific and technical communities. For these reasons, the author uses this acronym throughout this chapter.

3 Available at: https://www.cnil.fr/fr/conformite-rgpd-information-des-personnes-et-transparence [Accessed on April 19, 2022].

In this chapter, we propose to define and demystify XAI in the context of naturalist data. First, we present the characteristics of AI. We then describe the field of XAI and its specific features, before moving on to concrete examples of XAI applied to naturalist data. Finally, we discuss the importance of XAI and its impact on the dissemination of scientific and/or technical knowledge, and the link that this field creates between naturalist data, AI systems and individuals and societies.

5.2. Artificial intelligence, machine learning and deep learning definitions and challenges

In order to discuss XAI, we propose to first clarify the concepts of AI and machine learning before addressing the challenges of the field in terms of transparency.

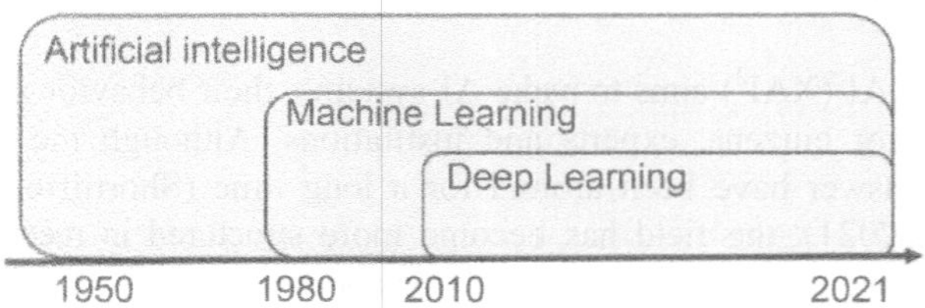

Figure 5.2. *Evolution of the AI field since the 1950s*

5.2.1. *Definitions*

In 1956, Marvin Lee Minsky, one of the founders of the AI field, defined AI as "the construction of computer programs that perform tasks that are, for the time being, more satisfactorily accomplished by human beings, because they require high-level mental processes such as: perceptual learning, memory organization and critical reasoning"[4].

AI is a field of computer science at the crossroads of the cognitive sciences[5]: psychology, mathematics, linguistics and philosophy. The field covers machine

4 COE (2020). History of artificial intelligence. Available at: www.coe.int/en/web/artificial-intelligence/history-of-ai [Accessed November 4, 2022].

5 Cognitive science is a research field that aims to describe, specify, explain and simulate cognitive processes, also known as mental processes, which correspond to all processes involved in acquiring, processing and using information. Cognitive science is itself at the crossroads of several sciences: philosophy, linguistics, anthropology, neuroscience, psychology and computer science.

learning, robotics, game theory, computer vision, natural language processing (NLP) and knowledge and reasoning representation (Lecue et al. 2020). Since the 2010s, the term AI has often been confused with *machine learning* and *deep learning*. However, it is important to distinguish between these three fields. AI is a field made up of sub-fields, each with its own specificities and temporality. Figure 5.2 illustrates the relationship between AI and the sub-domains described in this chapter, and how they appear over time. Note that there are other sub-domains of AI that are not covered here.

Machine learning is based on very general data transformation algorithms that are programmed implicitly from example data or a priori knowledge, enabling them to numerically adapt their parameters by machine learning, gradually reducing the prediction error of the calculation. In other words, it enables machines to learn complex mechanisms approximately, without being explicitly told what to learn. This field has mainly developed since the 1980s, with neural networks, computational architectures inspired by the highly simplified biological principles of the human brain. Artificial neurons are thus computational units inspired by biological neurons, which can be structured into networks, i.e. grouped together and arranged in different ways, so that they can communicate with each other (Rougier 2000). Since the 1980s, other types of computational units have been developed, such as long short-term memory (Hochreiter and Schmidhuber 1997) and its variants (Greff et al. 2016). In terms of architectures, several arrangements are possible (layered, clustered, etc.). The best-known architectures are recurrent networks, feed-forward networks, convolution networks and, since 2017, transformers (Vaswani et al. 2017; Lin et al. 2021).

The most common architecture are forward propagation networks, consisting of an input layer, one or more hidden layers and an output layer, as shown in Figure 5.3. Each layer can have any number of artificial neurons (or other types of computational units). The principle of operation of a neural network is the following: the network receives data on its input layer, propagates them through the hidden layers and provides an output response[6]. Each neuron and each connection is parameterized, and it is the adjustment of all of these parameters that enables extremely diverse and high-performance calculations. An example of this operating principle is the identification of a plant species from a photo. As input, the algorithm receives a photo and analyzes its digital representation through its various layers, in order to provide an output (response) for the species identified in the photo. The Pl@ntNet[7] mobile

6 For more details on how neural networks work, readers can refer to the articles on the Binary blog, an online science outreach blog. Available at: www.lemonde.fr/blog/binaire/2020/09/04/comment-saisir-ce-que-font-les-reseaux-de-neurones/ [Accessed November 17, 2022].

7 The Pl@ntNet project, launched in 2009 with the support of the Agropolis Fondation, is the work of scientists (computer scientists and botanists) within a consortium of several French

app, a free participatory science project on plant biodiversity from a consortium of French scientists, is based on this type of principle in order to perform what is known in AI as a classification task (Barthélémy et al. 2011).

Deep learning is a particular set of machine learning techniques and is distinguished by the fact that it requires more computational power and data for the learning phases as its architecture is heavier.

Indeed, the aim of deep learning methods is to model data at a high level of abstraction. To achieve this, this type of network is generally equipped with different layers of nonlinear processing units that facilitate the extraction and transformation of features, either from the data or from the layers of processing units. Put simply, a deep neural network is characterized by several hidden layers, as shown in Figure 5.3. Each layer performs computations on the basis of the information received and provides the next layer with a result to be analyzed.

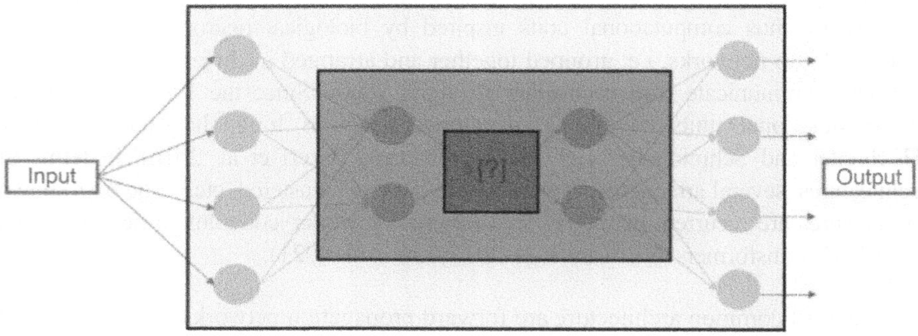

Figure 5.3. *Schematic representation of a neural network according to the "black box" principle: the greater the number of intermediate layers, known as hidden layers, between input and output, the deeper the neural network, i.e. the more complex and computationally demanding*[8]

Deep learning has enabled major advances in fields such as computer vision (facial recognition, image classification) and automated language processing (text

research institutes: the Institut de recherche pour le développement (IRD), the Centre de coopération internationale en recherche agronomique pour le développement (CIRAD), the Institut national de la recherche agronomique (INRA, now the Institut national de recherche pour l'agriculture, l'alimentation et l'environnement (INRAE)), the Institut national de recherche en sciences et technologies du numérique (INRIA) and the Tela Botanica network.

8 Image taken from a scientific outreach article for the general public: "How to grasp what neural networks do". Available at: www.lemonde.fr/blog/binaire/2020/09/04/comment-saisir-ce-que-font-les-reseaux-de-neurones/ [Accessed November 17, 2022].

recognition and interpretation, text generation). The result is more powerful algorithms, but less transparent, as it is very difficult to analyze the form of the calculations taking place in the depths of these networks.

Machine learning and deep learning can therefore be defined as a set of techniques used to learn from data using, among other things, neural networks and to support decision-making, for example, via recommendation, prediction or classification.

5.2.2. *More efficient but less transparent*

There is a real issue surrounding the collection and management of naturalist data (Fortier and Alphandéry 2017; Zucca 2019), especially as thousands of contributors are now involved in collecting and sharing these data.

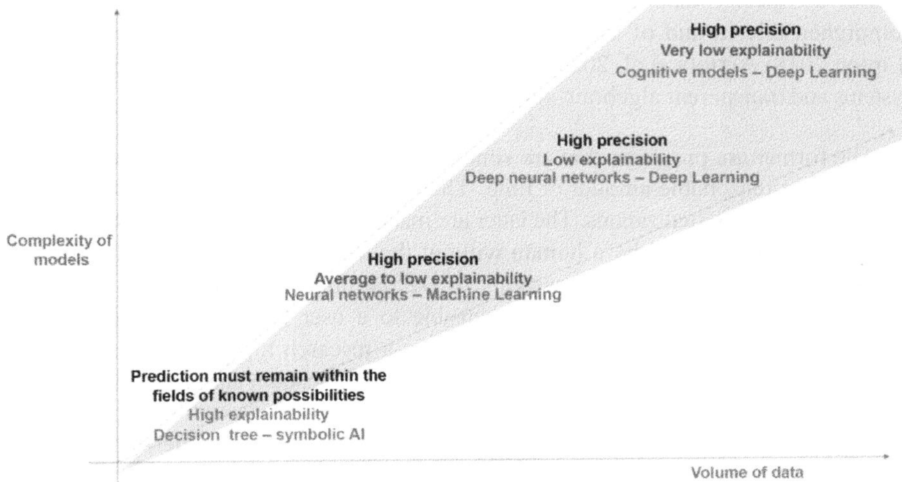

Figure 5.4. *Schematic representation of the evolution of algorithm explainability as a function of model complexity and data volume*[9]

The knowledge acquired through the analysis of these data allows the development and monitoring of public policies and the provision of information to citizens, enabling public debate (in particular through the publications of the National Observatory

9 Image extracted from a webinar for the general public reproduced with authorization: “Comment peut-on faire confiance à l’IA? De la boîte noire à l’IA explicable”, 2020. Available at: https://pixees.fr/comment-peut-on-faire-confiance-a-lia-de-la-boite-noire-a-lia-explicable/ [Accessed November 17, 2022].

biodiversity). This facilitates decision-making within a democratic framework; decompartmentalizes information between public authorities, citizens and economic players; and enables reporting in line with European and international commitments.

The development of the computing power of computer processors[10] and the significant increase in the volumes of data generated worldwide (this is also true in the field of biodiversity and naturalist data) have led to the development and adoption of these techniques, sometimes "personified" under the term AI, as well as infatuation with them, with their omnipresence in the media and the socio-economic landscape (OECD 2019; Bonab et al. 2021).

However, as the algorithms became more powerful, a loss of transparency became apparent, due to the complexity of the architectures and calculations involved. Figure 5.4 illustrates this phenomenon.

Let us specify that AI systems are considered to be transparent if they are comprehensible in and of themselves. There are different degrees of transparency (Lipton 2018; Arrieta et al. 2020): AI systems that can be simulated, decomposable AI systems and transparent algebraic systems.

The former are programs that are simple enough for a user to think and reason as a whole in a reasonable amount of time. They can be easily presented to a human by means of text and visualizations. The latter are made up of several parts, each of which can be easily interpreted by a human without the need for additional tools. Finally, the third category concerns AI systems where the process followed to produce an output from its input data is comprehensible to a user by means of analysis and mathematical methods. Algorithm transparency, a research topic in its own right, is one of the objectives of explainable AI that comes with its own challenges.

Regarding the explainability of an AI system, understanding the reasons for a prediction or behavior is not a mathematical or computer science question, since the IT and scientific community knows how to implement (code) these algorithms. It is more a question of the implicit functioning of the model: the why and the how. For example, what are the characteristics of the data on which the network has based its reasoning? How has the system extracted and processed the information present in the data?

This is all the more important when prediction errors occur and are noted by users (experts) or when the user, whatever their level of expertise, disagrees with a prediction

10 Processors are computing units that interpret, coordinate and execute the instructions defined by computer programming, while enabling the exchange of data between computer components.

made (without it being an error); for example, an image of an animal or plant classified in the wrong category or a category other than the one expected.

In theory, neophyte or expert users may be able to explain (verbalize) the reasons for their decisions or recommendations, but this is not the case with AI systems that have not been designed with this in mind. This lack of transparency can lead to a crisis of acceptability and trust in AI systems. It can lead to a rejection of such tools by users, or to a slower deployment of these technologies in institutions, for example, as illustrated in Figure 5.5.

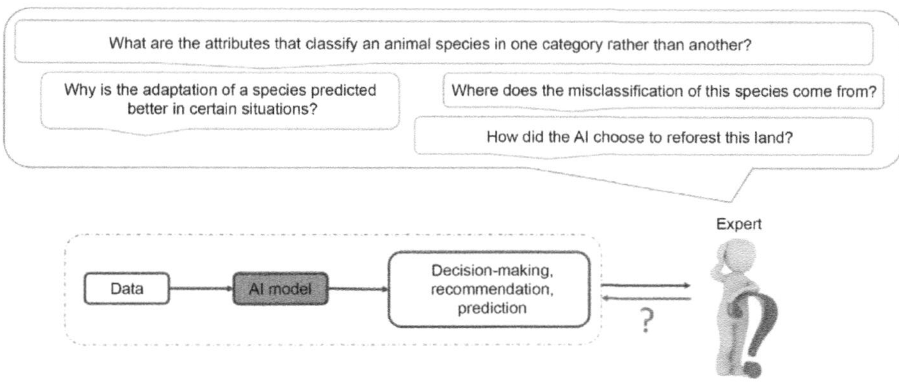

Figure 5.5. *Example of expert questioning of AI system results*

In certain scenarios, AI system prediction errors can have far-reaching consequences. In the field of smart farming, a plant species misclassified by an AI system may not receive the phytosanitary treatment it needs to thrive. Crops can then be damaged by this misclassification. In the field of animal species preservation, an AI system that fails to predict the geographical zones that are important for an animal species (breeding zone, for example) may allow the deployment of an urbanization policy in these zones instead of a preservation policy. The animal species may thus be endangered. A lack of explainability can therefore have a major societal, legal and financial impact on the companies and institutions involved.

In the field of biodiversity and naturalist data, such transparency is necessary to understand the reasons behind the behavior of AI systems, to enable informed decision-making and appropriate action. Beyond the case where an error occurs, providing explanations can help us to verify that the predictions made are for the right reasons according to the right data characteristics, and if necessary, enable the situation to be rectified.

The transparency of AI systems is one of the topical issues driving research and development into solutions for making AI systems explainable, transparent and high-performing.

The need for explainable, intelligible and accessible AI is therefore unavoidable if we are to develop trusted AI and enable the link between data, AI models, society and its citizens.

5.3. Explainable AI: general presentation

Although the field of XAI has become much more structured in recent years, the questions it raises have been studied by the scientific community since the beginning of AI (Lenca 2002). We propose to approach XAI from the perspective of human-centered AI before addressing the major characteristics of this field, namely the target audience, explanations and the different strategies available in XAI.

5.3.1. *Explainable AI: human-centric AI*

XAI aims to make AI models more intelligible and accessible, or to directly design models and results that are explainable for a target audience according to its context, expectations (questioning) and a priori knowledge of a domain (Chraibi Kaadoud et al. 2021). This definition underlines that XAI is an intrinsically multidisciplinary field at the crossroads of AI, ethics, human–computer interaction and social sciences, and is above all *human-centered*.

Human-centered AI is concerned with the design of algorithms and approaches that interact and collaborate with humans. The aim of these systems is to continually improve while offering a successful experience of the interaction between human and machine, from a human point of view. For example, by drawing inspiration from humans, their cognitive skills and the humanities and social sciences, human-centered AI seeks to foster human–machine interaction and the design of flexible, adaptable AI systems around human needs.

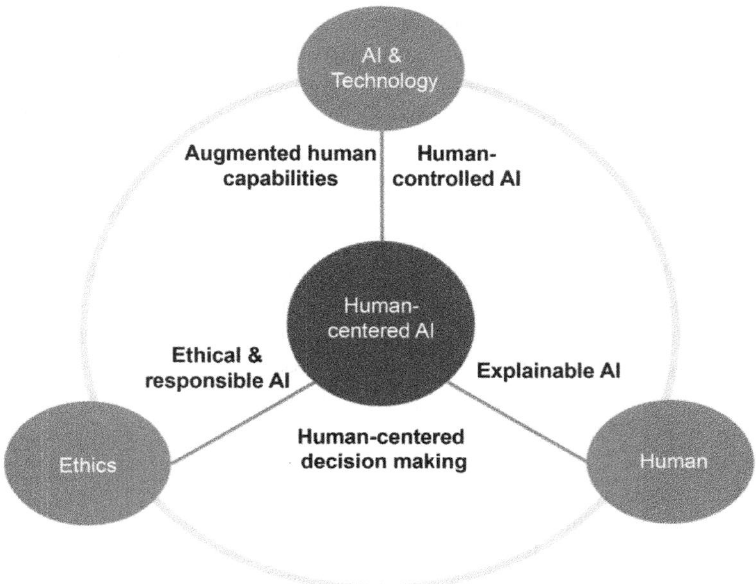

Figure 5.6. *Illustration of the field of human-centered AI, intrinsically multidisciplinary, at the intersection of ethics, humans and technology and its application cases. Illustration adapted from Xu et al. (2021)*

From a technical point of view, human-centric AI systems take advantage of data, as well as human expertise, to understand the needs, aspirations and deeper drivers (intrinsic motivations) that underpin people's behaviors in order to better anticipate them (Lenca 2002).

These contextual analyses combine data and knowledge from the humanities and social sciences to produce personalized and significantly enhanced human experiences. Such knowledge can enable the implementation (execution) of clear, explainable strategies to meet the expectations of a target audience.

5.3.2. *Target audience and explanation in XAI*

The XAI *target audience* is a very important concept. It can condition the choice of XAI methods used and the explanations to be generated. In the field of naturalist data, the concept of target audience can thus refer to *users* impacted by systems (either because they use AI systems or because they suffer the consequences of their results): neophytes, expert citizens or scientific experts (researchers, engineers) using AI tools for their work, such as naturalists and biologists.

Regulatory bodies are also a potential target audience. In the age of climate change and issues around biodiversity preservation, society needs concrete action (Rollnick et al. 2020). If regulatory bodies or agencies use AI systems upstream in their analysis, they need to understand these tools and their results, so they can adopt an informed action plan.

Board members of public institutions (UNESCO, the Système d'Informations Nature et Paysages (SINP, Biodiversity Information System on Nature and Landscapes), Ministry of Ecology, etc.) or companies are also a potential target audience. Without necessarily having a technical profile or being business experts, these people may be called upon to make decisions based on recommendations made by AI systems, amongst others. In order to assess regulatory compliance and understand AI systems or the results generated (why and how), they need XAI to ensure the sustainability of their project and/or company and to engage their responsibility.

Finally, the *scientific community* at large (data scientists, developers, IT researchers working in fields related to naturalist data, etc.) is also a potential target audience.

What is important to note here is that providing explanations to a target audience requires taking into account their prior knowledge, their acculturation to technology and their context. For example, if the target audience is technophilic, they may prefer a saliency map in terms of explanation (e.g. the "RISE" column in Figure 5.7), which is a simple and accessible visual explanation to explain the classification of an image into a particular category. In contrast, a neophytic target audience (unfamiliar with AI methods) or one that has a legal profile (e.g. government institutions) will potentially prefer a detailed natural language explanation of all of the data characteristics involved in the output of a classification AI system and their importance.

The target audience will therefore impact the choice of explanation, its generation, its format (visual, digital, text, etc.) and its semantic content (Walton 2004; Miller 2019; Arrieta et al. 2020; Ehsan et al. 2021; Chraibi Kaadoud et al. 2022; Delaforge 2022). An explanation is thus defined as an adapted and adaptable intermediary between an AI system that has learned from data and a target audience. To achieve this, an explanation needs to be intelligible in order to be accepted and perceived by the target audience (Ehsan et al. 2021). There is therefore a strong need for adaptability of explanation processes and also for flexibility, so that XAI can adapt to the dynamic nature of humans, their knowledge and their context.

5.3.3. *Dimensions and strategies in explainable AI: a technical aside*

In order to better grasp the examples of concrete applications of XAI methods in the fields related to naturalist data, a technical aside is essential to provide a better understanding of the field and the associated challenges.

Technically, it is worth pointing out that explainability generates several challenges. Firstly, we can *mention the multiple dimensions that can be explained.* These include:

– *explaining the data*, for example: "what are the determining features (temperature, sunshine rate) in the data that impact the performance and/or behavior of the AI system (prediction of a species' development)?";

– *explaining the result of* an AI system, for example, a prediction ("why was the photograph of a plant classified in a particular category (plant species) rather than another?") or a recommendation ("why does the network predict the adaptation of a species in a new ecosystem at 68.9%?");

– *explaining the AI system* and/or its internal mechanisms, for example: "how does the AI system visualize the difference between a whale shark and a basking shark, two species that are gigantic in size (18 meters) but threatened?".

Each time, the question posed concerns the link between the input data and the output results. The search for answers to these questions often leads to discoveries: the discovery of surprising or unexpected correlations or the questioning of widely accepted and established truths.

Thanks to XAI, the link between data, the AI algorithm and the human can be constantly reworked and requestioned.

There are two possible approaches to designing explainable AI systems. The first is the *ante hoc approach* (Rudin 2019). It consists of directly designing models and results that are explainable. They are said to be transparent by design, such as decision trees[11]. The second approach is called *post hoc*. It enables AI systems, not necessarily capable of producing legible results, already designed and in production (deployed and in use in a context), to be made more intelligible and accessible by delving into their internal workings, in order to provide an explanation to a target audience on a given question about the mechanisms and/or results of an AI model.

11 Decision-aid tool representing a set of choices in the graphic form of a tree. The leaves of the tree (branch tips) represent the different possible positions reached, depending on the decisions made at each stage (represented by the branches).

This approach is the one predominantly used to explain deep neural networks in deep learning (Guidotti et al. 2018; Arrietta et al. 2020).

The need for explanation is also a criterion affecting the choice of explainability strategy: is it *local or global*?

It is called local explainability when the need for an explanation arises at a specific moment concerning a specific result. For example, when an AI system delivers a result (a prediction, a recommendation or a classification), the XAI process will aim to provide a *local explanation* for a specific result, i.e. for a particular decision on a very small scale. This approach is particularly relevant when it is necessary to analyze a specific case for the needs of a target audience (Guidotti et al. 2018).

Global explainability, in contrast, is intended to provide an explanation of the network's overall behavior based on all of the data it has learned. By making the decision-making process transparent for all data, global explainability has been proven to be a valuable means of assessing the relevance of what the model has learned (Guidotti et al. 2018).

Let us illustrate this with an example. Imagine we have access to an AI tool for predicting the migration of African elephants, but we have lost the manual and do not know how it works. We can then always observe the tool's reaction while running different simulations as we go along, i.e. running the program several times to observe its behavior. In doing so, we associate a result (a prediction) with the arrival of information (temperature, rainfall, present population, presence of plants, etc.). This comes down to locally interpreting the AI tool's behavior in relation to incoming information, as we associate a precise action with a result via a function. We are then in a dimension of local explainability. Global explainability, in the context of this example, corresponds to a simple, global description of the complete operation of the predictive AI tool. In other words, it is a matter of outlining how it works: we will know which type of data makes it possible to obtain a high or, on the contrary, low prediction, which may or may not impact behavior (i.e. performance), and so on. However, we will not have direct access to precise behaviors, such as "to obtain a prediction of 88%, you need to give precise input information (precise data value)".

Figure 5.7 shows an example of local explainability in the explanation of image classification according to several XAI algorithms. It shows, in the second column from the left, an example of the global explainability of an AI system from Lee and Kim (2021) and, on the right, three examples of local explainable algorithms (RISE, LIME and Grad-CAM) for three predictions made by the same system.

Figure 5.7 has five columns: the first column represents the images fed to the AI system as input to be classified into a category (European goldfinch, California gull and Pacific loon), while the remaining columns represent the saliency maps generated using four local XAI methods to explain the classification achieved for each image. Therefore, for the same prediction, different local XAI methods can be used, each with its own precision, advantages and limitations.

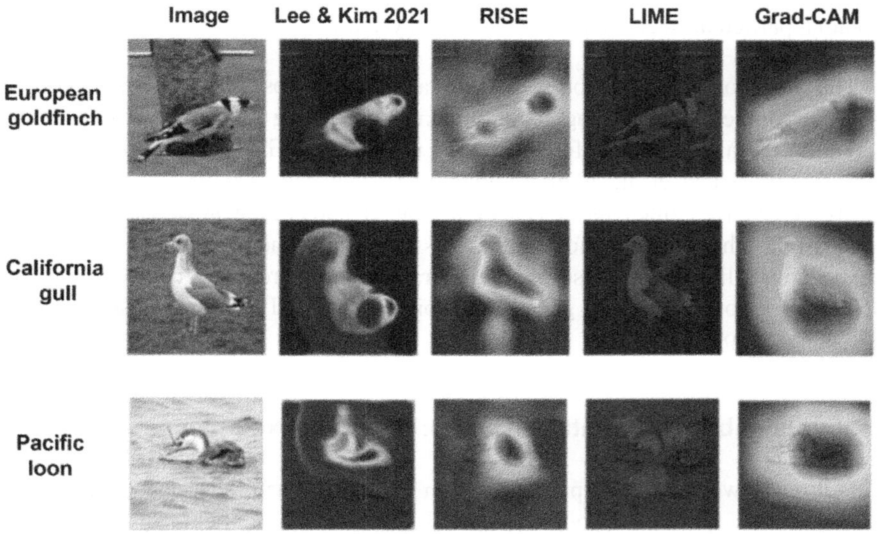

Figure 5.7. *Comparison of saliency maps[12] from four explanation methods generated for image classification provided as input to the AI model. Image adapted from Lee and Kim (2021). For a color version of this figure, see www.iste.co.uk/kohlmann/linking.zip*

COMMENT ON FIGURE 5.7.– Columns 1–5: the Lee and Kim (2021) method; the randomized input sampling for explanation, denoted RISE (Petsuik et al. 2018); the local interpretable model-agnostic explanations method, denoted LIME (Ribeiro et al. 2016); and the gradient-weighted class activation mapping method, denoted Grad-CAM (Selvaraju et al. 2017).

12 The saliency maps for each method use a heatmap, which maps the intensity of a variable onto a color chart. The redder (warm color) the zone, the more it plays a role in the AI model's output. Conversely, the bluer a zone is (cold color), the less important it is. This system efficiently and visually highlights the areas of an image that are important for the classification performed. The same classification algorithm, for the same data, can be explained using different methods, each with different characteristics and levels of performance. This image has been simplified and adapted to suit the purposes of this chapter. For more technical details, as well as the original image, the reader can refer to the original article by Lee and Kim (2021).

To summarize, just as there are a multitude of dimensions to explain in AI, there are also a multitude of XAI strategies: do we want a model-specific or model-independent approach? What type of AI task do we want to explain: a classification? A prediction? A clustering (partitioning of data into sub-groups)? Do we want to explain a particular prediction or model behavior? Or do we want to explain a particular decision or the whole AI system?

The choice of a XAI method is therefore a question whose answer depends on what the target audience is looking for and asking according to their needs. Although there are several scientific reference works in the field (Gilpin et al. 2018; Guidotti et al. 2018; Arrieta et al. 2020; Molnar 2020) that can help with this choice, the decisive element is often the needs of the target audience, who must be given an explanation. The latter, in formulating its questions and hypotheses (e.g. "does ocean depth allied to water surface temperature play a role in phenological events such as migration?"), strongly guides the choice of the XAI strategy, as shown in the following section.

5.4. Explainable AI for naturalist data: concrete examples

Is it really worth using explainable AI in the field of naturalist data? We propose to answer this question through three case studies in the fields of biodiversity, climate and smart farming. The work and approaches described are not exhaustive.

5.4.1. *Explainable AI and biodiversity*

Ryo et al. (2021) questioned the usefulness of XAI by looking at the behavior of African elephants over a period of the year. They used species distribution models (SDMs) to estimate the relationships between environmental variables and animal species occurrence data for a territory, with the aim of predicting the evolution of elephant populations in space and time. The authors performed an SDM analysis on the data related to these animals and their environment, and then used XAI tools to explain the model globally and specific predictions locally.

Figure 5.8, illustrating their results, presents, on the left-hand side, a global explanation of the SDM model ("which variables are important?") and offers, on its right-hand side, local explanations for three SDM predictions concerning the viability of three sites as habitat sites for the elephant population. These local explanations explain which characteristics of each site, such as rainfall or temperature, are involved in the model result.

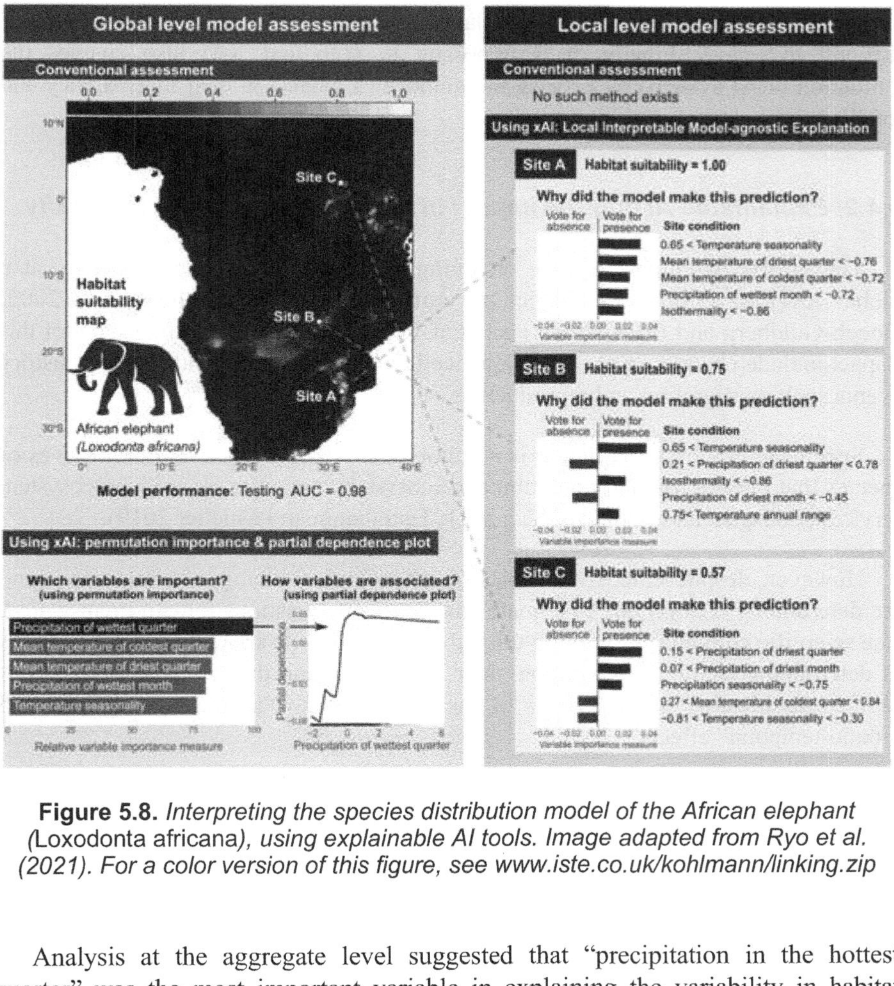

Figure 5.8. *Interpreting the species distribution model of the African elephant (*Loxodonta africana*), using explainable AI tools. Image adapted from Ryo et al. (2021). For a color version of this figure, see www.iste.co.uk/kohlmann/linking.zip*

Analysis at the aggregate level suggested that "precipitation in the hottest quarter" was the most important variable in explaining the variability in habitat suitability across the modeled region. However, this variable is not listed as a key variable at any of the three sites. This may indicate that other variables are more important (e.g. temperature seasonality) at the local (site) level. In other words, conclusions drawn at the global regional level do not automatically apply at the local level.

This XAI work, applied to the problem of monitoring elephant behavior in its natural habitat, allows questions to be asked, which may lead to the adoption of an informed action plan by local authorities to preserve the elephant species. In this case, XAI also makes it possible to perpetuate this knowledge, regardless of the presence and availability of experts, through a technological solution, and above all to deploy this "artificial expertise" in places where a human expert is unavailable or difficult to access. Finally, it is important to note that XAI also enables the validation of AI systems by experts and authorities, thanks to their transparency and intelligibility.

5.4.2. *Explainable AI and the impact of climate change on biodiversity*

The effects of climate change on living organisms, the fauna and flora, at a global level have been the object of numerous studies (Walther et al. 2002; Hoegh-Guldberg and Bruno 2010; Pecl et al. 2017; Liu et al. 2022). Indicators of this impact include changes in phenology, as well as the seasonal calendar of life-history events such as migration and reproduction.

Species migration in particular is monitored, as it is a major event in the lives of species that plays a role in population and ecosystem dynamics, as well as ecosystem services (Gallagher and Hammerschlag 2011; Teitelbaum and Mueller 2019).

However, despite extensive studies on phenological changes in migration (and the determining factors) due to climate change, many questions remain unanswered. The scientific community studying this subject knows little about the complex effects of determining factors for migration, their interactions and their nonlinearity, as well as the classification of the effects of these factors into "spatial", "temporal" and "spatio-temporal" effects.

Kanamori et al. (2022) investigated the migratory behavior of the Pacific dogfish *Squalus suckleyi* (hereafter "dogfish"), a common species of the shark family *Squalidae* and one of the world's most abundant shark species.

This species migrates south for the parturition period (term given to the giving birth of animals) and north to feed in the northwestern Pacific.

In order to elucidate migration patterns, as well as the determining factors in the context of climate change, the authors first examined long-term changes in the timing and geographical location of migration by applying a spatio-temporal model, known as *the barrier model* (Bakka et al. 2019), to time series[13] relating to five decades for the presence/absence of spiny dogfish in the northwestern Pacific.

13 A time series is a data format corresponding to a series of numerical values representing the evolution of a specific quantity over time (e.g. number of individuals) or the readings of a sensor (e.g. temperature).

The barrier model takes spatio-temporal changes in fishing grounds into account, as well as characteristics of the study area that could influence the study (e.g. the nearby presence of islands).

Kanamori et al. (2022) then assessed the spatial, temporal and spatio-temporal effects of the determining factors (sea surface temperature (SST), depth, productivity and magnetic fields) on the seasonal presence of spiny dogfish using gradient boosting, a machine learning method, and grouped permutation feature importance (GPFI), an interpretable machine learning technique.

Gradient boosting is a popular technique among data scientists due to its accuracy and speed, especially for complex and large data, used to create accurate predictive models (Shiferaw et al. 2019).

GPFI is a method for inspecting a machine learning model, recommended when data are tabular and highly correlated. The original idea behind this method is to calculate the importance of each feature in the data by permuting those that are correlated into a single set. This method makes it possible to break the relationship between features and the result of the model studied. In this way, the variation in prediction errors achieved by the model before and after the permutations indicates the extent to which the model depends on a studied feature for its performance.

In other words, a feature is important if reshuffling, or mixing, its values increase the model's error, because in this case, the model has relied on the feature for prediction. A feature is, conversely, unimportant if reshuffling its values leaves the model error unchanged, because in this case the model has not relied on the feature for prediction (Molnar 2020).

In the case of Kanamori et al. (2022), the permuted characteristics corresponded to the determining factors (SST, depth, productivity and magnetic fields) whose impact on the seasonal presence of spiny dogfish the authors wished to assess.

The work carried out showed that the migration area had not changed over the last five decades or so, while the migration time moved forward by one month after 2000. If the spatial effects of magnetic fields and depth were still significant, the spatial and spatio-temporal effects of SSTs increased during the migration season, although the temporal effect of SSTs was still small.

Such results suggest that the migration zone for spiny dogfish is stable over time, because its spatial distribution is determined by geographical features, while the timing of migration is determined by the search for a suitable SST location, which increased sharply after the 2000s.

Consequently, the use of interpretability methods in this case study highlighted that temperature as well as other factors simultaneously influence the migration of these animals and underline the importance of paying attention to biotic/abiotic factors, including temperature in the observation of phenological events.

These works – and more generally those in this line – show that machine learning methods offer various advantages (taking nonlinearity into account, detecting and learning from complex interactions between covariates[14]), even though they require large volumes of data which are often difficult to obtain in the fields of ecology and conservation. In this study, the use of an interpretable machine learning method enabled us to understand the process behind long-term changes in the seasonal migration of spiny dogfish: the migration area tended not to change due to the spatial effects of geographical features (magnetic fields and depth), but the moment of migration moved forward due to the search for the appropriate location of SST (i.e. the spatial effect) where it increased.

To conclude, this method provided a simple interpretation, more detailed information and a better understanding of the processes involved in the migratory behavior of this species. This ecological knowledge then makes it possible to predict the future impacts of climate change on future phenological events in marine fauna.

5.4.3. *Explainable AI and smart farming*

Intelligent agriculture, or smart farming, is a term used to describe agriculture that combines traditional techniques with innovative solutions based on information and communication technologies (ICT).

In concrete terms, technologies such as unmanned aerial vehicles (UAVs), unmanned ground vehicles (UGVs), image collection and processing technologies, machine learning, big data, cloud computing and wired and wireless sensor networks are being used to bring about significant changes in this field: increased production; lower costs by reducing necessary inputs, such as fuel, fertilizers and pesticides; reduced labor efforts; and finally improved quality of final products (Wolfert et al. 2017; Moysiadis et al. 2021). In short, the aim of smart farming is to enable intelligent farm management to achieve higher yields while respecting agricultural biodiversity.

The United Nations Food and Agriculture Organization (FAO) estimates that 50% more food will need to be produced by 2050 to feed the world's growing population

14 A covariate is a term used to designate any continuous variable that is generally not controlled during data collection.

(FAO 2017). However, ongoing efforts to increase food production are hampered by climate change, which has already impacted global average yields of major crops in recent decades and is expected to further negatively affect food security (FAO et al. 2018; Mbow et al. 2019). It is therefore crucial not only to accurately forecast crop yields but also to model and characterize the processes involved, including meteorological factors.

Predicting crop yields depends on a number of parameters: increasing soil erosion, temperature, radiation, water availability and other environmental conditions influencing crop growth and development, as well as final grain yield, in complex, nonlinear ways. Machine learning and deep learning techniques in particular can account for these nonlinear relationships between crop yield and its covariates. However, as mentioned above, these techniques generally lack transparency and interpretability, as the reasons behind the predictions made are not accessible.

Wolanin et al. (2020) addressed this issue and explored in their work the question of the interpretability of deep learning models.

To do this, they applied convolutional neural networks (CNNs, also known as ConvNet (Goodfellow et al. 2016)) to multivariate time series of vegetation and meteorological data in order to estimate wheat yields in India's wheat belt[15] (India's wheat-producing region).

CNNs are a class of deep learning models that take into account the large size of input datasets, nonlinear relationships and interconnections between several variables in order to learn features directly from the data without depending in any way on the manual selection of specific parameters by a human operator (Goodfellow et al. 2016). This class of neural networks is specialized for processing data with a grid-like topology, such as an image or time series.

After learning the CNNs, in order to understand the relationships implicitly learned by the model, the authors used the Regression Activation Mapping (RAM) method (Wang and Yang 2017) to visualize and study the features and performance factors learned by the model.

Activation maps are a visual representation of the activations of different network layers as a given image progresses, as a result of various linear algebraic operations. For a given prediction, activation maps essentially indicate the

15 The term "wheat belt" here refers to a large agricultural area in which corn is grown. These areas are known as wheat, corn or grain belts.

discriminating region of the image that has influenced the deep learning model for its prediction.

RAM, a sub-category of activation map methods, contains the immediate information for the final prediction, while maintaining correspondence with the input data in the temporal (or spatial) dimension and shows the contribution of each temporal (or spatial) instance to the final output.

In the work of Wolanin et al. (2020), the authors used deep learning to produce a high-performance model for predicting wheat yield, while focusing specifically on assessing the underlying factors responsible for the prediction made. This dual feature of performance and explainability enabled them to develop confidence in the model and gain a better understanding of the relevant conditions leading to crop yield variability.

The authors thus showed that the characteristics learned were mainly linked to the length of the growing season, as well as to temperature and light conditions during this period. For example, their results explained that high yields in 2012 were associated with low temperatures accompanied by sunny conditions during the growing season.

The advantage of the proposed methodology, which has proven to be effective on wheat crops, is that it can be used for other crops and regions to facilitate the development of different types of agriculture.

In summary, although machine and deep learning models are already widely used for a variety of problems in image and signal processing, their application to crop yield estimation is still under development. One reason for this is that transferring the tools available in the machine learning field to environmental applications requires adaptations that take into account the specificities of the data, which are not always possible (Goodfellow et al. 2016).

By extension, many XAI applications in the field of naturalist data have yet to be developed.

Other work unmentioned here also has highlighted the usefulness of XAI approaches as an artificial numerical simulation environment for testing hypotheses before launching laboratory experiments, which are generally costly and time-consuming (Rabinovich et al. 2021). XAI approaches thus have the potential to save time and money and also to improve the understanding of the links between species physiology, phenology and climate, the determining factors in the development of an animal or plant species, a subject of growing ecological importance.

5.5. Discussion: XAI to empower everyone in the field of naturalist data

The work presented above shows that XAI can be useful for understanding and determining the factors involved in a natural event linked to fauna, flora or habitats. These factors, which may be natural (e.g. changes in sea surface temperature) or due to human action (e.g. intensive agriculture), are often hidden by the complexity of AI tools. Thanks to XAI, it is possible to show an explicit link between an action and a consequence and thus identify the potential levers on which societies, individuals and institutions can act to preserve biodiversity.

More generally, at the level of civil society, XAI is a force for education and raising awareness of ecological issues and fields linked to naturalist data (biodiversity, environment). In theory, XAI is aimed at everyone – amateur or expert naturalists, biodiversity researchers or neophytes – making it easier to share knowledge. Explanations can be addressed to political decision-makers, administrative councils or concerned citizens, as well as industrialists or public institutions.

This role as an intermediary capable of interfacing with different categories of information makes the XAI a tool at the service of *the construction of a naturalist data –XAI system–human/society link* that is being built while being constantly put to the test.

Through the explanations it provides, XAI acts as a *scientific mediator*, enabling:

– *the knowledge discovered from naturalist data to be understood*;

– the reasons behind the behavior of an AI system and the factors that determine this behavior *to be demystified*;

– the availability for a target audience of information adapted to their knowledge, cognitive profile, culture and context, i.e. *a suitable explanation to be provided.*

Beyond this, highlighting the reasons behind an AI result (e.g. loss of yield or decrease in plant, animal or marine population) also contributes to understanding the impact of human activity on ecosystems, and conversely, the effect of the latter on human activities.

In the context of numerical simulations, beyond a simple result (e.g. the development or non-development of a species), XAI can be used to understand the factors involved in this result and to draw up recommendations for avoiding particular scenarios or favoring others.

By using visual explanations, for example, to explain the links between certain factors and their impact on areas linked to naturalist data, XAI can help to make the impact of government actions and policies more concrete for the target audience, even though the consequences are long-term (Luccioni et al. 2021; Fernández Galeote 2022).

In short, over and above its role as a technical tool, XAI can be a mediation tool for the preservation of biodiversity by informing and empowering all stakeholders, as well as a tool for acquiring the knowledge to better fight for this cause.

5.6. References

Arrieta, A.B., Díaz-Rodríguez, N., Del Ser, J., Bennetot, A., Tabik, S., Barbado, A., Herrera, F. (2020). Explainable artificial intelligence (XAI): Concepts, taxonomies, opportunities and challenges toward responsible AI. *Information Fusion*, 58, 82–115.

Bakka, H., Vanhatalo, J., Illian, J.B., Simpson, D., Rue, H. (2019). Non-stationary Gaussian models with physical barriers. *Spatial Statistics*, 29, 268–288.

Barthélémy, D., Boujemaa, N., Mathieu, D., Jean-François, M., Joly, A., & Mouysset, E. (2011). The Pl@ntNet project: Plant computational identification and collaborative information system. *Biosystematics 2011 – Digital Identification Methods in the Digital Age – Morphological and Molecular, Computer-Aided and Fully Automated, Research and Citizen Science*. February, Berlin.

Benet, B., Mårell, A., Boscardin, Y., Bonneau, M., Canario, L. (2020). Utilisation de techniques d'intelligence artificielle pour des opérations de détection et d'identification dans le domaine animalier. *Journée GDR Isis, Journée d'étude du CNRS* [Online]. Available at: https://hal.inrae.fr/hal-03079459 [Accessed 17 November 2022].

Bonab, A.B., Rudko, I., Bellini, F. (2021). A review and a proposal about socio-economic impacts of artificial intelligence. In *Business Revolution in a Digital Era*, Dima, A.M. and D'Ascenzo F. (eds). Springer Link, 251–270.

Bonnet, P., Joly, A., Faton, J.M., Brown, S., Kimiti, D., Deneu, B., Servajean, M., Affouard, A., Lombardo, J.C., Mary, L., Vignau C., Munoz, F (2020). How citizen scientists contribute to monitor protected areas thanks to auto-matic plant identification tools. *Ecological Solutions and Evidence*, 1(2).

Chraibi Kaadoud, I., Fahed, L., Lenca, P. (2021). Explainable AI: A narrative review at the crossroad of knowledge discovery, knowledge representation and represen-tation learning. *Twelfth International Workshop Modelling and Reasoning in Context (MRC)*, 19–20 August 2021 [Online]. Available at: https://ceur-ws.org/Vol-2995/paper4.pdf [Accessed 29 November 2022].

Chukkapalli, S.S.L., Mittal, S., Gupta, M., Abdelsalam, M., Joshi, A., Sandhu, R., Joshi, K. (2020). Ontologies and artificial intelligence systems for the cooperative smart farming ecosystem. *IEEE Access*, 8, 164045-64.

Delaforge, A. (2022) Visualisation pour l'interprétation et l'explicabilité des prédictions issues de modèles d'apprentissage profond en TAL. PhD thesis, University of Montpellier, Montpellier.

Ehsan, U., Passi, S., Liao, Q.V., Chan, L., Lee, I., Muller, M., Riedl, M.O. (2021). The who in explainable AI: How AI background shapes perceptions of AI explanations. arXiv preprint.

FAO (2017). The future of food and agriculture – trends and challenges. Report, FAO, Rome.

FAO, IFAD, UNICEF, WFP, WHO (2018). The state of food security and nutrition in the world 2018: Building climate resilience for food security and nutrition. Report, FAO, IFAD, UNICEF, WFP, WHO [Online]. Available at: https://docs.wfp.org/api/documents/WFP-0000074343/download/ [Accessed 14 November 2022].

Fernández Galeote, D., Legaki, N.Z., Hamari, J. (2022). Avatar identities and climate change action in video games: Analysis of mitigation and adaptation practices. *CHI Conference on Human Factors in Computing Systems*, 1–18.

Fortier, A. and Alphandéry, P. (2017). La maîtrise des données, un enjeu majeur pour les associations naturalistes à l'heure de la gouvernance de la biodiversité. *Revue française d'administration publique*, 163, 587–598.

Gallagher, A.J. and Hammerschlag, N. (2011). Global shark currency: The distribution, frequency, and economic value of shark ecotourism. *Current Issues in Tourism*, 14, 797–812.

Gilpin, L.H., Bau, D., Yuan, B.Z., Bajwa, A., Specter, M., Kagal, L. (2018). Explaining explanations: An overview of interpretability of machine learning. *IEEE 5th International Conference on Data Science and Advanced Analytics (DSAA)*.

Goëau, H., Lorieul, T., Heuret, P., Joly, A., Bonnet, P. (2022). Can artificial intelligence help in the study of vegetative growth patterns from herbarium collections? An evaluation of the tropical flora of the french guiana forest. *Plants*, 11(4), 530.

Goodfellow, I., Bengio, Y., Courville, A. (2016). *Deep Learning*. MIT Press, Cambridge [Online]. Available at: https://www.deeplearningbook.org/ [Accessed 22 November 2022].

Greff, K., Srivastava, R.K., Koutník, J., Steunebrink, B.R., Schmidhuber, J. (2016). LSTM: A search space odyssey. *IEEE Transactions on Neural Networks and Learning Systems*, 28(10), 2222–2232.

Guidotti, R., Monreale, A., Ruggieri, S., Turini, F., Giannotti, F., Pedreschi, D. (2018). A survey of methods for explaining black box models. *ACM Computing Surveys (CSUR)*, 51(5), 1–42.

Hochreiter, S. and Schmidhuber, J. (1997). Long short-term memory. *Neural Computation*, 9(8), 1735–1780.

Hoegh-Guldberg, O. and Bruno, J.F. (2010). The impact of climate change on the world's marine ecosystems. *Science*, 328, 1523–1528.

Joly, A., Vrochidis, S., Karatzas, K., Karppinen, A., Bonnet, P. (eds) (2018). *Multimedia Tools and Applications for Environmental & Biodiversity Informatics*. Springer, Berlin.

Kanamori, Y., Yano, T., Okamura, H., Yagi, Y. (2022). Spatio-temporal model and machine learning method reveal process of phenological shift under climate change of North Pacific spiny dogfish. *bioRxiv* [Online]. Available at: https://www.biorxiv.org/content/10.1101/2022.03.01.482455v1 [Accessed 22 November 2022].

Lecue, F., Gade, K., Geyik, S.C., Kenthapadi, K., Mithal, V., Taly, A., Guidotti, R., Minervini, P. (2020). Explainable AI: Foundations, industrial applications, practical challenges, and lessons learned. AAAI 2020 tutorial [Online]. Available at: https://xaitutorial2020.github.io [Accessed 22 November 2022].

Lee, H. and Kim, S. (2021). Explaining neural networks using attentive knowledge distillation. *Sensors*, 21(4), 1280.

Lenca, P. (2002). Human centered processes. *European Journal of Operational Research*, 136(2), 231–232.

Lin, T., Wang, Y., Liu, X., Qiu, X. (2021). A survey of transformers. arXiv.

Lipton, Z.C. (2018). The mythos of model interpretability. *Queue*, 16(3), 30–57.

Liu, Y., Duffy, K., Dy, J.G., Ganguly, A.R. (2022). Explainable deep learning for insights in El Nino and river flows. arXiv preprint.

Luccioni, A., Schmidt, V., Vardanyan, V., Bengio, Y. (2021). Using artificial intelligence to visualize the impacts of climate change. *IEEE Computer Graphics and Applications*, 41(1), 8–14.

Mamalakis, A., Ebert-Uphoff, I., Barnes, E.A. (2022). Explainable artificial intelligence in meteorology and climate science: Model fine-tuning, calibrating trust and learning new science. *International Workshop on Extending Explainable AI Beyond Deep Models and Classifiers*. Springer, Berlin.

Mbow, C., Rosenzweig, C., Barioni, L.G., Benton, T.G., Herrero, M., Krishnapillai, M., Liwenga, E., Pradhan, P., Rivera-Ferre, M.G., Sapkota, T. et al. (2019). *Climate Change and Land: An IPCC Special Report on Climate Change, Desertification, Land Degradation, Sustainable Land Management, Food Security, and Greenhouse Gas Fluxes in Terrestrial Ecosystems*.

Miller, T. (2019). Explanation in artificial intelligence: Insights from the social sciences. *Artificial Intelligence*, 267, 1–38.

Molnar, C. (2020). Interpretable machine learning: A guide for making black box models explainable. *Lulu.com* [Online]. Available at: https://christophm.github.io/interpretable-ml-book/ [Accessed 22 November 2022].

Moysiadis, V., Sarigiannidis, P., Vitsas, V., Khelifi, A. (2021). Smart farming in Europe. *Computer Science Review*, 39, 100345.

OECD (2019). *L'intelligence artificielle dans la société*. OECD Editions, Paris.

Pecl, G.T., Araujo, M.B., Bell, J., Blanchard, J., Bonebrake, T.C., Chen, I., Clark, T.D., Colwell, R.K., Danielsen, F., Evengard, B. & Robinson, S (2017). Biodiversity redistribution under climate change: Impacts on ecosystems and human well-being. *Science*, 355, 1389.

Petsiuk, V., Das, A., Saenko, K. (2018). Rise: Randomized input sampling for explanation of black-box models. arXiv preprint.

Rabinovich, J.E., Alvarez Costa, A., Muñoz, I.J., Schilman, P.E., Fountain-Jones, N.M. (2021). Machine-learning model led design to experimentally test species thermal limits: The case of kissing bugs (Triatominae). *PLoS Neglected Tropical Diseases*, 15(3), e0008822.

Ribeiro, M.T., Singh, S., Guestrin, C. (2016). Model-agnostic interpretability of machine learning. arXiv preprint.

Rolnick, D., Donti, P.L., Kaack, L.H., Kochanski, K., Lacoste, A., Sankaran, K., Slavin Ross, A., Milojevic-Dupont,N., Jaques, N., Waldman-Brown, A. et al. (2019). Tackling climate change with machine learning. arXiv preprint.

Rougier, N. (2000). Modèles de mémoires pour la navigation autonome. PhD thesis, Henri Poincaré University, Nancy.

Rudin, C. (2019). Stop explaining black box machine learning models for high stakes decisions and use interpretable models instead. *Nature Machine Intelligence*, 1(5), 206–215.

Ryo, M., Angelov, B., Mammola, S., Kass, J.M., Benito, B.M., Hartig, F. (2021). Explainable artificial intelligence enhances the ecological interpretability of black-box species distribution models. *Ecography*, 44(2), 199–205.

Sanchez-Pi, N., Marti, L., Abreu, A., Bernard, O., de Vargas, C., Eveillard, D., Maass, A., Marquet, P.A., Sainte-Marie, J., Salomon, J. et al. (2020). Artificial intelligence, machine learning and modeling for understanding the oceans and climate change. *NeurIPS 2020 Workshop – Tackling Climate Change with Machine Learning*.

Sanchez-Pi, N., Martí, L., Abreu, A., Bernard, O., de Vargas, C., Eveillard, D., Maass, A., Marquet, P.A., Sainte-Marie, J., Salomon, J., Schoenauer, M., Sebag, M. (2021). OcéanIA: AI, data, and models for understanding the ocean and climate change [Online]. Available at: https://hal.archives-ouvertes.fr/hal-03274323v2/document [Accessed 22 November 2022].

Selvaraju, R.R., Cogswell, M., Das, A., Vedantam, R., Parikh, D., Batra, D. (2017). Grad-cam: Visual explanations from deep networks via gradient-based localization. *Proceedings of the IEEE International Conference on Computer Vision*.

Shiferaw, H., Bewket, W., Eckert, S. (2019). Performances of machine learning algorithms for mapping fractional cover of an invasive plant species in a dryland ecosystem. *Ecology and Evolution*, 9, 2562–2574.

Shortliffe, E.H. (1977). Mycin: A knowledge-based computer program applied to infectious diseases. *Proceedings of the Annual Symposium on Computer Application in Medical Care.*

Teitelbaum, C.S. and Mueller, T. (2019) Beyond migration: Causes and consequences of nomadic animal movements. *TREE*, 34, 569–581.

Vaswani, A., Shazeer, N., Parmar, N., Uszkoreit, J., Jones, L., Gomez, A.N., Polosukhin, I. et al. (2017). Attention is all you need. *Advances in Neural Information Processing Systems*, 30, 5998–6008.

Walther, G.R., Post, E., Convey, P., Menzel, A., Parmesank, C., Beebee, T.J.C., Fromentin, J.-M., Hoegh-Guldberg, O., Bairlein, F. (2002). Ecological responses to recent climate change. *Nature*, 416, 389–395.

Walton, D. (2004). A new dialectical theory of explanation. *Philosophical Explorations*, 7(1), 71–89.

Wang, Z. and Yang, J. (2017). Diabetic retinopathy detection via deep convolutional networks for discriminative localization and visual explanation. ArXiv.

Wolanin, A., Mateo-García, G., Camps-Valls, G., Gómez-Chova, L., Meroni, M., Duveiller, G., Liangzhi, Y., Guanter, L. (2020). Estimating and understanding crop yields with explainable deep learning in the Indian Wheat Belt. *Environmental Research Letters*, 15(2), 024019.

Wolfert, S., Ge, L., Verdouw, C., Bogaardt, M.J. (2017). Big data in smart farming – a review. *Agricultural Systems*, 153, 69–80.

Xu, W. and Dainoff, M.J. (2021). Transitioning to human interaction with AI systems: New challenges and opportunities for HCI professionals to enable human-centered AI. ArXiv.

Zucca, M. (2019). La mise en commun des données naturalistes : des pratiques complexes. *Revue française d'administration publique*, 169, 195–206.

6

Pooling Biodiversity Databases: Linking Data, Linking Actors

Figure 6.1. *Identifying species in the field: linking beyond the data. Julie Polge (2021). For a color version of this figure, see www.iste.co.uk/kohlmann/linking.zip*

Chapter 5 defined the field of artificial intelligence (AI) and explainable AI (XAI) to improve understanding of the results produced by AI models. Explainable AI aims to put humans back at the heart of decision-making informed by AI models.

Chapter written by Camille BERNARD.

Through examples applied to the field of observations from the natural world, the importance of the readability of the results of predictive models has been demonstrated. It reinforces the acceptability and appropriation of results by actors and specialists in a given field, as well as by the general public. In the field of biodiversity or environmental data, a high degree of belief in simulation results is vital to counter any inaction on the part of decision-makers or citizens. Indeed, unless a clear and transparent approach is adopted, AI results could be met with a great deal of mistrust.

Alongside XAI, the opening up of biodiversity and environmental data is one of today's major challenges. Opening up data to citizens, researchers, businesses and local stakeholders promotes the transparency of results and their appropriation by all. First, data openness makes it possible to carry out cross-analyses based on multiple sources, which can be used for research purposes. Second, open data enable the construction of value-added services based on open data. As a result, many start-ups are emerging thanks to the Open Data Initiative. They exploit multiple sources of open data to meet new needs and generate not only profits, but also jobs. In the field of environmental data, for example, applications for tracking pollution by municipality have emerged in recent years, telling a user that it would be preferable to postpone a jogging session until tomorrow or giving the weather forecast[1] (i.e. weather data are another source of data retrieved from open data).

The opening up of public sector information is a regulated and legislated field. Numerous directives and laws have been passed over the last 20 years, all over the world, to ensure that data produced by government services are made freely available to all citizens. Alongside the opening up of public sector information, which is the result of a legal obligation on public sector institutions to open up their data, the Open Data Initiative is also emerging for data collected or constructed by private organizations, associations or even communities (using crowdsourcing methods[2], for instance). In the case of crowdsourcing initiatives, it should be noted that not all data are included in open data: some choose to include all or part of the data collected, while others decide not to open up any data outside the participating community.

In this way, some associations of naturalists enrich their databases (DBs) by way of free contribution, from experts and non-experts, using crowdsourcing platforms. These associations then choose to open up all or part of this data, depending on the species concerned and the protection issues associated with them. This opening up of

1 Example of the French Plume Air Report application, available at: https://plumelabs.com/fr/ [Accessed 7 August 2022].

2 Participatory production. Crowdsourcing refers to the division of a major task into sub-tasks carried out by a large number of people. The term is often reserved for the sharing of digital tasks carried out by Internet users.

the data collected by these communities of naturalists represents a rich source of information on a territory for researchers and the general public. For instance, based on community censuses of bird species, researchers can study the evolution of bird migration periods over time.

In the past, the challenge was to collect biodiversity data – a challenge met thanks to crowdsourcing platforms. Today, the challenge is to make the best use of these data, to cross-reference them with other data, to enable researchers and citizens to improve their understanding of the interactions taking place within a given territory. As noted by Groom et al. (2020, p. 1):

> Establishing explicit links between entities in biodiversity research is a goal of biodiversity informatics in the 21st century. [...] Creating these links allows us to describe biodiversity, provide evidence for theories, support prediction, underpin reproducibility, lend credence and, ultimately, underpin policy.

Therefore, the pooling of biodiversity databases and the interoperability of systems for better data sharing are major current challenges. While this sharing of data involves technical aspects, the fact remains that upstream of any sharing, the coordination of the actors is necessary, in order to establish unified data models by mutual agreement and to align some concepts.

The major challenges are:

– collecting biodiversity data;

– ensuring the quality of these data;

– carrying out cross-disciplinary, multi-thematic and multi-dimensional analyses of these biodiversity data, for a better understanding of the ecosystems and of their evolution over time.

In this chapter, we present the evolution over the last 20 years of platforms dedicated to the collection of observations from the natural world and their associated DBs towards standards and formats that enable data sharing. We show that those new forms of data collection (e.g. using crowdsourcing) and representation (e.g. linked open data) lead to communities emerging and, thus, the creation of links/connections between the actors sharing data. We also look at the limits and obstacles to the implementation of such tools and practices for sharing observations from the natural world.

6.1. Database developments in the field of biodiversity

6.1.1. *Increase in the volume of biodiversity data due to evolving practices and tools*

Today, we are witnessing a rapid increase in the volume of data available on the Web on the theme of biodiversity. This trend, which has been accelerating since 2016, is due to a combination of changes in practices and the digital tools available to contributors (Nature France 2021). Let us look to the past: databases of natural history observations did not wait for the digital era to exist. Paper records of species were the first databases in the field.

Then, with the advent of IT tools, the first spreadsheet databases appeared. Relational databases were then gradually introduced (from the 1980s to the 2000s), in most structures, in order to:

– implement more structured models;

– store more data;

– query these DBs.

Most organizations then implemented a data model designed in-house and specific to the data collected and processed by the organization.

Later, as a result of major environmental issues, among others, the need arose to pool these isolated silos of data, in order to better understand how widespread the phenomena were, on a wider scale than that of a study area. This pooling (which is still going on today) began with internal structures. For example, in the case of the Ligue pour la protection des oiseaux (LPO, French League for the Protection of Birds) association, several relational DBs exist, one for each departmental or regional section of the LPO. Currently, this association wishes to create a national relational DB from these multiple local DBs for improved knowledge sharing for species and their changing migration patterns, for example, due to global warming.

Another major change from the 2010s onwards was the advent of crowdsourcing platforms for collecting data. As mentioned in Chapter 4, these platforms developed as a result of the desire of institutions and associations to create or recreate a link with nature by using digital platforms. The result is a desire on the part of public bodies and associations not only to facilitate users simply reading data but also to get them involved in collecting observations from the natural world. For example, in 2012, the Muséum national d'histoire naturelle (MNHN, French Natural History Museum) set up the Les Herbonautes platform[3], a collaborative citizen digital herbarium. The aim of

3 Available at: http://lesherbonautes.mnhn.fr/ [Accessed 7 August 2022].

this platform is to appeal to the general public to decipher handwritten annotations inscribed on digitized plates from the MNHN's historical herbarium. Other similar initiatives have been launched by the MNHN as part of the Vigie-Nature project. For example, the "Observatoire de la biodiversité des jardins: Opération Papillons" to study butterflies was launched in 2006 by Noé and the MNHN. This crowdsourcing platform was one of the first on the theme of biodiversity to be offered to the public in France[4]. Internationally, we can cite the iNaturalist platform[5], an initiative of the California Academy of Sciences and National Geographic. This platform enables any citizen to record observations of plants and animals. These data can then be used by ecology researchers to study biodiversity.

This desire to involve the general public in the collection of observations led to the emergence of other problems relating to the management of the quantity of data collected, the quality of these data and finally whether or not to disseminate these data, which may be sensitive, uncertain or false.

6.1.2. *From quantity to quality: the need for data standardization?*

As noted by the MNHN (Muséum national d'histoire naturelle 2019), the proliferation of participatory biodiversity inventory programs has led to a considerable increase in the volume of data documenting the state of biodiversity in France and elsewhere in the world. These data, however, are highly heterogeneous, due to the use of different data formats and metadata. This is also due to the use (or non-use) of different experimental protocols when collecting data; they are highly heterogeneous and difficult to use for reliable analyses over time and space (Marsh and Trenham 2008). As it stands, these data can often not be pooled, due to the non-use of standard data collection protocols and data representation standards.

The use of digital tools based on standard protocols for large-scale biodiversity data collection is therefore essential. However, Legrand (2013) notes that the use of standards and procedures for data collection can be an obstacle to personal initiative and, more broadly, an obstacle to data collection by any citizen. The author presents feedback from the Vigie-Nature project[6], whose aim is to "better understand the dynamics of biodiversity on a large spatial and temporal scale" based on the contributions of volunteers who collect flora and fauna data throughout France. Vigie-Nature's ambition is not only to be an observatory of biodiversity in France, but also to reinforce the importance of biodiversity and its conservation among the general public, by encouraging them to observe the natural world around them. The data

4 Available at: www.vigienature.fr/fr/operation-papillons [Accessed 7 August 2022].

5 Available at: www.inaturalist.org [Accessed 7 August 2022].

6 Available at: www.vigienature.fr/fr [Accessed 7 August 2022].

collected by Vigie-Nature are obtained exclusively by professional or amateur volunteers. These volunteers carry out observations of populations, such as butterflies, for example. These observations are not standardized nor do they follow a standard protocol. They are called "opportunistic observations", as they are collected by volunteers during their walks. The members of Vigie-Nature then realized that this non-standard form of survey should not be restricted as it provides a wealth of data from a community that would certainly carry out fewer surveys if it had to follow very restrictive protocols. Furthermore, in a publication of the MNHN (Muséum national d'histoire naturelle 2019), the authors note that it is possible to correct certain biases through the mathematical processing of the data. The authors present the example of opportunistic observation data for a butterfly species in a given location that increases at certain times of the year, without it being possible to know whether it is the butterflies that are more numerous or the observers. Therefore, for each week of observation, the researchers divided the number of butterflies observed by the number of outings with observations to obtain an average number of butterflies per outing, per week. As far as standard survey protocols are concerned, we note that some scientists prefer to have plenty of surveys, even though they are opportunistic and do not follow standard protocols, because these surveys enable them to confirm the results of standardized monitoring, obtained with fewer data but remaining the reference. It is therefore preferable for some researchers in the field to have a lot of data with varying quality than to have limited data of high quality. These results must, however, be qualified as it has also been observed that most of the contributors to opportunistic surveys are enthusiasts, aware of the importance of capturing biodiversity data and respecting a protocol. Opportunistic surveys may therefore be of high quality.

Assessing the quality of observations from the natural world and their compliance with data collection protocols is essential but not the only criterion. In a publication of the INPN (2022), several data quality criteria for species are listed. We find the criterion relating to the collection protocol, "information on the acquisition context (transmission of metadata describing, in particular, collection protocols and methods)" alongside other criteria, such as "taxonomic, geographic and temporal precision", "traceability/sources (observer, determiner, validator)" and "use of reference systems (list of scientific names or descriptors), which is essential for homogeneous data processing and interoperability (notion of a common language to enable good communication between systems)". This last criterion is the one retained in the context of our study; that is, the pooling of various data for a better understanding of an area and of its evolution over time. This requires the use of standard thesauri, species taxonomies and data models. Indeed, harmonizing the vocabularies used to describe species and ecosystems, and more broadly, harmonizing data models and data exchange formats, guarantees the interoperability of information systems, which is the key to data pooling. Zárate et al. (2020) observe that scientists frequently collect biological and environmental information for years on end and store it in database systems to answer their own research questions, without exposing it in repositories that make it easy to find and retrieve. However, as soon as the need arises to pool several DBs or to open a DB (e.g. due to legal constraints such as the Open Data directive), these actors are faced with the issue of interoperability, which necessarily implies the use of standard data vocabularies or models.

Several standards for exchanging digitized information about biological diversity have emerged since the 2000s, such as Darwin Core, which is a standard for sharing data on biodiversity, in the sense of the presence of life on Earth and its links with the environment (Wieczorek et al. 2009). A first form of the standard was published in 1999, and then, thanks to successive working groups, various evolutions of this standard have emerged[7]. Today, this standard is widely used by natural history collection communities (in particular, the Taxonomic Databases Working Group (TDWG), now renamed Biodiversity Information Standards, was the initiator of this standard). It is even being increasingly adopted by more specialized groups, such as paleontologists, marine biodiversity researchers and the Nordic Genetic Resource Center[8], to share information on genetic resources (Wieczorek et al. 2012). The Darwin Core standard is based on other standards. It is an extension of the Dublin Core standard (DCMI Usage Board 2020), dedicated to describing the metadata of documents published on the Web. The motivation for this Darwin Core standard was that, to make effective use of existing biodiversity data for large-scale analyses of changes over time, coordination between different communities is required. The information must be in digital form, accessible, discoverable and integrated (Wieczorek et al. 2012). Other recognized standards and taxonomies exist in the field of information about biological diversity. Alongside the Darwin Core standard, the Biodiversity Information Standards group is developing other standards, data exchange protocols and vocabularies, such as the Audubon Core (AC). The latter consists of a set of vocabularies designed to represent the metadata of biodiversity resources and multi-media collections (TDWG 2022). Driven by directives – such as the European INSPIRE directive[9] or the European Open Data directive[10] – or out of necessity (e.g. to cross-reference multiple heterogeneous datasets), actors are increasingly adopting these standards.

However, as noted by Zárate et al. (2020), although in recent years biodiversity informatics has made significant progress in creating common shared vocabularies such as the Darwin Core and mechanisms for publishing these data, complete interoperability is still not attained and is currently limited to the aggregation of several datasets. Against this backdrop of still-isolated data silos, the authors draw

7 The latest and previous versions of the standard can be downloaded from http://rs.tdwg.org/dwc.htm [Accessed 7 August 2022].

8 Available at: www.nordgen.org [Accessed 7 August 2022].

9 Available at: www.ecologie.gouv.fr/directive-europeenne-inspire [Accessed 7 August 2022].

10 Available at: https://eur-lex.europa.eu/legal-content/EN/TXT/?uri=celex%3A32019L1024 [Accessed 7 August 2022].

attention to *Semantic Web technologies* that aim to transmit information to humans and also to machines, so that this information can be used autonomously by these machines for data integration and reuse across applications. Thus, in line with the adoption of standards and with a view to effective interoperability between information systems, it is pertinent and recommended to adopt Semantic Web technologies (also known as the linked data Web), in line with the Berners Lee five-stage approach[11] to open data and the FAIR principles: findable, accessible, interoperable, reusable.

The following section provides a brief introduction to Semantic Web technologies, also known as the linked data Web or linked open data Web (LOD Web), where the data are open.

6.1.3. *Towards open and linked data on the Web*

Public institutions have a long tradition of producing data. In France, for instance, the IGN[12] institute produces cartographic data, INSEE[13] produces statistical data for population analysis, the Météo France institute produces meteorological data, public transport agencies (RATP, TCL, RTM, etc.) produce public transport timetables and routes and environmental and biodiversity data are produced by research organizations. These data produced by public institutions are subject to directives in most countries and organizations around the world, such as the Open Data directive in Europe. This directive aims to encourage the opening up of public data to citizens, researchers, journalists, SMEs and start-ups, so that they can capture and reuse these data for public interest or commercial purposes. There are various ways of opening up data, but the solution most commonly used by institutions is to make them available on the Web through open data portals. From these portals, data are downloadable in various formats.

Berners Lee, the inventor of the Web, has published recommendations and a ranking of preferred data formats. Depending on the format chosen for data representation and storage, more or less advanced (automatic) data processing is possible. Berners Lee outlines a five-stage plan for opening up data on the Web (see Figure 6.2). At the very least, he recommends making data available on the Web (in PDF format, for example, a format that is not very usable by a computer program, but readable by a human). The next step is to make data available in a structured format, such as an Excel spreadsheet, which can be read by a computer program to automatically extract information. It is then recommended to publish data in an open, non-proprietary format (e.g. the open comma-separated values (CSV) format, rather

11 Inventor of the Web and initiator of the semantic Web.

12 Institut national de l'information géographique et forestière.

13 Institut national de la statistique et des études économiques.

than the proprietary Excel format). The last two levels are based on Semantic Web technologies, also known as the linked data Web. When a data producer chooses to publish its data according to Berners Lee's Tier 4 definition, each piece of data contained in a document becomes addressable by a uniform resource identifier (URI). This is a paradigm shift from the Web of documents to the Web of data (illustrated in Figure 6.3).

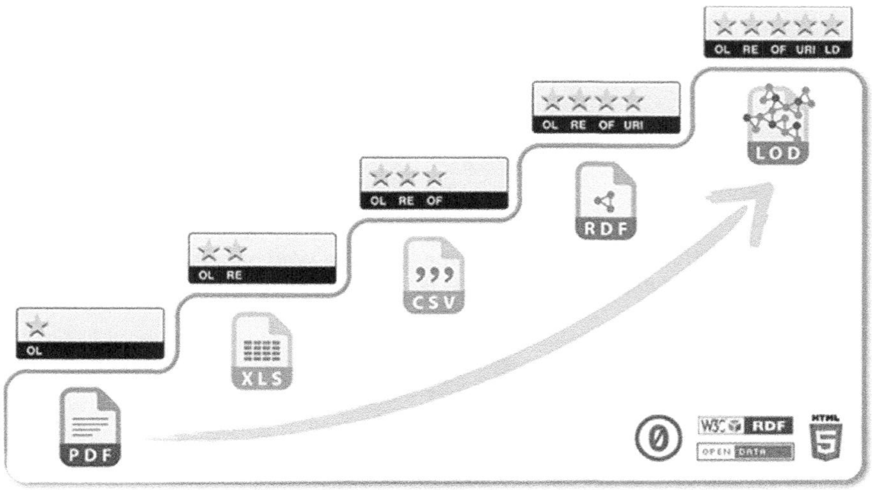

Figure 6.2. *Five-step program for deploying datasets with open data*[14]

COMMENT ON FIGURE 6.2.– The more datasets found in the formats (here, for example, PDF, XLS, CSV, etc.) that facilitate their exploitation by computer programs and whose specifications are open, the higher the level of data openness[15].

At this fourth level, data are written using the resource description framework (RDF) standard, a model for data exchange on the Web developed by the W3C (Cyganiak et al. 2014). RDF, in its simplest form, facilitates a relationship between two data items (also called *resources*) to be expressed in the form of a "subject, verb, object" triplet, with each element of the triplet identifiable by a URI. Figure 6.4 shows a Web of data RDF triplet expressing the "capital of" relationship between the data item "Helsinki" and the data item "Grand Duchy of Finland". Each element of the triplet has a URI that enables it to be referred to on the Web. A triplet is an embryonic

14 Figure taken from the website: https://5stardata.info/fr/ [Accessed 7 August 2022].

15 Image license: https://creativecommons.org/publicdomain/zero/1.0/deed.fr [Accessed 19 September 2022].

data graph made up of two nodes and an arc. Arcs (verbs in Figure 6.4) are essential elements for moving from one piece of data to another.

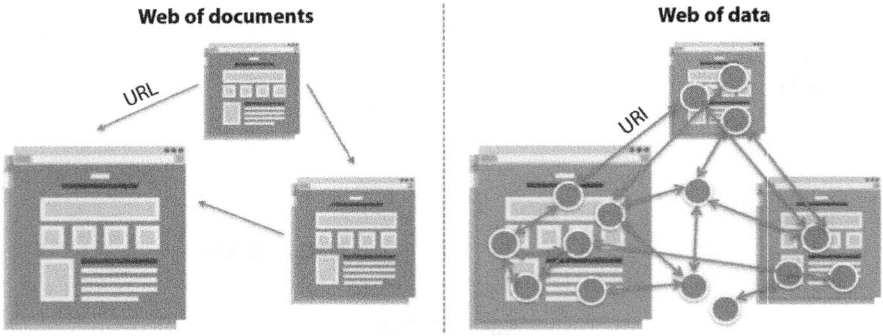

Figure 6.3. *From the Web of documents to the Web of data. For a color version of this figure, see www.iste.co.uk/kohlmann/linking.zip*

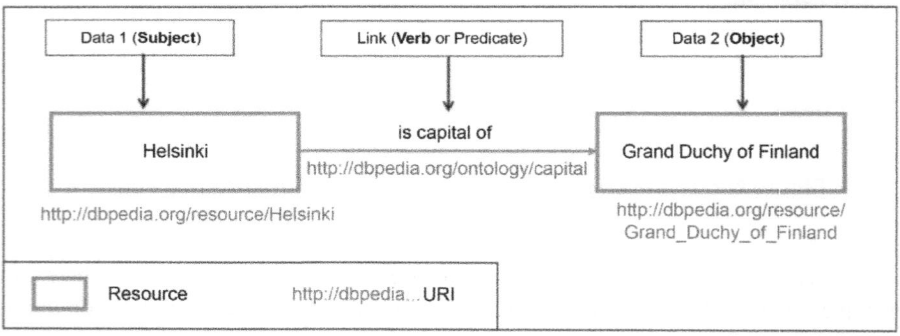

Figure 6.4. *RDF triplet expressing the fact that Helsinki is the capital of Finland. For a color version of this figure, see www.iste.co.uk/kohlmann/linking.zip*

The final level of data openness consists of linking together the RDF triplets defined as level 4 of data openness. In this way, the data published on one Web page are linked to other data on other Web pages, enabling them to be contextualized and enriched. Progressively, level 5 of data openness builds a graph of distributed data on the Web, also known as a knowledge graph. Figure 6.3 shows a schematic diagram, in orange, of a knowledge graph in the Web of data.

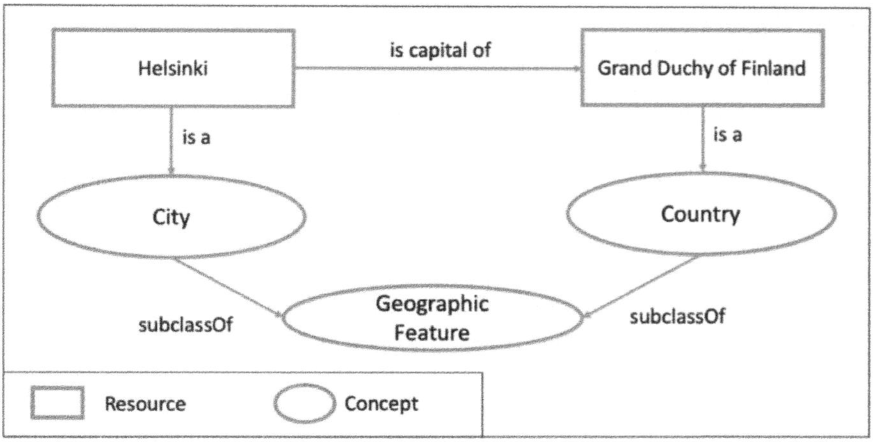

Figure 6.5. *RDF triplet linked to ontology concepts. For a color version of this figure, see www.iste.co.uk/kohlmann/linking.zip*

One or more concepts defining the resource are attached to each of these data items published on the Semantic Web. For example, when publishing a photo of a bird, we may associate concepts (tags) with this resource published on the Web, enabling a human and a machine to know that this resource is a "bird" and more specifically a "peony bullfinch". All these concepts, which specify membership sets, are defined in *ontologies*. The primary purpose of an ontology, in the IT sense, is to model the knowledge of a given domain in a form usable by a computer (Chaumier 2007). An ontology (sometimes also called a "vocabulary"), in the IT sense, is a (meta)data schema, providing a controlled vocabulary of concepts, each of which has explicitly defined, machine-usable semantics. By defining shared domain theories, ontologies help humans and machines to communicate precisely, by promoting the exchange of semantics and not only syntax (Maedche and Staab 2001). Figure 6.5 uses the example of Helsinki, the capital of Finland, to illustrate how, in the Semantic Web, this RDF triplet is linked to ontological concepts such as "city, country", enabling a human, and also a machine, to understand that behind these names lie geographic features of the world. Thanks to these concepts attached to resources published on the Web, it is then easy to automate processing. Therefore, it can be specified that all resources with which the geographic feature concept is associated will be displayed on a map automatically.

In the field of biodiversity data, numerous initiatives exist to publish data on the Semantic Web. For example, Zárate (2020) presents a method for integrating biodiversity data into the Semantic Web. Their approach consists first of extracting data describing species from the Global Biodiversity Information Facility

(GBIF)[16] database, converting these data into RDF and then contextualizing and describing them using other data present in the LOD Web: data from Wikidata, the NCBI Taxonomy, Springer Nature SciGraph or the OpenCitation corpus. The author demonstrates how biodiversity data can be better linked together when published on the Web as linked data. They also show how the Semantic Web makes it possible to contextualize these biodiversity data by linking them to other data available on the Web, enabling further data analysis. Another initiative is that of Penev et al. (2019), who present a knowledge graph called OpenBiodiv, made up of various biodiversity data collected from different data sources and transformed into RDF data published on the LOD Web. Thus, the authors explain that the RDF data contained in the OpenBiodiv knowledge graph were extracted from over 5,000 articles published in several open-access biodiversity journals, as well as from the Plazi Treatment Bank, which contains digitized taxonomic treatments from over 20,000 articles in around 80 academic journals. The scientific names used in this large group of texts have been mapped onto GBIF taxonomies, which have been converted to RDF and integrated into OpenBiodiv. The authors' aim is to demonstrate that, in the wake of earlier attempts to create systems and standards for sharing biodiversity knowledge (creation of the Taxonomy Database Working Group (TDWG) in 1985 and GBIF in 2001 to make biodiversity data accessible to all), the adoption of Semantic Web technologies has enabled us to go even further in opening up data and developing open scientific practices in the field of biodiversity.

Several advantages of using these technologies are highlighted:

– the transcription into RDF and publication on the LOD Web of data locked away in isolated silos have made it possible to open up the data and for any actor to easily reuse data from the biodiversity literature, including data previously available only in PDFs;

– the adoption of LOD technologies has enabled the integration of data from various sources in the field of biodiversity and federation with related green data from other fields;

– opening up the ontological model used in the OpenBiodiv graph to the Web of data, and opening up the source code, means that the principles of the Bouchout declaration[17] for open biodiversity data linked using recognized vocabularies, both in the field of biodiversity and in other fields, can be respected. In this way, the creators of OpenBiodiv rely on existing and standard vocabularies to describe the data contained in their knowledge graph. In particular, they use the Darwin Core standard.

16 Available at: www.gbif.org/what-is-gbif [Accessed 7 August 2022].

17 Available at: https://plazi.org/services/bouchout-declaration/ [Accessed 7 August 2022].

It should be noted that this Darwin Core standard is found in the vast majority of initiatives to publish biodiversity data in the Web of Data. It is a common pillar for all the data graphs created. This represents a gigantic step towards connecting these various RDF data graphs, all based on common concepts derived from the Darwin Core standard, which is itself published in RDF format and on the Web. These datasets are easily linked, and the pooling of data, for advanced spatio-temporal analyses, is made possible and facilitated by this process. This standard can establish links between different datasets that were previously isolated.

Numerous other initiatives exist to publish observations of biodiversity or the environment on the Semantic Web. These include those by Tran et al. (2020), Yacoubi et al. (2022) and a working group of the Open Geospatial Consortium (OGC) and the World Wide Web Consortium (W3C) studying the publication of Earth observations using the RDF Data Cube vocabulary[18]. What these projects have in common is the use of several ontologies, organized in a network, to describe observations and their evolution in time and space. For example, the Darwin Core ontology and Environment Ontology (EnvO[19]) describe biodiversity observations, and the W3C's OWL-Time and OGC's GeoSPARQL ontologies describe the spatial and temporal dimensions of these observations. Other standard ontologies used to describe observations made in a study area are the W3C and OGC ontologies: these include Sensor, Observation, Sampler, Actuator (SOSA) and Semantic Sensor Network (SSN), as well as the W3C's RDF Data Cube ontology[20], which enables the spatio-temporal analysis of data, based on an approach borrowed from business intelligence, a branch of IT that aims to help decision-makers by providing an overview of an activity.

After presenting the advantages of using Web data technologies, which enable data to be published on the Web and linked to other data to form knowledge graphs while respecting standards (and even several standards, by using several networked ontologies), we turn in the next section to the reality of the actors: i.e. data pooling and the use of common models require first and foremost that those responsible for the DBs to be shared agree on the concepts to be used to publish their data. We will see that aligning concepts requires meetings and agreements between actors, who weave links to better connect their data.

18 Available at: www.w3.org/TR/eo-qb [Accessed 7 August 2022].

19 Available at: https://bioportal.bioontology.org/ontologies/ENVO/?p=summary [Accessed 7 August 2022].

20 Available at: www.w3.org/TR/vocab-data-cube [Accessed 7 August 2022].

6.2. Linking actors in order to link data

In this section, we propose to examine the question of links in three stages. First, we study the different forms of linkage that are created between actors around biodiversity census issues. Then, in a second step, we see that alignments of concepts from different disciplines are sometimes necessary to document global trends in biodiversity evolution (NAS 2000). To carry out these alignments, computer scientists or knowledge representation theorists take on the role of mediators between different disciplines, in order to help establish a common frame of reference. In the third and final section, we look at the obstacles to linking data. We will see that the opening up and sharing of data have not yet been achieved, not least because of the problems inherent in the sensitive nature of this biodiversity data.

6.2.1. *Linking actors*

As already mentioned in this chapter as well as previous ones, digital platforms have multiplied over the period from the 2000s to the present day, coinciding with the emergence of crowdsourcing and collaborative platforms for data collection such as Wikipedia, which appeared in 2001. These digital nature mediatization platforms, initiated by local or national public policies, share a common goal: to sensitize the general public to nature and its preservation. The initial aim is therefore to (re)create a link between the general public and nature. If we consider the crowdsourcing platforms created by scientists, the use of the general public for nature observations is more opportunistic. The aim is not necessarily to raise awareness of nature, but rather to gain access to more data thanks to a public that is amateur, passionate and therefore often already aware of the changes that biodiversity is undergoing. In the first case, that of public policy initiatives, the collection of data by the general public is aimed more at raising public awareness of nature. In the second case, that of participatory sciences where experts and scientists rely on citizen participation to collect observations of biodiversity, the aim is more to help scientists in the difficult task of tracking the evolution of biodiversity over time. The Vigie-Nature participatory science program is an example of an initiative led by the MNHN (Julliard 2017). From its website, Vigie-Nature highlights these two aspects, political and scientific, of biodiversity study actions by the general public. Citizens are invited to take part in the study of biodiversity:

– with a scientific objective: to describe the changes undergone by biodiversity and understand the mechanisms that create these variations;

– with a political objective: to publicize the current biodiversity crisis (Muséum national d'histoire naturelle 2014).

In both cases, whether the aim is to raise public awareness of nature or to benefit from the surveys carried out by the general public, on-the-job training courses are offered to raise awareness of species among the amateur public, as well as of the protocols for carrying out observations from the natural world. These two types of initiatives involve experts in flora and fauna, who accompany the amateur public, train them and raise their awareness of nature. A tripartite link between the general public, expert and nature is being attempted. For researchers and biodiversity analysts, these training initiatives for the general public are of vital importance. Their aim is to enable more people to make high-quality observations, respecting the protocols that will then enable researchers to mobilize these data when analyzing complex phenomena and their underlying mechanisms, requiring the pooling of different sources of information. The links created here between researchers and the general public are necessary to guarantee the quality of the observations collected, an essential criterion when pooling these data for a global understanding of the changes at work.

Subsequently, during this phase of sharing DBs for a global understanding of biodiversity, it is the experts responsible for each of these DBs who must make contact, in order to pool their data. During an interview we conducted with the LPO, a volunteer in charge of the Isère database remarked:

> We had to set up gateways to exchange information between partners – there are perhaps fifteen different sources in Isère alone, between municipalities, communities of municipalities, and the metropolis, which collects information on parks and gardens, etc. – the aim being to try and present a somewhat unified vision of biodiversity in Isère, so that decisions can be taken with full knowledge of the facts.

In the case of these shared DBs covering the same territory, actors from different backgrounds (associations, municipalities, national parks, etc.), each experts in their own database, are thus brought together to pool their observations of biodiversity, and this without too many difficulties, according to the LPO volunteer with whom we spoke. It is when it is necessary to pool data from different territories that things become complicated:

> Already, there are population differences between east, west, north and south: there are species that are common here and rare in the west, and vice versa. So the perception of what is rare is different. There are species that breed in the north and not in the south, and vice versa, so this frame of reference is based on their habits, their rarity and their protection. Some of our species are protected; they're at the limit of their range, so we try to protect them. There are others for which this is not an issue, because they reproduce easily. That's where the debate

> lies: we only want to have one head at French level, and each region, department or smaller geographical entity is a special case.

So, as mentioned above, the pooling of DBs implies the use of a common model, which will tend to erase local particularities. This is not always desired by actors, or even desirable, since as this LPO volunteer points out, knowledge of locally protected species could be lost. In such cases, it is vital to design and build common models capable of accounting for local particularities. In such cases, knowledge representation experts can act as mediators between different communities of experts, helping to pool databases without loss of information. In the following section, we propose to analyze these DB alignments in the specific context of data publication on the Semantic Web.

6.2.2. *Aligning concepts in order to link data*

The pooling of biodiversity DBs and system interoperability for improved data sharing are among today's major challenges. While this sharing of data involves technical aspects, the fact remains that upstream of any sharing, the coordination of actors is necessary in order to establish unified data models, by mutual agreement, and to align certain concepts. Establishing standards facilitates data sharing. However, the very construction of these standards first and foremost requires multiple exchanges between specialists in a given field, a sharing of knowledge and mutual agreement on how a domain should be represented. In most cases, the process of creating standards involves bringing together different experts in a given field in a working group. The W3C, and also the OGC, for example, are standardization organizations that opt for this type of standard construction. This ultimate outcome, the creation of a standard, is therefore often the result of many years of (sometimes fruitless) exchanges between stakeholders (Dreal Bretagne et al. 2016). What is more, as Zucca (2019) points out, the standardization of local DBs sometimes results in a loss of information, a loss that is necessary for the pooling of data on a larger scale. As a result, some actors and communities are reluctant to share data and data models.

In this context, it is interesting to look at the Semantic Web. As actors adopt different models to reflect the particularities of their study context, and as it is sometimes impossible to get these actors to share a common model, Semantic Web specialists have come up with solutions for the automatic alignment of data models, enabling each community to retain the specific features of its chosen representations. Euzenat and Shvaiko (2007) present different methods for aligning concepts present in ontologies, approaches that come under the heading of ontology matching. They explain that these approaches are also applicable to the matching of relational or Extensible Markup Language (XML) data models. The aim of ontology matching is to find correspondences between semantically related entities in different ontologies. These correspondences can represent equivalence links or other relationships, such as consequence, subsumption or disjunction. In this way, links between different ontological data models are automatically constructed and, what is more, this discipline of ontology matching seeks to characterize the nature of these links. Automated solutions therefore exist to try and align concepts in the Semantic Web. However, the most common solution for representing domain data is to establish a common data model. These pivotal data models are created within working groups where, in the context of the Semantic Web, computer scientists sometimes find themselves taking on the role of mediator between different communities wishing to pool their data.

Unlike the world of relational DBs or XML schemas, the work of this computer mediator is facilitated in the world of the Semantic Web by the very specific organization of data models. Indeed, the Semantic Web differentiates three types of ontologies:

– *high-level ontologies*, defined as domain-independent ontologies. The concepts defined in these ontologies are fundamental and universal, in order to guarantee generality and expressiveness for a wide range of domains (Schmidt et al. 2019). High-level ontologies describe very general concepts, such as space, time, matter and object, which are independent of a particular problem or domain (Guarino 1998);

– *domain ontologies* describe the vocabulary related to a generic domain (such as medicine or the automotive industry) or a generic task or activity (such as diagnostics or sales), by specializing the terms introduced in the high-level ontology (Guarino 1998);

– *application ontologies* describe concepts that depend on both a particular domain and a particular task (Guarino 1998).

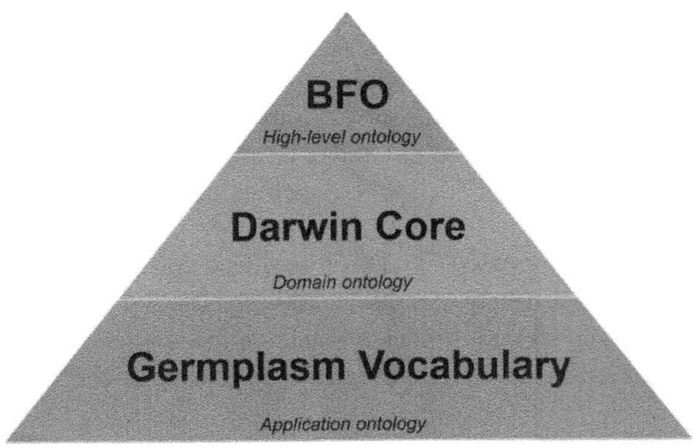

Figure 6.6. *Example of pyramid-shaped ontology organization*

Figure 6.6 shows an example of the pyramid-shaped organization of ontologies. At the center is the Darwin Core domain ontology already mentioned. This ontology inherits highly abstract concepts defined in the high-level ontology called Basic Formal Ontology (BFO)[21]. This ontology is presented as a data model designed for use in scientific research, analysis and information integration. By inheriting concepts from BFO, the creators of the Darwin Core ontology are not obliged to redefine notions specific to information integration already defined within other ontologies. The same applies to the Germplasm Vocabulary application ontology: this ontology inherits concepts defined within the Darwin Core standard and proposes an extension of them, in order to more specifically describe plant genetic resources, focusing on germplasm seed samples held by gene banks worldwide[22].

This pyramid-shaped organization of data models in the Semantic Web makes it possible to respect, in terms of the application ontology, the particularities of an application context. This model is linked, by concept inheritance, to less specific domain ontologies and, even higher up, to highly generalist high-level ontologies. In this way, the Semantic Web makes it possible to organize these three types of ontology into a network, while preserving the particularities of each application domain and respecting high-level standards. In this case, the mediating role of the computer scientist, an expert in knowledge representation, is to work with domain specialists to define which high-level ontologies to use, and which domain ontologies already exist. It is often necessary to make a selection, as several ontologies may have been defined to represent the same domain. It may then be necessary, for the particularities of the study, to create an application ontology.

The high-level ontologies most often used are Geosparql (OGC standard) and Owl-Time (W3C standard). The Geosparql ontology is used to represent the spatial dimension of data (e.g. the study area). The OWL-Time ontology, on the contrary, represents the temporal dimension of data. In fact, as noted by the OGC/W3C Spatial Data on the Web working group[23] (a group that brings together OGC and W3C members), these spatial and temporal dimensions are commonly shared by the vast majority of data present on the Web; thus, through these dimensions, it will be possible, in the Web of data, to link all Web data together.

The Semantic Web approach is therefore ideal for creating networked data models based on several different standards, and thus linking different DBs together, thanks, for example, to a shared dimension such as the spatial dimension. However, it should be noted that the use of this technology is still at the margins. While the

21 Available at: https://basic-formal-ontology.org/ [Accessed 7 August 2022].

22 Available at: https://code.google.com/archive/p/darwincore-germplasm/ [Accessed 7 August 2022].

23 Available at: www.w3.org/TR/sdw-bp [Accessed 7 August 2022].

Semantic Web is now widely used by major Web actors such as Google and LinkedIn, for example, to improve data linking and searching of data and associated metadata, in practice, the pooling of domain or application DBs has yet to be undertaken. Very often, relational DBs remain the most widespread form of database available to domain actors, as the transition to Semantic Web technologies and the paradigm shift towards data graphs have a significant entry cost, hence the reluctance to change. The following section looks in more detail at this and other obstacles to the pooling of nature observation DBs.

6.2.3. *Obstacles to the sharing and opening up of databases*

A major obstacle to data pooling in the field of biodiversity remains the fear of associative actors seeing their expertise and the quality of their observations disappear in a standard data model, erasing the particularities of their field of study or the species observed. However, this fear of standardization needs to be mitigated as progress is being made, as Zucca (2019, p. 203) notes: "The standardization of surveys is increasingly emanating from the associations themselves", in order to facilitate collaboration between different associations or different local bodies of the same association, and in order to "prove phenomena that were only felt by naturalists: the considerable decline in common birds, bats and butterflies" (Zucca 2019, p. 203), for example.

For some naturalists, sharing their own data can feel like an act of dispossession. "Obtaining these data is the result of many years of experience and many hours of observation: the observer must be considered worthy of their work" (Zucca 2019, p. 199). There is the individual data collector, and also the group, a community of experts who may, by mutual agreement, lock up their data for various reasons. Some communities of experts remain closed and "claim the capacity for expertise in the work of analyzing and understanding their data" considering that they are "best able to analyze the data they themselves have produced" (Zucca 2019, p. 196).

Another obstacle to the opening up and sharing of DBs, which should not be overlooked in these associative communities, is the desire to protect species. For example, a volunteer interlocutor at the LPO mentioned in 2020 that "in the case of the wolf, initially, when it came back everyone wanted to note that they had seen the first wolf in Isère, but now no one does, because everyone is afraid the hunter will shoot it".

Zucca (2019) summarizes various obstacles to sharing natural data linked to different "things in the world" that need to be protected. These include the desire to protect species or data (under copyright law) or associations (and their grants, for example). Reasons for not sharing biodiversity data may include:

– wishing to preserve the monopoly of a place or its tranquility;

– fearing that this sharing will harm certain species;

– fearing that these data could be misinterpreted or misanalyzed;

– fearing that these data will be used by engineering firms;

– fearing a loss of visibility for the associative structure.

Added to this is a technical obstacle, as opening up your data can prove to be very time-consuming: it means having a quality database that is maintained and, ideally, compliant with standards. What is more, aligning with other DBs can be even more restrictive and difficult to implement, especially when this alignment results in a loss of precision concerning the study area.

Adopting Semantic Web technologies and networked ontologies (which are technically the best current solutions for sharing DBs, while retaining the specificity of each territory, thanks to application ontologies) is technically difficult to implement, and the result (data graphs) is often difficult to exploit for actors who are inexperienced in the field. There are mixed feelings about Semantic Web technologies.

Some find them too complex, and note that "the Semantic Web is currently losing interest in the scientific community", but that "it will probably come back in another form. Because of the challenge of interoperability" (Rovellotti 2019, p. 21). Others, on the contrary, believe that the current challenge is to "reconcile data representing the complexity of living things at multiple levels (molecule, protein, gene, cell, phenotype, species, ecosystem, etc.)" and that it is thanks to research into the Semantic Web that we will be able to "create the tools needed to explore this interdisciplinarity" (Rovellotti 2019, p. 21).

6.3. Conclusion

In conclusion, it is now essential to raise public awareness of nature and re-establish a link with it, with the political aim of publicizing the current biodiversity crisis and ensuring its preservation. Bringing this crisis to light on a large scale requires the pooling of databases produced at different territorial scales and by different actors.

We have found that there are currently technical solutions in the Semantic Web, based on standards such as the Darwin Core, to facilitate the pooling of biodiversity databases, while respecting the local particularities of a territory or community. What is more, we have noted that the development of these solutions brings actors from different communities together, creating links between data and actors. However, these Semantic Web technologies are still at the margins and are complicated to implement.

Another way of reaching out to the general public and re-establishing a link with nature is to provide access to a service that enables the user to learn about nature and thus to better understand/increase interest it in and potentially safeguard it. In recent years, we have seen a rapid progression in the development of such services, based on big data and artificial intelligence technologies. One example is the service offered by Pl@ntNet, which uses big data technologies to help ordinary users identify species. This application is presented in Chapter 8, after a closer look at the LPO database in the next chapter.

6.4. References

Biodiversity Information Standards (2022). Standards [Online]. Available at: https://www.tdwg.org/standards/ [Accessed 3 May 2022].

Chaumier, J. (2007). Les ontologies : Antécédents, aspects techniques et limites. *Documentaliste Sciences de l'information*, 44, 81–83 [Online]. Available at: https://doi.org/10.3917/docsi.441.0081 [Accessed 7 August 2022].

Cyganiak, R., Wood, D., Lanthaler, M. (2014). RDF 1.1 concepts and abstract syntax. *W3* [Online]. Available at: https://www.w3.org/TR/rdf11-concepts/ [Accessed 28 April 2022].

DCMI (2020). Usage board. Dublin Core [Online]. Available at: https://www.dublincore.org/specifications/dublin-core/ [Accessed 28 April 2022].

Dreal Bretagne, Conseil régional de Bretagne, GIP Bretagne environnement (2016). Standard d'échange des données naturalistes. GeoBretagne [Online]. Available at: https://cms.geobretagne.fr/sites/default/files/documents/modele_architecture_table_naturaliste_v3.pdf [Accessed 28 March 2022].

Euzenat, J. and Shvaiko, P. (2007). *Ontology Matching*. Springer, Berlin.

Groom, Q., Güntsch, A., Huybrechts, P., Kearney, N., Leachman, S., Nicolson, N., Page, R.D.M., Shorthouse, D.P., Thessen, A.E., Haston, E. (2020). People are essential to linking biodiversity data. *Database* [Online]. Available at: https://doi.org/10.1093/database/baaa072 [Accessed 28 April 2022].

Guarino, N. (1998). Formal ontologies and information systems. *FOIS'98*. Trente.

INPN (2022). Données d'observation sur les espèces. Principes de qualité [Online]. Available at: https://inpn.mnhn.fr/programme/donnees-observations-especes/references/qualite?lg=fr [Accessed 28 April 2022].

Julliard, R. (2017). Science participative et suivi de la biodiversité : l'expérience Vigie-Nature. *Natures Sciences Sociétés*, 25(4), 412–417.

Kohlmann, É. and Cambone, M. (2021). Plateforme Nature-Isère. In *Humains et Données : Création, Médiation, Décision, Narration, Actes Du Colloque "Document Numérique et Société", Nancy, 2020*, Simonnot, B., Broudoux, E., Chartron, G. (eds). Boeck Supérieur, Brussels [Online]. Available at: https://hal.archives-ouvertes.fr/hal-03242713 [Accessed 4 March 2022].

Legrand, M. (2013). Vigie-Nature : Sciences participatives et biodiversité à grande échelle. *Cahiers des Amériques latines*, 72(73), 65–84 [Online]. Available at: https://doi.org/10.4000/cal.2805 [Accessed 28 April 2022].

Maedche, A. and Staab, S. (2001). Ontology learning for the Semantic Web. *IEEE Intelligent Systems*, 16(2), 72–79 [Online]. Available at: https://doi.org/10.1109/5254.920602 [Accessed 4 March 2022].

Marsh, D.M. and Trenham, P.C. (2008). Current trends in plant and animal population monitoring. *Conservation Biology*, 22(3), 647–655.

Michel, F., Faron-Zucker, C., Gandon, F. (2018). Integration of biodiversity linked data and web APIs using SPARQL micro-services. *Biodiversity Information Science and Standards*, 2, e25481 [Online]. Available at: https://doi.org/10.3897/biss.2.25481 [Accessed 4 March 2022].

Muséum National d'Histoire Naturelle (2014). Du citoyen à la recherche scientifique. Vigie-Nature [Online]. Available at: https://www.vigienature.fr/fr/programme-vigie-nature-2877 [Accessed 3 May 2022].

Muséum National d'Histoire Naturelle (2019). Données naturalistes : Le pouvoir des grands nombres. Vigie-Nature [Online]. Available at: https://www.vigienature.fr/fr/actualites/donnees-naturalistes-pouvoir-grands-nombres-3630 [Accessed 3 May 2022].

National Academy of Sciences (2000). *Grand Challenges in Environmental Sciences* [Online]. Available at: https://doi.org/10.17226/9975 [Accessed 3 May 2022].

Nature France (2021). Évolution du volume de données disponibles sur la biodiversité [Online]. Available at: http://naturefrance.fr/indicateurs/evolution-du-volume-de-donnees-disponibles-sur-la-biodiversite [Accessed 3 May 2022].

Penev, L., Dimitrova, M., Senderov, V., Zhelezov, G., Georgiev, T., Stoev, P., Simov, K. (2019). OpenBiodiv: A knowledge graph for literature-extracted linked open data in biodiversity science. *Publications*, 7(2), 38 [Online]. Available at: https://doi.org/10.3390/publications7020038 [Accessed 3 May 2022].

Rovellotti, O. (2019). Open-data et biodiversité. Pourquoi et comment publier ses données de biodiversité en opendata ? *GeoNature* [Online]. Available at: https://geonature.fr/documents/2019-04-biodiversite-opendata.pdf [Accessed 3 May 2022].

Schmidt, D., Trojahn, C., Vieira, R. (2019). Aligning top-level and domain ontologies. Report.

Tran, B.H., Aussenac-Gilles, N., Comparot, C., Trojahn, C. (2020). Semantic integration of raster data for earth observation: An RDF dataset of territorial unit versions with their land cover. *ISPRS International Journal of Geo-Information*, 9(9), 503 [Online]. Available at: https://doi.org/10.3390/ijgi9090503 [Accessed 25 April 2022].

Wieczorek, J., Döring, M., De Giovanni, R., Robertson, T., Vieglais, D. (2009). Darwin Core [Online]. Available at: http://www.tdwg.org/standards/450/ [Accessed 3 May 2022].

Wieczorek, J., Bloom, D., Guralnick, R., Blum, S., Döring, M., Giovanni, R., Robertson, T., Vieglais, D. (2012). Darwin Core: An evolving community-developed biodiversity data standard. *PLOS One*, 7(1) [Online]. Available at: https://doi.org/10.1371/journal.pone.0029715 [Accessed 25 April 2022].

Yacoubi, N., Faron, C., Michel, F., Gandon, F., Corby, O. (2022). A model for meteorological knowledge graphs: Application to Météo-France observational data. *ICWE 22nd International Conference on Web Engineering*. June, Bari [Online]. Available at: https://hal.inria.fr/hal-03619869/document [Accessed 25 April 2022].

Zárate, M., Zermoglio, P., Wieczorek, J., Plos, A., Mazzanti, R. (2020). Linked open biodiversity data (LOBD): A semantic application for integrating biodiversity information. *Biodiversity Information Science and Standards*, 4 [Online]. Available at: https://doi.org/10.3897/biss.4.58975 [Accessed 25 April 2022].

Zucca, M. (2019). La mise en commun des données naturalistes : des pratiques complexes. *Revue française d'administration publique*, 169, 195–206.

7

The Challenges and Implementation of the LPO Auvergne-Rhône-Alpes Naturalist Information System

Figure 7.1. *Faune-France, the new digital naturalist "community"? Julie Polge (2021). For a color version of this figure, see www.iste.co.uk/kohlmann/linking.zip*

Chapter written by Daniel THONON.

Biodiversity information systems (BISs) manage naturalist data and are widely used by public bodies and nature protection associations. The work carried out by the Ligue pour la protection des oiseaux Auvergne-Rhône-Alpes (LPO AuRA, Auvergne-Rhône-Alpes League for the Protection of Birds)) to protect species, sites and habitats requires a sound knowledge of the fauna. This knowledge comes from the collection of observations made by naturalists and professionals, as well as the contextualization of these data. To manage the acquisition and enhancement of the fauna data entrusted to it, it has set up a BIS. The LPO also works to raise awareness of the challenges of biodiversity loss, and the collection of observations is a rewarding entry point for contributors. The LPO is thus in a position to lead a crowdsourcing network comprising some 150,000 observers in France[1] and numerous partner associations. Finally, the LPO manages the controlled transmission of data to government departments[2], local authorities, research organizations, etc.

This chapter is the testimony of a contributor to this BIS. It presents both the system's functionalities and the way in which contributors use these tools and communicate with other stakeholders. This information comes from exchanges between the author and other BIS administrators, validators and contributors.

In section 7.1, we present the evolution of observation management systems, from the paper forms collected since the 1970s to the current information system. In section 7.2, we describe in detail how the various players use the information system: network management, observation collection, validation and data exchange with other BISs.

7.1. The evolution of naturalist data management

In their work, Montagne (2011) and Charvolin et al. (2022) present the genesis of VisioNature, which refers to the BIS developed by the Swiss company Biolovision and used in France, and then that of Faune-France a few years later. The following sections illustrate this evolution through the case of Isère.

1 Available at: https://cdnfiles1.biolovision.net/www.faune-france.org/userfiles/FauneFrance/FFnews/FauneFrance100millionsV5WEB.pdf [Accessed 25 October 2022].

2 Voluntary deposit of volunteer contributors and legal deposit of biodiversity data produced as part of publicly funded studies since the 2016 law "de reconquête de la bio-diversité". Available at: https://depot-legal-biodiversite.naturefrance.fr/ [Accessed 25 October 2022].

7.1.1. *Data collection before computerization: 1973–2000*

Since its creation in 1973, the Centre Ornithologique Rhône-Alpes (CORA), which later merged with the LPO, has been collecting observations from its members and employees.

These were paper forms providing the minimum information required for observation: observer, date, species, number/sex/age, nesting index and notes. Figure 7.2 shows such a form.

The paper files were centralized at CORA Isère and could be consulted by other members. They could also be used as a basis for studies and protection measures, such as red lists of endangered species, the creation of protected areas or atlases of the species observed.

From the outset, this approach illustrated the association's founding principles: to know, share, mobilize and safeguard.

ANNEE : 2009 OBSERVATEUR(S) :

COMMUNE(S) : 38320 ETBENS

LIEU-DIT : La Tuilerie

D'après carte IGN 1/25000

DATE Jour	DATE Mois	ESPECES CONTACTEES	NBR / SEXE / AGE	NIDIF.	NOTES
27	03	Col-Vert	1 f A	7	verderet
29	03	Mésange bleue	1 A	7	nichoir
30	03	Col Vert	3 M A	2	Verderet
31	03	Rougequeue Noir	1 f A	2	
1	04	Mésanges bleues	2 H/f A	14	Nichoir
2	04	Bergeronnette Ruis	2 M/f A	2	Verderet
4	04	Merle Noir	1 M A	3	sur le site
5	04	Merle Noir	1 f A	16	sur le Site
5	04	Rougequeue Noir	1 M A	3	alentour
5	04	Rouge-gorge fam.	1 M A	3	Site et Alentour
5	04	Pinson des Arbres		3	site et alentour
5	04	Verdier d'Europe		3	site et alentour
5	04	Pic-Vert		3	bois du château d'Eybens

CORA ISERE, MNEI 5 PLACE BIR HAKEIM 38000 GRENOBLE

Figure 7.2. *Example of a handwritten observation form. Species are listed down the left (2009)*

Until the early 1990s, the primary purpose of these data was to provide a better understanding of the department's fauna and its dynamics. The use of these data for species protection was initially limited, for example, the protection of raptor nesting sites by volunteers. The use of these data in studies on the impact of human activity on wildlife[3] followed the introduction of this approach. In a large number of cases, the aim was to provide contradictory studies as part of litigation aimed at overturning authorization to carry out an urban, road, commercial or other development project with potential or proven effects on the environment.

This notion of naturalist data enabling us to decide on a development emerged gradually and remains an important motivation for the contributors with whom we have had the opportunity to exchange views.

However, there were a number of difficulties associated with collecting data on paper. Since entering data was unrestricted, observers sometimes did not respect the official nomenclature. For example, in the form shown in Figure 7.2, the mallard duck was named "*col-vert*" (green collar in English). The geographical precision was that of the locality, which could vary from less than 100 meters to more than a kilometer depending on the case. Sharing involved consultation in the association's premises, which nevertheless offered opportunities for direct exchanges between observers. Last but not least, the use of the data meant consulting paper archives that were ill-suited to information retrieval.

7.1.2. *The beginnings of computerization: early 2000s*

To overcome these difficulties, the CORA association began to computerize data collection. In the early 2000s, Excel spreadsheets were made available to observers, enabling them to enter information in a more controlled way. In addition to capturing new information, these files enabled the digitization of paper data sheets. The digitization of the data sheets was largely carried out by volunteers.

The list of species included several taxonomic groups: birds, mammals, reptiles, etc.

This computerized version avoided many data entry errors and was much easier to use, both faster and with more complex queries. However, geographical precision remained at the locality level. These files were not distributed and could only be consulted on the association's premises.

3 Available at: www.ecologie.gouv.fr/levaluation-environnementale [Accessed 25 October 2022].

Date * (champ	Observateur *	Nom de Commune (brut) *	Lieu-Dit (brut) *	Localisation (brut)	Espèce français *	Nombre	Male	Femelle	Nombre Sexe	Statut	Code Nidificat	Notes
30/09/2000		VATILIEU	Vatilieu	Cimetière	Busard cendré	1	1					Depuis 1 mois au même endroit
30/09/2000		VATILIEU	Vatilieu	Cimetière	Torcol fourmilier	1					12	Nichoir
30/09/2000		CRAS		Etang de Chantes	Grand-duc d'Europe	1						Chasse en vol sur étangs
21/05/2000		GRENOBLE		Maison du tourism	Sittelle torchepot	1						Choquée, relachée à Seysinnet Village
02/06/2000		FONTANIL-CORNILLON	Station d'épuration	Canal EDF, près :	Aigrette garzette	2						
02/06/2000		FONTANIL-CORNILLON	Station d'épuration	Canal EDF, près :	Cygne tuberculé	7			2 adulte		19	
04/06/2000		SAINT-LATTIER	les Econdues	A49	Cigogne noire	1						Vol au-dessus de l'A49, 21h20 (encore jour)
24/07/2000		ECHIROLLES		Toit du Casino	Guêpier d'Europe	1						Grosse pluie
18/03/2000		MONESTIER-DE-CLERMONT		D34 vers Pont de	Faucon pèlerin	1						En piqué sur proie
09/03/2000		NANTES-EN-RATIER	le Marais	Sentier	Bruant des roseaux	3	3					
09/03/2000		NANTES-EN-RATIER	le Marais	Sentier	Bruant proyer	2						
09/03/2000		NANTES-EN-RATIER	le Marais	Sentier	Grive litorne							
09/03/2000		NANTES-EN-RATIER	le Marais	Sentier	Lièvre variable (des al	1						
03/03/2000		MARCIEU	Route Forestière de Marcieu		Aigle royal	2						Adultes volant ensemble
03/03/2000		MARCIEU	Route Forestière de Marcieu		Mésange noire							

Figure 7.3. *Example of an observation entry screen (computer entry via spreadsheet)*

7.1.3. *An initial centralized system: 2007–2009*

In 2007, CORA launched a new website, the fruit of reflection on the theme of participatory ecology, using the Internet to publicize and share knowledge about French natural heritage.

The site was intended to be an information system on wildlife, useful to provide elected officials, managers, companies and citizens with all of the information necessary (indicators, maps, data, assessments) for the protection of wildlife. The site offered the possibility for anyone, CORA member or not, to transmit their observations, contributing to the common effort of biodiversity conservation by sharing their knowledge.

The site is now open to the general public, making it easier to enter observations and to consult. The level of geographical precision and the list of species remain identical to those in the Excel files.

As with the other systems, this site did not offer the possibility of contacting observers directly by email to ask for clarification of their observations, particularly if they posed reliability problems.

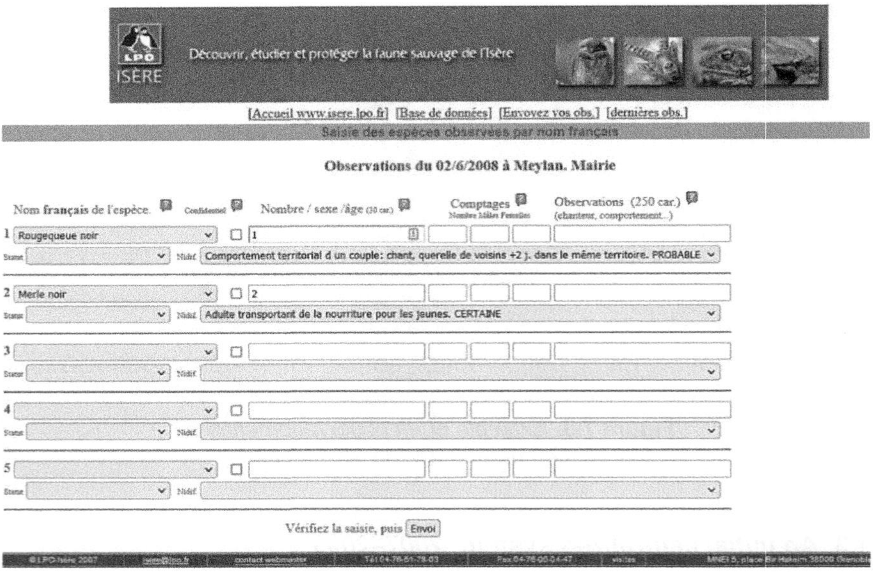

Figure 7.4. *Example of an observation entry screen from the LPO Isère's first naturalist information system (now obsolete)*

7.1.4. *The current system: since 2009*

Parallel to these developments in Isère, the Swiss ornithological station of Sempach[4] developed a site for collecting observations based on the same principle of participation of the general public[5]. The software was developed by the Swiss company Biolovision and is now used in over a dozen other European countries, including Italy, Germany and Poland.

In France, this system was first set up by the LPO Haute-Savoie in 2006 and gradually spread to various local LPOs: PACA, Loire, Vienne and Isère during 2009. This spread of the LPO led to the creation in 2011 of VisioNature[6]. Montagne (2011) describes the system's development and operation in his master's thesis. In France,

4 The Sempach ornithological station is a Swiss association for the study and protection of birds based in Sempach, in the canton of Lucerne. Available at: www.vogelwarte.ch/en/station/ [Accessed 25 October 2022].

5 Available at: www.ornitho.ch [Accessed 25 October 2022].

6 This platform is presented in the tutorial. Available at: https://youtu.be/fpP2sOK3pD4 [Accessed 25 October 2022].

this diffusion has culminated in the establishment of 36 local portals, one national generalist portal and five specialized portals[7].

The desire of other French naturalist associations to join this approach led to the creation of Faune-France in 2017. This collective approach currently brings together more than 50 naturalist associations in France. When it went live, the site offered a national naturalist data portal with over 50 million observations. Today, more than 100 million observations have been collected[8] for 30 taxonomic groups (birds, butterflies, mammals, etc.) and nearly 13,000 species. These data cover around 99% of French communes. It is accessible via a national portal[9] and regional portals.

Compared with the portal described in section 7.1.3, this system offers several particularly useful features:

– entry of geolocated observations: users can click on a map to indicate the precise location of their observation;

– form-based data entry: the ergonomics allow multiple data entry masks, according to different protocols that were previously managed by heterogeneous applications, such as the FEPS software for the temporal monitoring of common birds (STOC-EPS). An observer therefore has just one website to use, but several different input masks depending on the protocols followed;

– data validation: a validator can communicate with the observer via messaging to ask for details of the observation and validate it scientifically.

These functions are described in more detail in section 7.2.

7.2. Functions of the naturalist information system

7.2.1. *General presentation*

Today, the BIS is therefore the result of several concomitant developments: firstly, technological possibilities and their acceptance by the contributor community have enabled the implementation of widely accessible databases. At the same time, Zucca (2019) and Charvolin et al. (2022) note that the motivations and numbers of contributors have led to a very significant increase in the volume of data. Finally, the

7 The list and description of these sites can be consulted on the portal. Available at: www.ornitho.fr [Accessed 25 October 2022].

8 Available at: www.faune-france.org/index.php?m_id=1164&a=2180#FN2180 [Accessed 25 October 2022].

9 Available at: www.faune-france.org [Accessed 25 October 2022].

evolving relationship between the LPO AuRA and the French government, as described by Fortier and Alphandéry (2017), has led to greater use of the data. Managing multiple databases and applications was no longer viable and led to the generalization of a more efficient information system. This BIS is now the support for naturalist data management processes, aiming to ensure that the data collected by contributors are validated and made available to all stakeholders (the general public, consultancies, researchers, government departments, etc.).

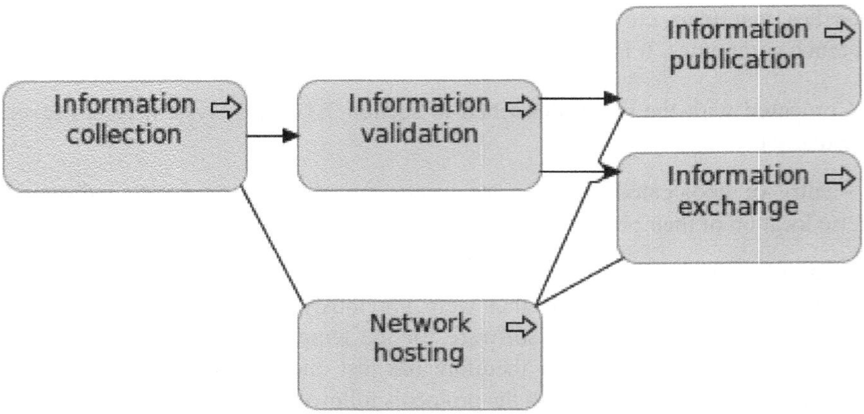

Figure 7.5. *The main BIS acquisition and enhancement processes*

The processes directly linked to the acquisition and enhancement of naturalistic data are as follows:

– the "collect information" function allows observers to enter their observations. Several collection modes are available;

– the "validate observations" section enables validators to exchange information with contributors about doubtful or incomplete observations. It guarantees the reliability of the information and considerably increases the possibilities for exploiting the natural data collected;

– the "data enhancement" section covers all activities aimed at enhancing the value of naturalist data for different audiences. This may involve the presentation of maps, sensitivity studies, atlases, etc.;

– "data exchange" enables the LPO to transmit data, according to defined agreements, to various partners, which may include consultancy firms, research organizations, local authorities, government departments, etc. Reciprocally, it enables the LPO's partners to transmit data to it on a large scale.

Other processes are involved in managing the BIS:

– the "network coordinator" is responsible for liaising with observers and partners. This makes it possible to recruit new observers and partners and to support them in the process of collecting and promoting knowledge;

– the "steering the information system" function enables the LPO to define the objectives and orientations of the approach. It also ensures coordination with the steering bodies of partners and other interested parties. This mission is carried out, by delegation from the LPO AuRA board of directors, by the SIN Steering Committee made up of LPO employees in charge of naturalist data, plus a volunteer referee. This steering committee works in conjunction with the naturalist committee (scientific body) and the company Biolovision;

– "managing repositories" cover the management of reference data, such as species lists, their conservation status[10] (the state of a species' populations at a given time), their characteristics, geographical locations, etc. It also ensures consistency with other repositories, such as TAXREF provided by the Inventaire national patrimoine naturel (INPN).

– the term "information system administration" covers the various activities required to keep the system running smoothly.

The main processes are detailed below.

7.2.2. *Animating observer networks: the human link*

The profiles of contributors are very varied, from novices taking part in a bird count in their garden for an hour a year to experienced naturalists who transmit tens of thousands of observations a year. It is important that these different audiences can participate according to their possibilities and desires. Facilitating networks of contributors is an important part of the BIS organization. It enables them to recruit new observers, train them, upgrade their skills and show them the value of their participation.

There are several ways of recruiting new observers. The annual Garden Bird Count in France (ODJ), organized by the LPO and the Muséum national d'histoire naturelle (MNHN), enables many private individuals to pass on information about birds seen in their gardens, thus familiarizing themselves with the basic principles of observation. Some bird-watching observers continue to pass on their observations

10 Available at: www.iucn.org/fr [Accessed 25 October 2022].

throughout the year. Others go beyond the perimeter of their garden to observe and transmit data in other environments.

Training is provided by volunteers who lead introductory outings for the use of the various tools. These may be dedicated outings, introductory sessions during another outing or training undertaken while manning a stand. Training is also provided to introduce protocol-based data entry.

It is also important that contributors know what their participation is for. Feedback to observers can take the form of presentations of studies carried out with the data, publication of articles, theme days, etc. They can also consult the maps presented on the site.

7.2.3. *Gathering information: public input*

Information is collected in several ways: observers enter their observations into the BIS, and data from partner BISs is imported en masse, along with data from digitized paper archives.

Figure 7.6 shows the various players involved in data collection in relation to the tool's main functions:

– the top rectangles represent different types of observers. There are several categories of users:

- bird-watching participants, who take part in the observation campaigns of the Vigie-Nature program[11],

- observers contributing via the Naturalist mobile app, whose level of naturalistic knowledge varies greatly,

- observers using the Web interface, who are generally quite experienced and prefer this mode of entry to using the Naturalist application,

- partners: these are naturalist associations, protected area managers and local authorities with whom the LPO AuRA has signed a data exchange agreement;

– the rectangles with rounded edges represent the services provided by the BIS, described in more detail below;

– the rectangles at the bottom of the figure represent different types of records in the database.

---

11 Available at: www.vigienature.fr/fr/observatoire-des-oiseaux-des-jardins (Accessed 25 October 2022).

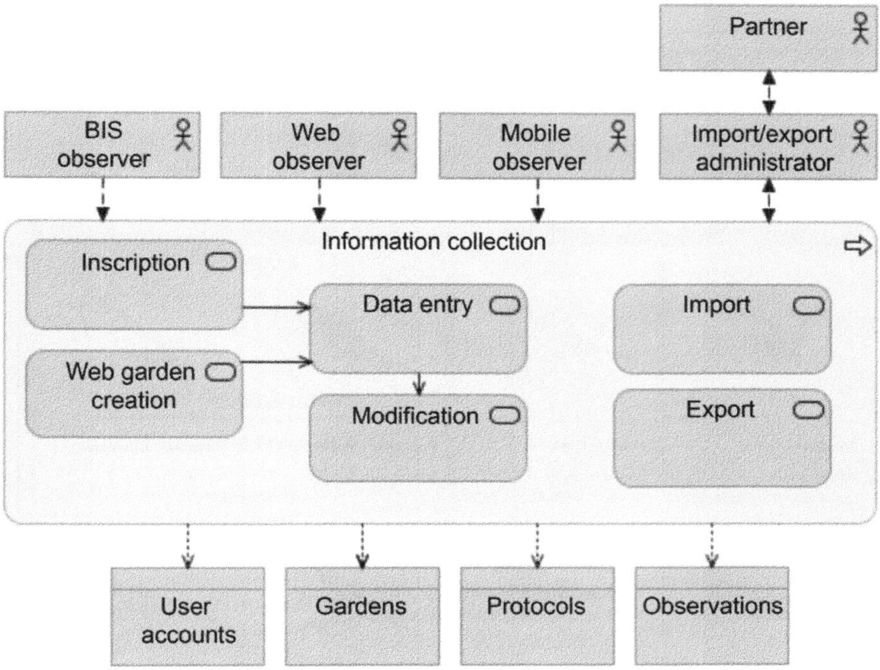

Figure 7.6. *Observational data collection process and flow*

Different categories of users may have different links with the BIS. In their study on the sociology of observers, Charvolin, Pietropaoli and Joliveau (Charvolin et al. 2022) distinguish seven classes of observer. These different classes are reflected in part in the mode of information transmission: annual bird count, punctual entry and protocol entry.

7.2.3.1. *Simplified Web entry*

This input mode is designed for garden bird-watchers, most of whom are beginners with little ornithological knowledge. It allows a guided entry of species on a page presenting a drawing of common species. The observer enters the duration of the session (1) and then designates the species seen (2).

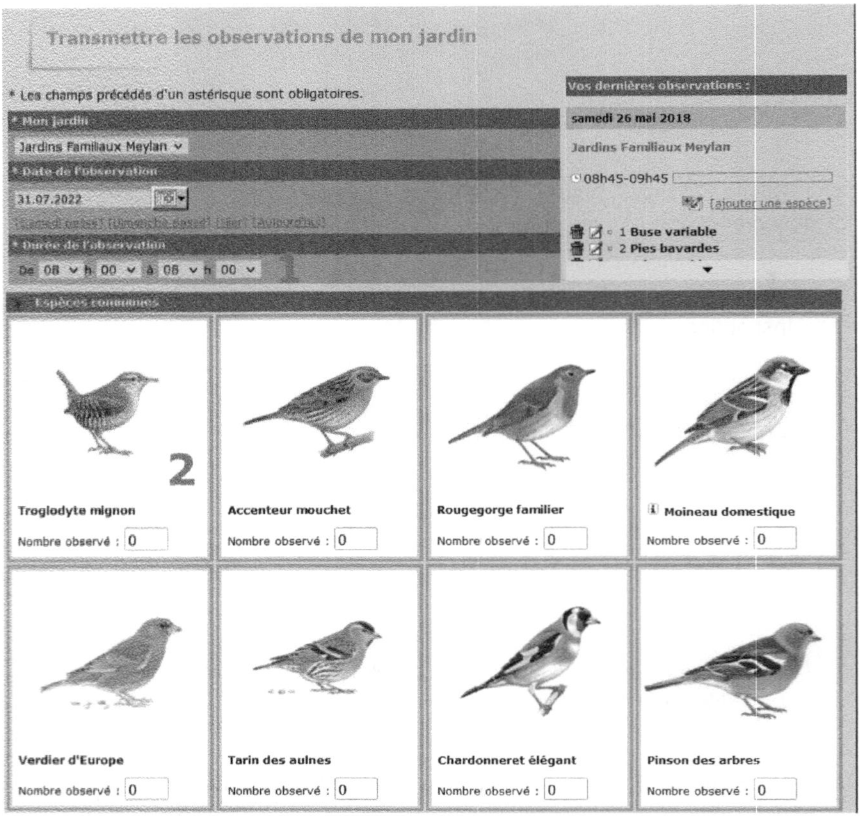

Figure 7.7. *The simplified Web portal entry screen used by contributors to the "garden bird" surveys*

This input mode is easy to use for beginners. It also makes it possible to quantify the prospecting effort, as the duration of the entry is memorized in the entry form. The advantage is that observations are recorded over time (minimum one hour). In general, regular observers no longer use this input mode, preferring to enter data on a one-off basis or with a general list.

7.2.3.2. *Punctual Web entry*

This mode allows an observer to enter a single observation, as opposed to a list or protocol. In addition to entering basic information, more detailed information can be entered if required.

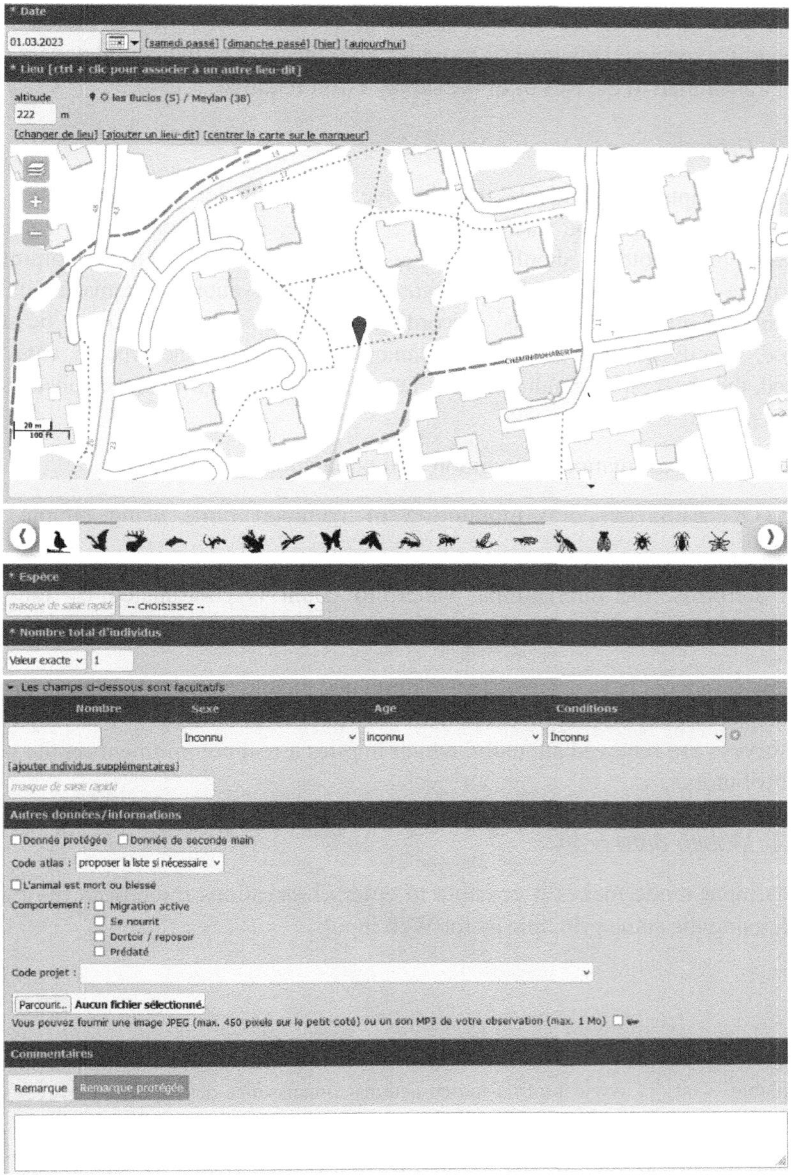

Figure 7.8. *The Web portal punctual-entry screen*

This type of spot observation is simple to use and well-suited to indicating the presence of a species. However, it provides no indication of the completeness of the species transmitted to the BIS or of the survey effort required.

7.2.3.3. *Protocol-based Web entry*

The data capture methods described above pose methodological difficulties when it comes to exploiting the data. Whenever possible, observations made within the framework of a protocol should be better exploited by the scientific community. These more advanced modes of data capture enable observations to be made within the framework of different protocols[12] according to a methodology that must be strictly followed, specifying the prospecting techniques to be used, the type of data to be collected, the observation conditions, etc. For example, the BIS manages observations made as part of:

– EPOC-FF: estimation of common bird populations[13];

– STOC EPS: temporal monitoring of common birds using simple point sampling[14];

– Waterbirds: the international waterbird count is coordinated by the NGO Wetlands International[15].

These protocols have a scientific vocation and enable contributors to get involved in participatory science programs (Julliard 2017; Bœuf et al. 2021). The majority of these surveys are renewed annually, which implies a real commitment on the part of the contributors.

7.2.3.4. *Mobile data entry*

This input mode makes it possible to enter observations directly in the field or offline, using the same principle as for Web input.

12 Available at: www.lpo.fr/la-lpo-en-actions/connaissance-des-especes-sauvages/suivis-ornithologiques [Accessed 25 October 2022].

13 Launched in 2017 by the LPO and the MNHN, it is based on a very simple, low-impact protocol: a five-minute listening point, with no constraints on spatial sampling.

14 This is an annual count, coordinated by the MNHN and LPO, involving 10 listening points located in a 2 km grid.

15 This is an annual simultaneous count in five geographical regions (the Africa–Eurasia, Asia–Pacific, Caribbean, Central American and Neotropics regions) and takes place over one or two days around mid-January. Further information available at: www.wetlands.org [Accessed 25 October 2022).

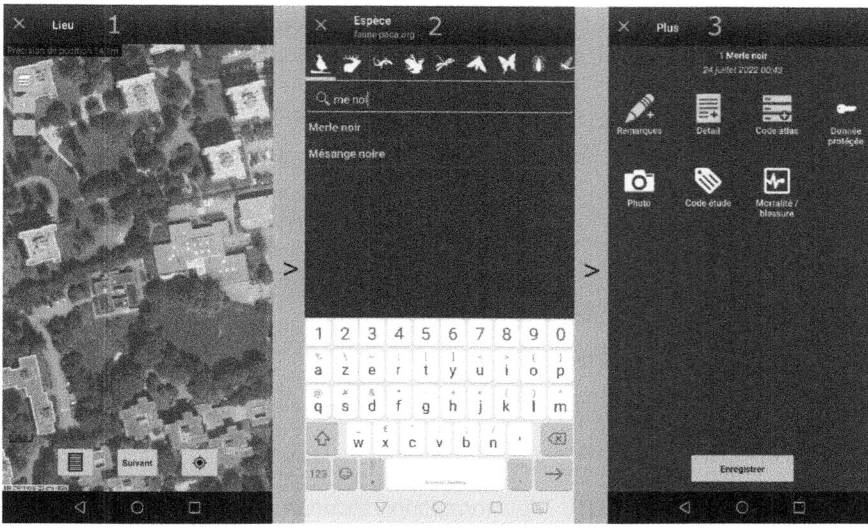

Figure 7.9. *Mobile location and observation entry screens in the iNaturalist app*

For step one, the observer indicates the position of the individual observed, then for step two, they select the species observed and the number of birds. Additional information can then be entered: text remarks, details of sex, age, behavior, nesting signs, etc.

The mobile application also enables data to be entered according to several protocols, simplifying the work of observers who no longer have to copy paper forms onto a computer.

7.2.4. *Validating data: the link between experts and observers*

The aim of validation is to encourage the collection, in the best possible conditions, of a maximum amount of information that can be put to good use, because it has been verified and is therefore credible. It is a compromise between the need to have a dataset that is as usable as possible for the players involved and the need to mobilize observers as effectively as possible.

Data reliability is also a prerequisite for the input of information, in raw or aggregated form; for example, into the INPN reference database via the Nature and Landscape Information System (*système d'information nature et paysages*, SINP)[16].

16 Available at: https://naturefrance.fr/ [Accessed 25 October 2022].

Data are subject to a series of processing and control procedures, detailed on the INPN website[17]. Data exchanges are dealt with in section 7.2.6.

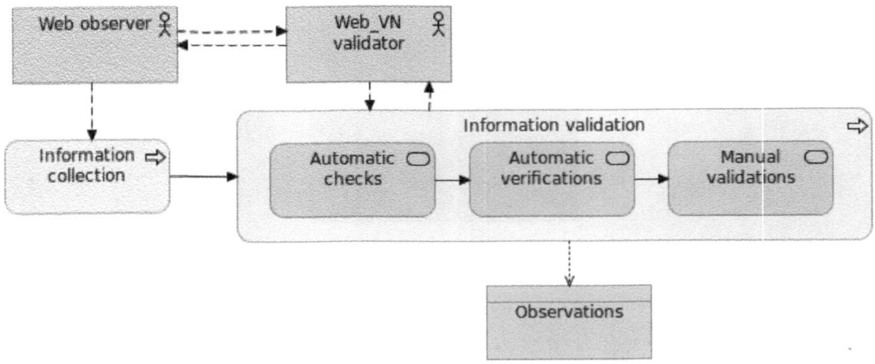

Figure 7.10. *The information validation process*

Firstly, the conformity and consistency of the data entered are ensured by controls and restrictive choices (drop-down menus) during data entry. For example, the total number of individuals cannot be less than the sum of the number of males, females and juveniles.

Secondly, scientific validation is assured at several levels:

– *automatic data consistency checks*: presence of the species in the biogeographical zone, date and location of photographs compatible with the observation, date not later than the present moment;

– *automatic plausibility checks*, based on a number of filters, aimed at highlighting out-of-spec observations as early as possible. Filters can be applied for altitude, periods of presence and numbers;

– *manual validations* by a validator, who checks the validity, conformity and consistency of the data entered and contributes to their improvement. The validator acts as part of a validation committee, facilitating collective decision-making. The BIS enables validators to mark data upstream as "to be verified" or "to be completed". A message can be sent to the observer requesting clarification. If the validation process is unsuccessful, the data can then be marked as "invalid" and excluded from further use.

17 Available at: https://inpn.mnhn.fr/programme/donnees-observations-especes/references/validation [Accessed 25 October 2022].

At the end of the validation process, which can sometimes be quite lengthy depending on the responsiveness of the observers, observations can be either accepted, possibly after modification, or invalidated.

This process also reassures observers that their data will be verified. It also enables them to make progress, as messages from validators to observers often specify the species identification criteria to be used. The vast majority of regular contributors appreciate this control over their data. Some annual bird-watching contributors do not always respond to these requests, most likely because they are unfamiliar with the principle of validation. Some contributors do not accept the principle and leave the network, but this is rare.

7.2.5. *Data enhancement*

By using this BIS, contributors accept that the LPO and partner associations may use the naturalist data within the framework of their missions related to awareness, knowledge and protection of nature. However, Noucher and Gautreau (2013), Fortier and Alphandery (2017) and Zucca (2019) clearly show that the use of data is a sensitive subject. Any use of naturalist data at a national level is subject to approval by the Faune-France steering committee. At a local level, the associations define the rules of use according to similar principles and adapt to the context.

The use of data[18] can take many forms and meet a variety of needs:

– various cartographic outputs, for the public and contributors, presenting the distribution of a species, its migration routes, wintering or nesting areas, etc.;

– publications, for contributors, of news, newsletters on follow-up campaigns, etc.;

– targeted consultations according to different criteria concerning location, species and dates.

In addition to the information provided directly by the VisioNature portal, the LPO also offers complementary sites. For example, the Atlas of the Birds of France has a dedicated website[19] which maps the survey effort (observation density), as well as randomly drawn grids for a detailed count. This enables observers to direct their surveys towards less well-known areas.

18 Available at: www.faune-france.org/index.php?m_id=20029 [Accessed 25 October 2022].

19 Available at: https://oiseauxdefrance.org/ [Accessed 25 October 2022].

Figure 7.11. *Example of a map available on the faune-aura.org Web portal, showing the location of nesting red kites*

These publications help to animate the network of contributors by highlighting certain aspects of biodiversity, such as the arrival of migrants, the distribution of an emblematic species, the temporal progression of nesting and so on.

7.2.6. *Exchanging with other information systems: linking different databases*

Naturalist data are transmitted to third parties with which the LPO signs an agreement defining the terms and conditions of these exchanges. There are many recipients: government departments, museums, local authorities, other associations, consultancy firms, etc. This provision of data supports government environmental policies and research partnerships (dissertations and theses, scientific publications, etc.).

Even more so than for data enhancement on LPO sites, it is the exchange of data with third parties that is the subject of sometimes impassioned debates within decision-making bodies. Certain issues, such as the risk of destroying certain species, commercial use and the lack of appreciation of the work of volunteers, have been studied by Noucher and Gautreau (2013), Fortier and Alphandery (2017) and Zucca (2019). However, data exchange is rapidly evolving towards being open to all, both through the growing acceptance of the usefulness of open data as well as the LPO's position as a key player in the field of wildlife knowledge. Discussions focus on the pertinence of data transmission, the list of species concerned and the geographical precision of data provided (the more precise, the more the species may be potentially disturbed). Forms[20] are filled in by applicants, so that they can specify their request as precisely as possible, which is accepted in the majority of cases. In cases of uncertainty, the request is validated by the steering committee or even by the board of directors in cases concerning politically sensitive subjects (large predators). For example, data on the presence of wolves and lynxes were systematically concealed. In view of the controversy surrounding the estimated number of wolves present in France, the LPO AuRA board of directors finally decided that it was more useful to pass on the data, so as not to give the impression of hiding information.

On both national and international levels, Faune-France contributes data to the EuroBirdPortal[21], the SINP, several Vigie-Nature observatories[22], national action plans, etc. On a regional level, Faune-Aura participates in the Observatoire régional de la biodiversité (ORB)[23], the *Atlas de la biodiversité communale* (ABC), road mortality monitoring, etc. The aim of the ORB's reports is to publicize biodiversity issues at the local level, so as to encourage their inclusion in development projects governed by regulations (green and blue framework, etc.).

In Isère, data are transmitted daily to the Museum of Grenoble to update the animal presence maps on the Nature-Isère website.

In practice, these exchanges can range from a single file to automatic computer links, updating sites several times a day. The sharing of naturalist databases is discussed in Chapter 6.

20 Available at: www.faune-france.org/index.php?m_id=20030 [Accessed 25 October 2022].

21 Available at: www.eurobirdportal.org/ebp/fr/ [Accessed 25 October 2022].

22 Available at: www.vigienature.fr/ [Accessed 25 October 2022].

23 Available at: www.biodiversite-auvergne-rhone-alpes.fr/ [Accessed 25 October 2022].

7.2.7. *Managing repositories*

The BIS is based on the use of several reference systems:

– *the species repository*, which is based on a list of species specific to VisioNature sites. Local management of this repository consists of defining the species that can be entered, their rarity by biogeographical zone, the sensitivity (hidden data), verification filters, approval committees and colonial status. It is also possible to create descriptive sheets;

– *the location repository*, covering administrative zones, regions, departments, communes and localities. Administrative zones, supplied by the Institut national de l'information gographique et forestire, are managed globally for all sites in France. Each local site can add, modify or delete localities;

– *the project repository*, which characterizes groups of data captured within a particular framework.

Having started in Switzerland, the species repository is different from TAXREF, the INPN taxonomy repository, which is the reference in France. The development and updating of these repositories are essential to ensure the exchange of relevant information between BISs. This is one of the main technical obstacles encountered when importing and exporting data.

The species repository also manages "hidden data", i.e. observations whose visualization and/or use are restricted. This masking can be chosen by the contributor or imposed by the system. Hidden data remain visible to the observer and the holders of viewing rights, whose number is voluntarily restricted. It is invisible to other users. Determining the list of species to be hidden is the subject of sometimes heated discussions between administrators. However, the general tendency is to limit the number of hidden species and to align with the lists of sensitive species currently being defined at regional level by various public players and associations. Currently, less than 7% of data are hidden.

7.3. Conclusion

The LPO's BIS has rapidly evolved from the initial handwritten data entry still in use in the 2000s to an information system with numerous functionalities, enabling tens of thousands of observers to contribute to wildlife knowledge. This growth has been driven by developments in technology, in the motivations of contributors and in the links between the LPO and other parties involved in naturalist knowledge and the preservation of biodiversity.

Beyond this growth, there are still important issues to consider. These include:

– recruitment, training and motivation of contributors, validators and administrators;

– managing exchanges between different BISs, which are increasingly complex and numerous;

– maintaining consistency between the various, rapidly evolving reference systems.

Beyond the technical challenges, the LPO's role in terms of knowledge and protection of biodiversity is changing through the evolution of its BIS.

7.4. References

Alphandéry, P. and Fortier, A. (2011). Les associations dans le processus de rationalisation des données naturalistes. *Natures Sciences Sociétés*, 19, 22–30 [Online]. Available at: https://www.cairn.info/revue--2011-1-page-22.htm [Accessed 25 October 2022].

Bœuf, G., Allain, Y.M., Bouvier, M. (2012). L'apport des sciences participatives à la connaissance de la biodiversité en France. *La Lettre de l'OCIM*, 144 [Online]. Available at: http://journals.openedition.org/ocim/1119 [Accessed 25 October 2022].

Charvolin, F., Pietropaoli, K., Joliveau, T. (2022). Sociologie des Observateurs de Faune-france Territorialisés (SOFT). Research report, Centre Max Weber.

Fortier, A. and Alphandéry, P. (2017). La maîtrise des données, un enjeu majeur pour les associations naturalistes à l'heure de la gouvernance de la biodiversité. *Revue française d'administration publique*, 163, 587–598 [Online]. Available at: https://doi.org/10.3917/rfap.163.0587 [Accessed 25 October 2022].

Julliard, R. (2017). Science participative et suivi de la biodiversité : l'expérience Vigie-Nature. *Natures Sciences Sociétés*, 25, 412–417 [Online]. Available at: https://doi.org/10.1051/nss/2018008 [Accessed 25 October 2022].

Montagne, D. (2011). Les données localisées en accès libre sur la biodiversité en France : variation géographique de disponibilité et principales logiques de constitution. Report.

Noucher, M. and Gautreau, P. (2013). Le libre accès rebat-il les cartes : Nouvelles perspectives pour les données géographiques. *Les Cahiers du numérique*, 9, 57–83. Available at: https://www.cairn.info/revue--2013-1-page-57.htm [Accessed 25 October 2022].

Zucca, M. (2019). La mise en commun des données naturalistes : des pratiques complexes. *Revue française d'administration publique*, 169, 195–206 [Online]. Available at: https://doi.org/10.3917/rfap.169.0195 [Accessed 25 October 2022].

PART 3

Gains and Losses: Questioning the Link to Nature

8

Complementarity of Big Data and Citizen Participation in Monitoring Plant Biodiversity

Figure 8.1. *Pl@ntNet enriches its database thanks to its many users. Source: Julie Polge (2021). For a color version of this figure, see www.iste.co.uk/kohlmann/linking.zip*

Chapter written by Pierre BONNET, Alexis JOLY and François MUNOZ.

8.1. Introduction

The rise in the world's population and the resulting needs are increasing the pressures on natural resources and ecosystems. These new pressures, exerted as a result of human activities, require us to rethink the way in which we manage and conserve biodiversity on a large scale. The aim is to limit the impacts on it and maximize the many contributions of nature to the sustenance of humankind. The regions with the highest biodiversity are often the most threatened, but also those where knowledge of biodiversity is least advanced. The spatio-temporal species dynamics are difficult to understand without intensive and regular monitoring, which is complex to implement. The emergence, over the past decade, of initiatives based on participatory approaches and the potential of big data and machine learning in ecology (Hampton et al. 2013; Peters et al. 2014; Hallgren et al. 2016; Soltis and Soltis 2016; Christin et al. 2019), and more specifically for biodiversity monitoring, have profoundly transformed the way we carry out this monitoring. For example, the five largest datasets now contributing to the global biodiversity monitoring system (through the GBIF platform[1]) are the output of extensive citizen science programs in Europe and North America, based on advanced data management and artificial intelligence technologies.

These new approaches have considerable potential to increase contributions in terms of both the quantity of data and number of contributors. However, this is only possible if there is a long-term investment by the users of these platforms. A better understanding of participants' uses and expectations is therefore essential to guide their future development and identify the levers for participation and support for these initiatives.

To this end, we looked at the uses of the Pl@ntNet platform[2] (Joly et al. 2016), a citizen observatory that relies on artificial intelligence technologies to help people identify plants with their smartphones, focusing on users participating in groups, a feature offered since summer 2021. After a brief introduction to the platform and the technical modalities for implementing Pl@ntNet groups, we analyze their objectives and modes of operation in order to understand their dynamics. This work helps us to identify the current benefits and limitations of this type of approach and to formalize recommendations for their development in other thematic, geographical or societal contexts.

1 Available at: www.gbif.org [Accessed August 26, 2022].

2 Available at: https://plantnet.org/ [Accessed August 26, 2022].

8.2. The Pl@ntNet platform

8.2.1. *Origin and operation*

The Pl@ntNet computer platform (Affouard et al. 2017) is the result of a research project initiated over a decade ago with the aim of facilitating the identification of plant species thanks to innovative image analysis algorithms. The results obtained were soon made available to the general public and have led to the widespread adoption of the Web and mobile tools developed. It is currently one of the world's largest biodiversity observatories, with several million contributors in over 200 countries. Today, the platform is best known for its mobile application (Goëau et al. 2013), which enables anyone to take a photo of a plant and send it to a server to get the recognition performed by a convolutive neural network. Visual observations can be shared by observers, who thus help to improve visual knowledge of species, as well as the extent of the areas in which they are observed. The network of users has submitted almost 570 million identification queries, of which almost 10 million are published on the GBIF intergovernmental platform[3] and used in various ecological research projects.

8.2.2. *Individual use*

An impact study conducted by Morin (2015) surveyed over 700 users of the Pl@ntNet platform with a user account: 12% said they used it professionally, mainly in the fields of training/education and the management of natural or anthropogenic ecosystems. The creation of an account enables the users to access the platform's services through:

– the contribution of new observations for species already illustrated or those not yet listed on the platform;

– collaborative reviews of data quality (with the possibility of voting on the quality of proposed determinations, images and common names);

– a dashboard of their own observations allowing their mass export, enabling them to be analyzed with tools other than those offered.

Individual use of Pl@ntNet as a field tool for capturing and managing botanical observations has been supplemented over the years by collective use, based on the

3 Available at: www.gbif.org/publisher/da86174a-a605-43a4-a5e8-53d484152cd3 [Accessed August 26, 2022].

ability of users to exchange information in text form in order to interact around the subject of an observation (in particular to help determine the species illustrated in an image, or to discuss the type of photograph to produce to ensure the best possible identification). Spot analysis of individual uses enabled us to highlight collective uses, notably by detecting groups of observations produced at the same time and located on the same site.

8.2.3. *Pl@ntNet "groups"*

The platform has also been used for prospecting groups of people in the natural environment, and for educational activities in schools and training courses. Analysis of these uses led to the development of new functionalities designed to encourage interaction between users who already physically knew each other or who wished to develop new collective activities through this virtual environment. The concept of user "groups" was then defined and implemented, first on the Web version in the spring of 2021, then on the mobile version in the autumn of the same year. Pl@ntNet[4] "groups" can be set up by any user with an account. Figure 8.2 shows an example of a group layout. Creating a group includes:

– identification of the group by a name, succinctly indicating its purpose and enabling it to be quickly found among all existing "groups";

– a potential description, enabling the creator to indicate the objectives sought and the type of observations expected of potential members;

– setting whether the group is "public" or "private". As this cannot be updated at a later date, the group creator must define whether they want all authenticated Pl@ntNet users to be able to join the group ("public group") or only members approved by an administrator;

– deciding whether or not to display the map of geolocated plant observations shared within the group. If the group creator agrees to display it, shared observations will be visible on the group map, and an alert will be displayed to users before they share their observations within the group to inform them of this;

– the option of limiting the group to a geographical area defined by the creator, either by drawing a polygon on a map, or by uploading a shapefile at the time of creation. If a geographic zone is specified, only observations located in this zone will be displayed in this group.

4 Available at: https://identify.plantnet.org/fr/groups [Accessed August 26, 2022].

Figure 8.2. *Presentation of the Pl@ntNet group for the Semur-en-Auxois communal biodiversity atlas (Côte-d'Or), showing (i) the title with a brief description of the objectives; (ii) the list of members; (iii) the cartography of geolocalized observations; and (iv) at the bottom, details of two observations from this group*

8.3. Diversity of uses and implications

8.3.1. *Quantitative analysis of Pl@ntNet "groups"*

By May 31, 2022, a total of 9,568 different groups had been created. Approximately 44.5% of these were public, enabling all users to view aggregated botanical observations. The largest group in terms of members and observations has 1,123 members and 10,004 observations. Of the ten largest groups created (with 415–1,123 members), the first nine are public, the last being private. Only 12% of groups are restricted to a specific geographical area. Of these, the most numerous are in Europe, followed by America, Asia, Africa and Oceania. Group creators initiated groups via interfaces in almost 18 different languages, with English, French and Spanish represented by 28%, 20% and 16% of cases respectively. Groups with more than 100 members (53 groups in total) are mainly interested in sharing observations within large geographical areas (such as a continent, sub-continent, country or large biogeographical zones), or on large groups of highly attractive plant organisms (such as trees, cacti or useful plants). Groups with fewer than 100 members, on the other hand, are often interested in much more targeted geographical and/or thematic contexts, as in the example shown in Figure 8.2 (a group of nine people working on the atlas of biodiversity in Semur-en-Auxois (Côte-d'Or)). Figure 8.3 illustrates the very wide geographical distribution of the groups on all continents, from New Zealand in the southern hemisphere to northern Norway. Desert zones (in Africa, Asia and Oceania), where Internet connectivity is limited, are where the development of these groups is least significant.

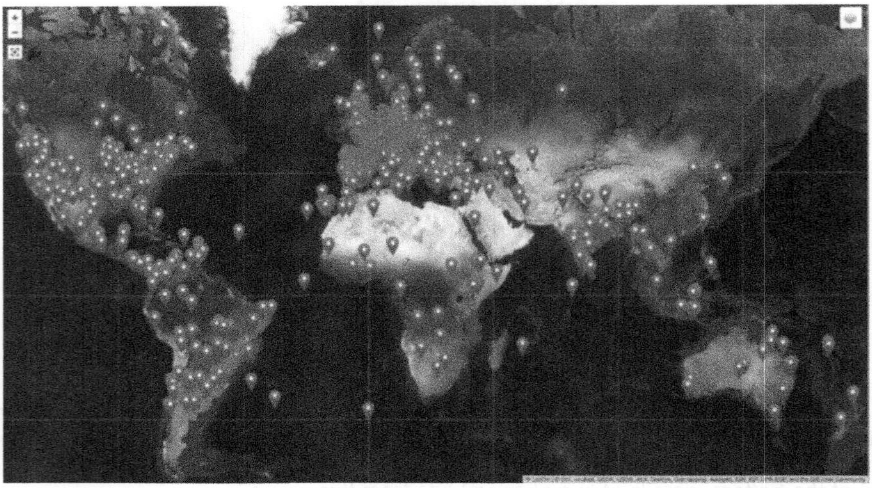

Figure 8.3. *Location of groups restricted to one geographical area*

8.3.2. *Qualitative analysis of uses*

Among the main motivations of group creators (expressed in the textual descriptions introducing the objectives of each group), we note the following two main interests:

– the desire to share observations to facilitate the recognition of species belonging to plant groups about which the members are passionate, such as orchids, cacti, succulents and ferns;

– surveying species in a given area, be it a protected natural zone, an urban or peri-urban area, for educational purposes (e.g. species surveys in schools), for land management (e.g. municipal biodiversity atlas) or for scientific inventories.

Group dynamics can vary widely. Some are very short-lived, created to mark a particular event or field mission, as in the case of the "Living Laboratory at Lewa". This group was set up to aggregate 146 observations of 81 different species via Pl@ntNet during an expedition by members of the Kenyan National Herbarium to the Lewa Nature Reserve. Other groups present an activity over a few weeks, as in the case of groups used for school activities, where pupils carry out a census of the plant biodiversity observed within their school grounds; for example, at the Lycée Saint-Joseph in Gap, France[5], or the Turkish university Tekirdağ Namık Kemal. The activity of groups developing communal biodiversity atlases (*Atlas de la biodiversité communale*, ABC) generally extends over several months, as with the ABC of Semur-en-Auxois, in the Côte-d'Or department[6], or that of the municipality of Beaulieu, in the Hérault department[7].

It is also worth noting the individual use of certain groups, since many have only one member. In some cases, this may be a matter of user testing, but we can also see this feature being used by single users to facilitate the regrouping and sharing of observations relating to a specific area or theme. While the majority of group administrators have created only one group, some have created more than a dozen. This is the case for users wishing to structure the collection of observations on the flora of regional parks or nature reserves in a more systematic way.

8.4. Discussion

8.4.1. *Current limitations*

Although functional on mobile devices since 2013, the Pl@ntNet platform has only facilitated the grouping of observations through "groups" since spring 2021. The new possibilities offered by this functionality allow us to identify new uses, reinforcing collective capacities for the discovery and inventory of species present in natural or anthropized environments. Although it is not yet possible to analyze the use of these "groups" over several years, the dynamics are sufficiently sustained to suggest long-term activity. The maintenance and development of these digital spaces could contribute to improving the performance of species identification for the benefit of all users, thanks to the availability of new learning data for automated visual classification models. Such spaces could also facilitate the discovery of local biodiversity for new users or group members, by giving them access to species

---

5 Available at: https://identify.plantnet.org/fr/groups/24002860001 [Accessed August 26, 2022].

6 Available at: https://identify.plantnet.org/fr/groups/23586754601 [Accessed August 26, 2022].

7 Available at: https://identify.plantnet.org/fr/groups/21796884046 [Accessed August 26, 2022].

previously recorded around them or at the same time of year. As can be seen from the above examples, this spatial and temporal contextualization of botanical information can make a major contribution to promoting a territory's natural heritage, on a wide variety of spatial scales and in a wide variety of sociological contexts.

As moderation of group creation is deliberately reduced, some groups may appear redundant, with overlapping themes or geographical areas. This fragmentation of aggregated knowledge can potentially make it more difficult to identify relevant groups for a potential new member. Implementing mechanisms to encourage collaboration or group mergers could help us to limit this fragmentation. Another limitation also identified in the functioning of the groups analyzed concerns those with a pedagogical vocation. In fact, the platform was initially developed for adults, with no notion of hierarchy between users. However, teachers need to be able to keep a close eye on their students' activities, the help they have received and the skills they have acquired. The management of accounts of this type needs to evolve, to better meet the pedagogical challenges for which the platform is used.

However, much remains to be done to facilitate this promotion in areas where access to mobile data is still limited, whether in deserts or mountains or far from major urban centers. Access to image-based automatic species recognition services is often data-intensive, and their offline use could open up new opportunities for less-connected populations or in surveys in more isolated areas.

8.4.2. *Perspectives*

More systematic use of this type of platform and service in educational contexts could encourage young people to use this type of technology for discovering their natural environment. In this way, urban populations could gain a better understanding of the biodiversity present in the spaces they travel through, and estimate the benefits. The ecosystem services provided by the various species that surround us are measurable on a finer scale when they are associated with specific species communities rather than natural habitat typologies.

The use of this type of service by professionals in research, management and education, as well as novices, allows us to build bridges between communities and social groups that would be difficult to build without these platforms. The introduction of a wider range of roles than those currently available through Pl@ntNet could, for example, facilitate these bridges and extend the range of possible uses. Although the maintenance and development of this type of platform cannot be guaranteed over the long term, the very large number of users and the benefits they derive from it make it reasonable to envisage mobilizing this community to participate in its sustainability.

8.5. Conclusion

Growing access to visual, sound and audiovisual sensors is opening up new opportunities for the development of more widely accessible approaches to the surveying and characterization of biodiversity. Their combination with participatory data collection and analysis methods has enabled the emergence over the last 10 years of large-scale platforms used on a planetary scale to produce and exchange data and knowledge about our environment. Although relatively recent, these platforms have generated exceptional volumes of new data, requiring not only appropriate IT infrastructures but also social organizations to optimize their use. Their longevity will largely depend on their widespread appropriation, which will require further research at the boundary between computer and social sciences.

8.6. References

Affouard, A., Goëau, H., Bonnet, P., Lombardo, J.C., Joly, A. (2017). Pl@ntnet app in the era of deep learning. *ICLR: International Conference on Learning Representations*. Toulon.

Christin, S., Hervet, É., Lecomte, N. (2019). Applications for deep learning in ecology. *Methods in Ecology and Evolution*, 10(10), 1632–1644. doi: 10.1111/2041-210X.13256.

Goëau, H., Bonnet, P., Joly, A., Bakić, V., Barbe, J., Yahiaoui, I., Selmi, S., Carré, J., Barthélémy, D., Boujemaa, N., Molino, J.F. (2013). Pl@ntnet mobile app. *Proceedings of the 21st ACM International Conference on Multimedia*. doi: 10.1145/2502081.2502251.

Hallgren, W., Beaumont, L., Bowness, A., Chambers, L., Graham, E., Holewa, H., Laffan, S., Mackey, B., Nix, H., Price, J. et al. (2016). The biodiversity and climate change virtual laboratory: Where ecology meets big data. *Environmental Modelling & Software*, 76, 182–186. doi: 10.1016/j.envsoft.2015.10.025.

Hampton, S.E., Strasser, C.A., Tewksbury, J.J., Gram, W.K., Budden, A.E., Batcheller, A.L., Duke, C.S., Porter, J.H. (2013). Big data and the future of ecology. *Frontiers in Ecology and the Environment*, 11(3), 156–162. doi: 10.1890/120103.

Joly, A., Bonnet, P., Goëau, H., Barbe, J., Selmi, S., Champ, J., Dufour-Kowalski, S., Affouard, A., Carré, J., Molino, J.F. et al. (2016). A look inside the Pl@ntNet experience. *Multimedia Systems*, 22(6), 751–766. doi: 10.1007/s00530-015-0462-9.

Morin, T. (2015). Les espoirs socio-environnementaux d'une approche innovante pour la production, l'agrégation et la diffusion de données botaniques : une analyse quantitative et participative. Master's thesis, Clermont Auvergne University, Clermont-Ferrand.

Peters, D.P., Havstad, K.M., Cushing, J., Tweedie, C., Fuentes, O., Villanueva-Rosales, N. (2014). Harnessing the power of big data: Infusing the scientific method with machine learning to transform ecology. *Ecosphere*, 5(6), 1–15. doi: 10.1890/ES13-00359.1.

Soltis, D.E. and Soltis, P.S. (2016). Mobilizing and integrating big data in studies of spatial and phylogenetic patterns of biodiversity. *Plant Diversity*, 38(6), 264–270. doi: 10.1016/j.pld.2016.12.001.

9

New Automatic Identification Tools: An Aid for Botanists and Nature Managers?

Figure 9.1. *Automatic identification tools and field trips. Source: Julie Polge (2021). For a color version of this figure, see www.iste.co.uk/kohlmann/linking.zip*

Chapter written by François MUNOZ and Pierre BONNET.

9.1. Introduction

Citizen science has contributed to the development of knowledge in the environmental sciences, particularly concerning the ecological study of biodiversity (Dickinson and Bonney 2012). These contributions take three forms:

– generating knowledge;

– creating opportunities to teach and learn;

– enabling civic participation (Turrini et al. 2018).

Citizen science contributes to conservation efforts, natural resource management and environmental protection (McKinley et al. 2017; Bonnet et al. 2020a) at multiple spatial scales (Mahecha et al. 2021). Citizen participation is voluntary and expresses the values and desires of participants to engage in the preservation of nature (Larson et al. 2020). The observations gathered by citizens can be used to characterize the threats and conservation status of biological species (Devictor et al. 2010) and complement the data acquired by professional ecologists (Young et al. 2019).

Citizen science is booming thanks to the development of new computer tools and new media. This has contributed to the emergence of a new field of research named "iEcology" (Jarić et al. 2020). There are many ways in which citizen data can contribute to research programs. Historically, the first citizen observatories followed precise observation protocols to ensure the scientific rigor of the analyses they produced, for example, on plant phenology (Chuine 2005). More recently, systematic and automated computer content analysis methods have enabled remarkable advances in the exploitation of opportunistic observations, such as the visualizations and contributions on Wikipedia pages (Guedes-Santos et al. 2021; Mittermeier et al. 2021). Massive observations from social networks allow us to monitor plant populations (Marcenò et al. 2021) and study their phenology (Reeb et al. 2022). Thanks to increasingly sophisticated technological solutions, the stakes are shifting from the computer and statistical limitations of data exploitation to the question of public support and the dissemination of knowledge (Larson et al. 2020; Maund et al. 2020). Here, we approach this issue from the angle of the involvement and participation of professionals and citizens in citizen science actions using an automated plant recognition tool, Pl@ntNet (Joly et al. 2018).

Computer-aided identification applications use new information technologies and artificial intelligence for fast, efficient recognition of organisms from photographs, sounds or videos (Bonnet et al. 2020b). With these tools, users can easily identify photographed plants and gain access to botanical knowledge that traditionally requires meticulous learning. The Pl@ntNet application uses artificial intelligence that compares a submitted image with a knowledge database compiled and validated elsewhere, usually by experts (Joly et al. 2018). The identification proposed by the application is associated with a score that represents the degree of confidence of the best answer given. A list of possible identifications is then provided in descending order of confidence scores. In this way, the user does not necessarily get a single, certain identification but rather a list of the most plausible identifications. Biases in use may possibly emerge from a lack of knowledge of this principle of uncertainty, as not all users have the same expectations of this service.

Using the application, managers of natural areas can participate in the inventory of the biodiversity of these areas (Bonnet et al. 2020b). The opportunistic data collected can also be used to monitor and track exotic and invasive plants (Botella et al. 2018; Groom et al. 2019; Johnson et al. 2020), particularly present in anthropized areas where Pl@ntNet is widely used. However, the question arises as to the extent to which the developed tools replace or complement more traditional tools, such as field books and guides (Austen et al. 2016) or even professionals trained and experienced in botany (Bonnet et al. 2016). To address this question, we here study the testimonies of Pl@ntNet users and professionals involved in botanical data acquisition, knowledge sharing and management of natural areas.

The chapter is organized as follows:

– a presentation and analysis of interviews and testimonials on the use of Pl@ntNet to acquire, share and mobilize botanical knowledge for conservation purposes;

– a discussion of the strengths and limitations of the current tool, and an outline of the prospects for improvement in the context of the expected growth and evolution of citizen science.

9.2. Interviews and testimonials

9.2.1. *Interviews*

We spoke to two people who had tested the tool on a personal basis and were interested in using it as part of their professional activities in nature. Cédric Dentant (CD) is a botanist in the scientific department of the Ecrins National Park. Sophie Lovato (SL) is a mountain guide.

CD has expressed interest in developing a project with Pl@ntNet to study high-elevation plants. The idea would be to encourage hikers and mountaineers traveling at high altitudes to take photos and feed the Pl@ntNet application with their geolocated observations of plants characteristic of this particular environment.

In addition to its educational value for users wishing to learn more about high-altitude plants, the initiative would help to clarify the still poorly known distribution of very-high-altitude species, as demonstrated by the recent discovery of several new species of *Androsace* in France (Boucher et al. 2021). This would also make it possible to assess the phenology of high-altitude species, the sentinels of climate change (McDonough MacKenzie et al. 2017). Another potential audience would be farmers in the Alps, an option also discussed with CD and the National Alpine Botanical Conservatory. Farmers could identify weeds in their crops, some of which have become rare and need to be protected. Conversely, identifying the weeds as most harmful to crop yields could help guide management courses.

CD also points out that learning botany is a long process, which can be discouraging for many novices. Pl@ntNet represents an intermediary tool in this learning process, enabling users to progress in their botanical learning. The act of naming begins to make the diversity of plants encountered intelligible. Regular use of the application allows for a gradual appropriation of names, rather than, dependent on trainers, being confronted with a flood of names that are difficult to grasp and quickly forgetting them. CD constantly encourages people to use Pl@ntNet, knowing that it does not replace a botanist but simply helps in the process of discovering living things. CD therefore emphasizes the value of Pl@ntNet as a tool for mediation with nature.

SL does not use Pl@ntNet with her customers. In the event of a successful determination, the app can communicate basic taxonomic information such as the botanical family, but for the moment it does not provide information on determination criteria (morphological, phenological, ecological characteristics, etc.). The app can therefore be used to “clear up” plant identification but cannot be used on its own to develop educational content that can be shared with customers. Links integrated into the application to collaborative descriptive sheets or complementary external educational resources can meet this need. SL notes that reaching greater pedagogical value would require further integration of additional information about plants, taking the example of a tree identification guide from the Office National des Forêts, whose purpose is “learning to look”.

Another difficulty noted by SL is that the application works well on the most obvious and common species but poses problems when similar species are differentiated on tenuous criteria that are poorly captured by the application, as in the case of mountain gentians (Figure 9.2). There could be an advantage in taking into account additional information for identification, such as the precise location of the plant or the nature of the soil. SL also regrets that a fairly large number of poor-quality photographs appear in the results to illustrate the different species. She wonders whether it would be possible to display only the best-quality photographs.

Figure 9.2. *Example of uncertainty in Pl@ntNet image-based identification: the case of blue trumpet gentians in the French Alps*

The species photographed (left) is *Gentiana alpina*, which appears in the results (right) in the first position with a score of 35.31%. This score pales in comparison to those of the following species, which are visually very similar but all belong to the correct genus *Gentiana*. This query was carried out on July 20, 2022, for the flora of Western Europe[1].

9.2.2. *Social networks*

Secondly, we examined mentions of Pl@ntNet in Facebook groups whose members represented a wide range of botanical expertise. We used the keyword "Pl@ntNet" to search Facebook posts, groups and members. From the results obtained, we selected two exchanges representative of the diversity of the threads examined.

Pl@ntNet was mentioned in exchanges concerning two major themes:

– "Wild Plant Identification" group: how reliable are the identifications provided by Pl@ntNet?

1 Available at: https://identify.plantnet.org/weurope/identify [Accessed on August 26, 2022].

- *user 1*: Wild plant identification: the Pl@ntNet application is just incredible;

- *user 2*: This app makes a lot of mistakes;

- *user 3*: User 2, no, it makes suggestions. It also depends on the photo and the database. I personally think it's an extraordinary tool that will improve with time and use;

- *user 4*: User 3, yes, it's quite impressive, but you do need a good photo. But don't take everything at face value!;

- *user 5*: User 2, I find that Pl@ntNet gives the best possible results most of the time. Beyond that, the app is for roughing it out, nothing beats human verification.

This exchange is representative of the hiatus that can exist between an expectation of the unique and unambiguous determination of the plant photographed and the fact that the application actually provides a list of visually similar and probable species, each with an identification score that takes into account numerous sources of uncertainty.

– "Botany and Flora of France" group: what are the scientific values and interest of opportunistic data provided by Pl@ntNet users?

- *user 1*: Botany and Flora of France: do any of you contribute to the open-source flora on Pl@ntNet?;

- *user 2*: I think it's a great "tool" (I'm going to incur the wrath of our beloved user 3...). On the contrary, lots of botanists use it, but mostly for horticulture! 😂 The problem is therefore always the same, quality versus quantity... Is it better to have little data or lots of data? That is the real question... A lot of data, even with the errors we know about, is always better than little or no data at all, in fact, it depends a lot on the context in my opinion, on the issues faced... That's what citizen science is all about! Pl@ntNet is a real democratization, but it's still based on artificial intelligence algorithms, and science without conscience... But I see the positive side. It's a gateway into this wonderful world, and is helping to move things forward a little by raising a lot of awareness! But would it really make a difference if all high-level botanists entered their data? For it to be efficient, we'd have to "clean up" the quantity of poor-quality obs, which seems totally illusory to me. So, let's make the most of what's here, and not knock those who don't want to participate! ☺ [...] This tool would need to be accompanied by keys to fully achieve its objective...;

- *user 3*: User 2, there is no "wrath", because we've both said the same thing: it democratizes botany, and that's great. On the other hand, I'm still not at all convinced of the value of citizen science when there's no "expert" control behind it, as with some people... In this group, we can already see how difficult it is for "professional" botanists to determine the species from photos, so delegating this job to ordinary citizens who, with a simple click, can enter their data into a database is not a solution, it's a problem.

The question of the scientific interest and use of user data is likely to evolve thanks to technological advances in the application. For example, the recent creation of a sharing interface (Figure 9.3) enables users to fine-tune the visibility of the information they wish to make public, which will feed Pl@ntNet's geo-referenced database thanks to the increasingly systematic and precise GPS locations of smartphones. These data are all the easier to aggregate, process and visualize for scientific purposes in the sharing interface and to render simply and quickly for the user. The question then arises as to how to manage the uncertainty and heterogeneity of observations feeding the database. This raises the more general question of how to integrate opportunistic observation data (without a standardized observation protocol) into the reference databases used by decision-makers and scientists.

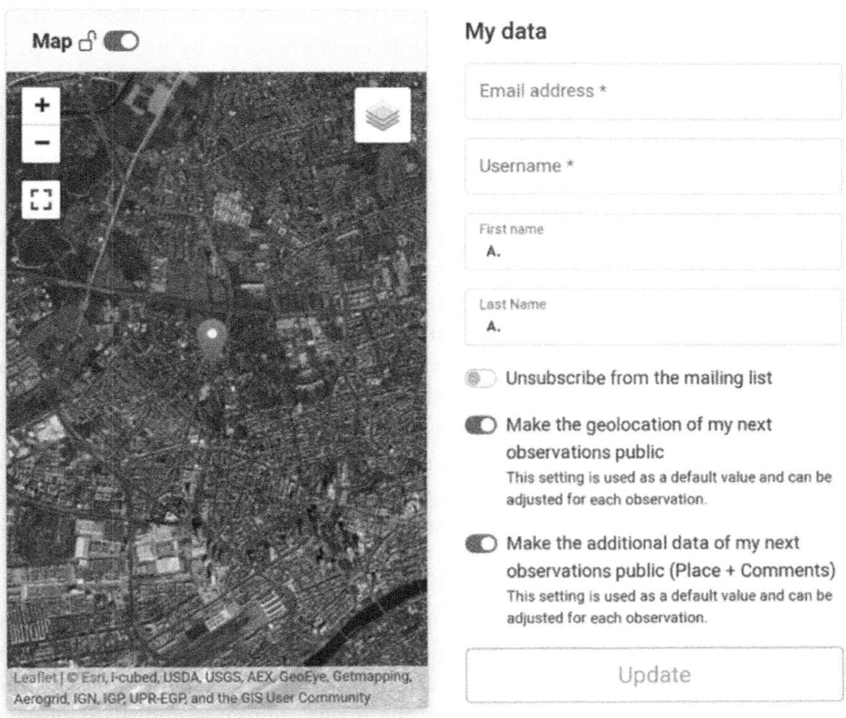

Figure 9.3. *Geolocation interface for observation data integrated into Pl@ntNet. Users can contribute to the global database of observations available online. Screenshot posted by A.A. on Facebook on December 15, 2021*

9.3. Discussion

Using the example of the Pl@ntNet application, we have examined the uses and relationship to nature that the tool enables among botanist users (amateur or professional) and nature professionals. We have highlighted a paradigm shift in botanical learning and plant observation. The application makes it possible to name plants even without any prior knowledge of plant biology. This not only broadens the scope of users interested in botany but can also prove to be an interesting tool for experienced botanists. In the following sections, we identify the major challenges posed by the use of the application and possible future developments, both technical and in terms of uses and our relationship with nature.

9.3.1. *Challenges and opportunities of uncertainty*

A long-standing debate on the use of Pl@ntNet concerns the performance of plant identification from photographs. A plant, or a photo of a plant, does not always allow for identification at a specific level with certainty, even by the best botanists. Indeed, depending on the season, the age of the plant, the level of wilting or any other factor influencing the quality of the visual information contained in the photo illustrating a plant (level of humidity, wind, etc.), its identification at the species level may prove to be impossible due to the visual inaccessibility of the distinctive criteria. This explains why the app is not intended to give a definitive answer, and why it provides a list of species ranked in descending order of confidence score. The confidence score is calculated using a computer classifier that discriminates between the species most similar to the photo(s) supplied by the user. It is then up to the user to establish whether the identification is sufficiently reliable or not. In particular, the user can choose and validate a species from among the ones proposed, and contribute to the application's knowledge base. The fact that the application sometimes gives a very rich result in terms of the number of possible species may be at odds with the expectations of a user in search of a unique and certain identification. This does, however, highlight the diversity of the plant world and the difficulty sometimes faced in differentiateing with certainty between two species that are visually very similar.

There is therefore a real cognitive and cultural challenge in taking uncertainty into account in the use of automated IT tools. The only certainty is the deterministic operation of the application: Pl@ntNet is a tool providing the best possible response given the available photographic database, the image submitted and the parameters of the algorithm applied. In this respect, Pl@ntNet can in no way be considered as a substitute for the botanist's expertise; it is a digital tool to help analyze visual content. The score attributed by the application to each result can be seen as an indication of the confidence associated with the identification of visual content. The uncertainty of an identification can have multiple origins: the quality of the visual image submitted, the nature and precision of the organs observed, the existence of taxa that are very close or for which the identification criteria are not apparent or not sufficiently clear from a simple image. This uncertainty should not be seen as the tool's inability to provide a reliable answer, but as an assessment of the nature and quality of the information that the submitted image can provide for identification.

What consequences does this uncertainty have for Pl@ntNet users? It can be seen as an obstacle for users wishing to employ the tool to contribute to the systematic inventory of a protected area, for example, or for educational use as part of group activities. However, knowing how to take uncertainty into account and communicating its nature also offers opportunities. In the case of systematic inventories of protected areas, the confidence score is used to filter the data which, above a certain threshold, are retained for inclusion in reference databases. By examining the data according to this score, it is possible to classify and potentially clean up the data to be retained in the end, depending on the use (whether for inventories of areas to be protected or for research programs). For educational purposes, learners can be shown the existence of similar species and how they differ from the target species, thus introducing notions of botany and plant biology.

There remains a sticking point for some opponents to the use of Pl@ntNet, more of a psychological nature: the idea that an algorithm can take the place of a human being for a task that until now has only been possible by trained personnel. A number of botanists who are reluctant to use Pl@ntNet fundamentally fear that systematic and massive use of the application could ultimately jeopardize the jobs and expertise of botanists. However, given the necessarily limited range of functions offered by the app, and the uncertainty associated with identification, this fear appears to be largely unfounded. Pl@ntNet cannot decide on the identification of a plant, only the user can, with the possible help of the confidence scores provided by the application. Due to the agnostic nature of automated identification, Pl@ntNet is not a botanist, nor is it intended to replace one. Pl@ntNet does not know, nor does it learn, the morphological characters essential to plant classification. In fact, Pl@ntNet's identification performance is highly correlated with the volume, diversity and quality of learning data provided by amateur or professional botanists. Other computer-aided identification tools offer an intermediate approach where users are invited to select characters sequentially, to arrive at a determination with a certain confidence score. These tools may be useful for teaching botany, but they do not provide as immediate and easy an answer as Pl@ntNet's automatic identification.

9.3.2. *Diverse expectations and uses*

Interviews with professionals and the examination of Facebook discussion threads revealed heterogeneous expectations, as well as a number of general facts. Beyond the uncertainty inherent in the analysis of a visual medium with limited information content, the most notable criticism concerns the existence of photographs of heterogeneous quality in the results returned by the application. The application's philosophy is to take into account the diversity of shooting conditions and qualities in the knowledge base. The photographs associated with a proposed identification reflect this heterogeneity. In this way, the assessment provided by the application concerns not only the taxonomic identity of the plant photographed, but also the nature and quality of the photograph taken. The user can use different shots, with different organs and different field depths, to improve the identification quality provided by the application and thus reduce uncertainty.

Professionals have expressed a desire to use the application for ecotourism activities in particular. Whether in the context of guiding nature trips, with schoolchildren (nature immersion), amateurs (image hunters) or managers of natural areas (e.g. land managers or farmers), the application makes it possible to integrate and disseminate naturalist knowledge in the context of ecotourism. Although expectations and frustrations about the uncertainty inherent in automatic identification remain, the existence of the application opens up new prospects for access to naturalist knowledge for a wide range of users. The application's playful nature and ease of use in the field are sources of motivation for users who would not otherwise be inclined to observe plants. There are also the application's benefits to those involved in education and nature management and to those developing the application and its data infrastructure. The Pl@ntNet project is thus based on the establishment of a virtuous circle between the various users and developers, collectively contributing to a better understanding and integration of botanical knowledge in the many activities related to nature. It helps to change the way people relate to nature by offering new opportunities for learning and communicating about nature.

9.3.3. *Citizen science*

One of Pl@ntNet's fundamental assets is its ability to produce a large volume of plant identification and location data. These data can be used for studies on plant ecology, phenology and biogeography, provided that the heterogeneity, biases and uncertainty of the data produced are properly managed. A recurring point of criticism or doubt as to the value of Pl@ntNet is the highly heterogeneous quality of the data produced. However, new digital technologies, in particular those based on artificial intelligence, make this heterogeneity intelligible: the algorithms currently used to study plant distribution with Pl@ntNet can take into account both user behaviors and ecological differences between species (Botella et al. 2021). The latter approach evaluates the density of observation by users in different meshes of the territory studied, and distinguishes variations in this density from the ecological preferences of species. It therefore provides information on both species ecology and user observation behavior.

The question of how to integrate Pl@ntNet into citizen science initiatives involves establishing a link between scientists and citizens through the application. The motivation of users, seduced by the application's practicality and playfulness, is an essential prerequisite, but the success of scientific research carried out using Pl@ntNet can also help to overcome the skepticism of some about the heterogeneity and quality of the data. Another important benefit of Pl@ntNet is the ability to unite different players around common projects. The example of modeling potential species distributions using geolocated data, mentioned above, involved the participation of researchers from INRIA and CIRAD and members of the Tela Botanica association. These players have been involved in the development of the Pl@ntNet application from the outset. In addition, the data produced feed the GBIF international database, enabling it to be used by scientists all over the world. The *GeoLifeClef challenge* is an example of an initiative encouraging the involvement of scientists from different areas in the development of species distribution models, in the form of an evaluation to obtain the best possible predictions (Lorieul et al. 2021). Other forms of citizen science actions are possible, thanks in particular to the possibility of creating thematic groups within the Pl@ntNet community (see Chapter 8): these groups can be led by managers or researchers aiming to improve knowledge and monitoring of biodiversity for determined groups (e.g. invasive plants, crop weeds) and/or specific areas (e.g. a protected natural area).

9.3.4. *Perspectives*

A fundamental objective of Pl@ntNet is to contribute to the development of citizen science initiatives. This field is constantly evolving, thanks in particular to the development of numerous digital tools (Ellwood et al. 2017). Beyond the opportunities offered by new tools, citizen science actions can only emerge and be sustained if:

– volunteers are motivated by the organizers to participate over the long term;

– volunteers are helped to identify the species observed;

– regular feedback is provided on how their contributions are being used to generate new scientific knowledge (Bíl et al. 2020).

Although Pl@ntNet is a powerful lever for fulfilling the second condition, it remains essential that the scientists are involved in the development of actions and communicate sufficiently in advance of their implementation, and that there can be feedback and communication to volunteers valuing their participation. These issues are at the heart of our policy of developing a network of collaboration and project groups around the Pl@ntNet platform.

In terms of new resources, the visual content of photographs can provide information other than the image of the focal plant. These may include elements of the mineral and plant (vegetation) context. Analysis of these additional visual contents can also contribute to better ecological knowledge and management of the species. Moreover, plant images can capture the presence of pollinators, and the coupled observation of plants and their pollinators can provide essential information about ecosystem functioning and pollination services (Groom et al. 2021; Pernat et al. 2022). The development of visual content analysis and associated metadata (conditions and location of observations, user profiles) contributes to the development of the *iEcology* field (Jarić et al. 2020). In addition, the information acquired by many means from massive ecological data contributes to the recent development of the culturomics field. This originally concerned the systematic lexical study of digital content representing human behaviors and cultural aspects (Michel et al. 2011), later extended to ecological data to meet the challenges of biodiversity conservation (Ladle et al. 2016; Jaric et al. 2021). This approach thus makes it possible to enrich the purely visual and taxonomic data derived from automated identification. The integration of botanical and cultural knowledge beyond the taxonomic identity of the plant meets a central expectation expressed in the survey conducted here. Access to the diversity of botanical knowledge and the development of communities of curious or passionate users, notably via social networks, are contributing to the current botanical boom (Burke et al. 2022). We can only hope that this development will offset the concomitant decline in teaching botany at schools and universities (Stroud et al. 2022).

9.4. Conclusion

By means of the testimonies from professionals and an analysis of Facebook discussions, we have identified a diversity of uses and expectations for the Pl@ntNet app. This tool fundamentally influences users' relationship with nature, making it quick and easy to name plants. This asset is at the heart of the application's uses, both among curious non-botanists and among professionals. Knowing how to name species changes our relationship with nature by making its diversity intelligible. However, the application is not a substitute for the knowledge of botany and plant biology. It is a gateway, an auxiliary facilitating and encouraging users to go further, by means of flora, trainers or traditional works and by seeking complementary information among the multiple resources offered by new media. In short, Pl@ntNet is an open window on plant diversity, and a useful aid to the implementation of participatory inventories of this diversity at different spatial and temporal scales.

9.5. References

Austen, G.E., Bindemann, M., Griffiths, R.A., Roberts, D.L. (2016). Species identification by experts and non-experts: Comparing images from field guides. *Scientific Reports*, 6, 33634.

Bíl, M., Heigl, F., Janoška, Z., Vercayie, D., Perkins, S.E. (2020). Benefits and challenges of collaborating with volunteers: Examples from National Wildlife Roadkill Reporting Systems in Europe. *Journal for Nature Conservation*, 54, 125798.

Bonnet, P., Joly, A., Goëau, H., Champ, J., Vignau, C., Molino, J.F., Barthélémy, D., Boujemaa, N. (2016). Plant identification: Man vs. machine. *Multimedia Tools and Applications*, 75, 1647–1665.

Bonnet, P., Goëau, H., Hopkins, F., Véla, E., Sahl, A., Affouard, A. et al. (2020a). Contribution citoyenne au suivi de la flore d'un parc national français, un exemple remarquable à l'échelle du parc national des Cévennes. *Carnets Botaniques*, 1–9. doi: 10.34971/zaz0-n247.

Bonnet, P., Joly, A., Faton, J.M., Brown, S., Kimiti, D., Deneu, B. et al. (2020b). How citizen scientists contribute to monitor protected areas thanks to automatic plant identification tools. *Ecological Solutions and Evidence*, 1. doi: 10.1002/2688-8319.12023.

Botella, C., Joly, A., Bonnet, P., Monestiez, P., Munoz, F. (2018). Species distribution modeling based on the automated identification of citizen observations. *Applications in Plant Sciences*, 6. doi: 10.1002/aps3.1029.

Botella, C., Joly, A., Bonnet, P., Munoz, F., Monestiez, P. (2021). Jointly estimating spatial sampling effort and habitat suitability for multiple species from opportunistic presence-only data. *Methods in Ecology and Evolution*, 12(5), 933–945. doi: 10.1111/2041-210X.13565.

Boucher, F.C., Dentant, C., Ibanez, S., Capblancq, T., Boleda, M., Boulangeat, L. et al. (2021). Discovery of cryptic plant diversity on the rooftops of the Alps. *Scientific Reports*, 11, 1–10.

Burke, R., Sherwood, O.L., Clune, S., Carroll, R., McCabe, P.F., Kane, A., Kacprzyk, J. (2022). Botanical boom: A new opportunity to promote the public appreciation of botany. *Plants, People, Planet*, 4, 326–334.

Chuine, I. (2005). Un réseau d'observations phenologiques pour la gestion du changement climatique. *De l'observation des écosystèmes forestiers à l'information sur la forêt*. 2–3 February, Paris.

Devictor, V., Whittaker, R.J., Beltrame, C. (2010). Beyond scarcity: Citizen science programmes as useful tools for conservation biogeography. *Diversity and Distributions*, 16, 354–362.

Dickinson, J.L. and Bonney, R. (2012). *Citizen Science: Public Participation in Environmental Research*. Cornell University Press, New York.

Ellwood, E.R., Crimmins, T.M., Miller-Rushing, A.J. (2017). Citizen science and conservation: Recommendations for a rapidly moving field. *Biological Conservation*, 208, 1–4.

Groom, Q., Strubbe, D., Adriaens, T., Davis, A.J., Desmet, P., Oldoni, D., Reyserhove, L., Roy, H.E., Vanderhoeven, S. (2019). Empowering citizens to inform decision-making as a way forward to support invasive alien species policy. *Citizen Science: Theory and Practice*, 4(1), 1–11.

Groom, Q., Pernat, N., Adriaens, T., de Groot, M., Jelaska, S.D., Marčiulynienė, D. et al. (2021). Species interactions: Next-level citizen science. *Ecography*, 44, 1781–1789.

Guedes-Santos, J., Correia, R.A., Jepson, P., Ladle, R.J. (2021). Evaluating public interest in protected areas using Wikipedia page views. *Journal for Nature Conservation*, 63, 126040.

Jarić, I., Correia, R.A., Brook, B.W., Buettel, J.C., Courchamp, F., Di Minin, E. et al. (2020). iEcology: Harnessing large online resources to generate ecological insights. *Trends in Ecology & Evolution*, 35, 630–639.

Jarić, I., Bellard, C., Correia, R.A., Courchamp, F., Douda, K., Essl, F., Jeschke, J.M., Kalinkat, G., Kalous, L., Lennox, R.J. (2021). Invasion culturomics and iEcology. *Conservation Biology*, 35(2), 447–451.

Johnson, B.A., Mader, A.D., Dasgupta, R., Kumar, P. (2020). Citizen science and invasive alien species: An analysis of citizen science initiatives using information and communications technology (ICT) to collect invasive alien species observations. *Global Ecology and Conservation*, 21, e00812.

Joly, A., Vrochidis, S., Karatzas, K., Karppinen, A., Bonnet, P. (2018). *Multimedia Tools and Applications for Environmental and Biodiversity Informatics*. Springer, Berlin.

Ladle, R.J., Correia, R.A., Do, Y., Joo, G.J., Malhado, A.C., Proulx, R., Roberge, J.M., Jepson, P. (2016). Conservation culturomics. *Frontiers in Ecology and the Environment*, 14, 269–275.

Larson, L.R., Cooper, C.B., Futch, S., Singh, D., Shipley, N.J., Dale, K. et al. (2020). The diverse motivations of citizen scientists: Does conservation emphasis grow as volunteer participation progresses? *Biological Conservation*, 242, 108428.

Lorieul, T., Cole, E., Deneu, B., Servajean, M., Bonnet, P., Joly, A. (2021). Overview of GeoLifeCLEF 2021: Predicting species distribution from 2 million remote sensing images. *Working Notes of CLEF 2021 – Conference and Labs of the Evaluation Forum*. 1451–1462.

Mahecha, M.D., Rzanny, M., Kraemer, G., Mäder, P., Seeland, M., Wäldchen, J. (2021). Crowd-sourced plant occurrence data provide a reliable description of macroecological gradients. *Ecography*, 44, 1131–1142.

Marcenò, C., Padullés Cubino, J., Chytrý, M., Genduso, E., Salemi, D., La Rosa, A. et al. (2021). Facebook groups as citizen science tools for plant species monitoring. *Journal of Applied Ecology*, 58, 2018–2028.

Maund, P.R., Irvine, K.N., Lawson, B., Steadman, J., Risely, K., Cunningham, A.A. et al. (2020). What motivates the masses: Understanding why people contribute to conservation citizen science projects. *Biological Conservation*, 246, 108587.

McDonough MacKenzie, C., Murray, G., Primack, R., Weihrauch, D. (2017). Lessons from citizen science: Assessing volunteer-collected plant phenology data with Mountain Watch. *Biological Conservation*, 208, 121–126.

McKinley, D.C., Miller-Rushing, A.J., Ballard, H.L., Bonney, R., Brown, H., Cook-Patton, S.C. et al. (2017). Citizen science can improve conservation science, natural resource management, and environmental protection. *Biological Conservation*, 208, 15–28.

Michel, J.B., Shen, Y.K., Aiden, A.P., Veres, A., Gray, M.K., Pickett, J.P., Hoiberg, D., Clancy, D., Norvig, P., Orwant, J. et al. (2011). Quantitative analysis of culture using millions of digitized books. *Science*, 331, 176–182.

Mittermeier, J.C., Correia, R., Grenyer, R., Toivonen, T., Roll, U. (2021). Using Wikipedia to measure public interest in biodiversity and conservation. *Conservation Biology*, 35, 412–423.

Pernat, N., August, T., Groom, Q., Memedemin, D., Reyserhove, L. (2022). An iNaturalist-Pl@ntNet-workflow to identify plant–pollinator interactions – a case study of *Isodontia mexicana*. *BioHackrXiv*. doi: 10.37044/osf.io/em3rk [Accessed 29 November 2022].

Reeb, R.A., Aziz, N., Lapp, S.M., Kitzes, J., Heberling, J.M., Kuebbing, S.E. (2022). Using convolutional neural networks to efficiently extract immense phenological data from community science images. *Frontiers in Plant Science*, 12, 3148.

Stroud, S., Fennell, M., Mitchley, J., Lydon, S., Peacock, J., Bacon, K.L. (2022). The botanical education extinction and the fall of plant awareness. *Ecology and Evolution*, 12, e9019.

Turrini, T., Dörler, D., Richter, A., Heigl, F., Bonn, A. (2018). The threefold potential of environmental citizen science – Generating knowledge, creating learning opportunities and enabling civic participation. *Biological Conservation*, 225, 176–186.

Young, B.E., Dodge, N., Hunt, P.D., Ormes, M., Schlesinger, M.D., Shaw, H.Y. (2019). Using citizen science data to support conservation in environmental regulatory contexts. *Biological Conservation*, 237, 57–62.

10

The Contribution of New Technologies to Our Experiences of Nature

Figure 10.1. *Gamers sensitive to nature thanks to video games. Source: Julie Polge (2021)). For a color version of this figure, see www.iste.co.uk/kohlmann/linking.zip*

Chapter written by Minh-Xuan TRUONG.

10.1. Introduction

Against the backdrop of biodiversity and the climate crisis, the way we encounter and communicate about the natural world is changing. Increased technological capabilities, accessibility and connectivity have enabled the expansion and widespread adoption of digital platforms and media consumption in the most developed countries (O'Dea 2021). Coupled with an increasingly urban and sedentary lifestyle, this technologization of our relationship with the world is leading to a significant change in the way people, and children in particular, interact with their daily environment, communicate with each other and spend their free time. In just a few decades, we have thus gradually shifted from societies where children spent a lot of time outdoors to societies where they increasingly interact with screens (Rideout et al. 2010; Larson et al. 2018). However, it is not just the proportion of time spent with technology that has changed; the types of technology and the ways in which people interact with it are also transforming. The new generations, born into a connected world enhanced by all of these technologies, and in particular by smartphones, will grow up immersed in this digital and technology-mediated environment, where many if not all sectors of their social life, their leisure, their education and their openness to the world will incorporate a technological medium. In this environment, traditional media – television, radio and the press – are complemented by new digital and social media that provide instant access to entertainment, virtual sociality, information and knowledge (Moreno et al. 2016). In this way, any information obtained from traditional or digital media can be completed, enriched and discussed instantaneously, which was not the case before. So, unlike traditional media, in which users are mainly spectators and consumers of finished content, these new digital types also offer users the opportunity to actively consume and create content, making them actors in their experience rather than just spectators (Reid Chassiakos et al. 2016). In this way, users of the Instagram social network can both share their photographs and enjoy those of others. They can also, as is the case on the Twitch platform, react to videos broadcast live and act on what they see on screen.

When it comes to relationships with nature, given the increasing amount of time it occupies in our daily lives, digital media is often placed in competition with so-called nature or outdoor activities in expert reports and scientific publications (Larson et al. 2018). Furthermore, the proliferation of new technologies is also cited as contributing to a decline in individual interactions with natural environments and their associated biodiversity, described as a gradual extinction of nature experiences (Pyle 2011; Soga and Gaston 2016). There is also growing concern that this move away from unstructured outdoor activities for children (Ulset et al. 2017) or outdoor sports and recreation for adults may have consequences for individual health and well-being (Loureiro et al. 2013; Hughes et al. 2019). It could also lead to a loss of interest in nature and environmental issues, such as global warming or the biodiversity crisis, which could ultimately cause a weakening of environmental attitudes and pro-environmental behavior (Bratman et al. 2019).

In this chapter, based on the work of Kellert, we consider that there is more than one type of nature experience[1]. In *Birthright: People and Nature in the Modern World* (2012), Kellert emphasizes the need to acknowledge the fact that children today can experience nature in a wide variety of ways; and these are not simply limited to involvement in *direct* experiences (involving actual physical contact), but also include *indirect* or *vicarious* experiences (involving realistic, as well as symbolic and fantastical representations of nature without any real, physical contact with natural environments), such as through magazines, books, films, TV programs and websites. Also, following the work of Clayton et al. (2017a), we take a broader view of what constitutes an experience of nature and define it as a process that includes three components:

– interactions, especially sensory ones between individuals and natural entities, which involve more emotions and create a personal history and memories that are more meaningful than mere observation;

– a social and cultural context, which often plays an important role in the meaning of the experience and the memory it leaves behind;

– a transformative phenomenon of personal enrichment in the acquisition of new knowledge and skills and behavioral changes.

Moreover, as Crowley et al. (2021) develop in their work on the potential of nature experiences in an adventure video game as a means of learning about North American wildlife, if it is likely "that the ratio of direct to vicarious experiences has shifted in post-industrial societies where people can now live with few direct interactions with 'nature'", this does not mean that all interactions with places of nature and biodiversity have necessarily been lost. On the other hand, it is possible that some of them have been transformed into more technologically mediated experiences. With increasing urbanization and the use of digital technologies, technological or virtual vicarious representations of nature and biodiversity can increasingly replace direct experiences. New technologies thus offer a whole new range of experiences, depending on the degree of mediation they provide. For example, an experience in the forest with a plant identification application such as Pl@ntNet[2] will be very different from the entirely

1 We do not define here what we consider to be nature. Indeed, just as experiences of nature are placed in an environmental, personal and socio-cultural context (Clayton et al. 2017), we consider nature as a personal, cultural and social construct that can vary greatly from one person to another, depending on their history and their own experiences. For someone urban-born, an urban park may define nature in all the memories, experiences and personal contributions these places may have brought, whereas this will not be the case for someone else, for whom only wild, isolated and preserved nature can be defined as real.

2 Available at: https://plantnet.org/ [Accessed November 10, 2022].

virtualized experience of an adventure video game in which the player is not physically present in the field. Thus, these new technologies can also be differentiated according to the embodiment and degree of involvement of the body and senses in the experience. As Truong and Clayton (2020, p. 2) wrote, “we need to consider the consequences such a change might have on people’s lives in the long term”. The expansion of technologies and their democratization in the most developed countries are indeed phenomena from which it is now impossible to turn back. It is therefore important to understand the social, ecological and experiential impacts of these technologies, so that we can take them into account in our societies, particularly in terms of environmental education and connection to nature.

10.2. From embodied experience to techno-mediated experience

Humans are sentient beings, living in interaction with environments, natural or otherwise, that are rich in stimuli and information that are picked up and recognized by their senses (see, for example, Ingold 2000). It is through this relationship between the sensory body and the environment that people develop their relationships with natural environments, their environmental knowledge as well as their understanding and ability to commit to the conservation of nature and biodiversity (Truong 2018). In this sensory and embodied dimension, the senses are not isolated from each other but function together (Pink 2015) as a combination of images, sounds, textures, smells and tastes, as well as thermal and atmospheric conditions (Thibaud 2011; Bull and Howes 2016). This interaction enables us to have a coherent awareness and representation of our environment (Fulkerson 2014), as well as to connect to and identify with places (Casey 2009). So, if the place where we experience nature anchors the human connection to the natural environment, it is through our bodies in motion and the embodied dimension of our sensory experiences that we place ourselves in the living world (Kothencz et al. 2017). To this, Lumber et al. (2017) add that there are different modalities available in the way we can experience nature: through emotion, the senses, knowledge or even aesthetics. They add that considering these different pathways rather than just the one pathway could be a way of enhancing, diversifying or creating connections between humans and nature, while monotony of stimulation can conversely be a source of stress (Stuster 2000). As new technologies take on an ever-greater importance in our lives, we are entitled to ask whether relationships with nature through these technologies still allow us to have this richness and diversity of ways of relating to nature. Likewise, it is important to question the impact they could have on the way we learn, build and interact with natural environments. This technological mediation of our experiences of nature can take place along a gradient ranging from a real experience lived with the help of technologies to completely virtualized experiences. These different experiences could have different implications and consequences for our relationship with nature and biodiversity.

10.3. The smartphone, a multifaceted mediator of our experiences of nature

Of all the technologies developed since the beginning of the 21st century, the smartphone is the fastest-growing, with the number of devices connected to the Internet rising from 3.6 billion in 2016 to over 6 billion in 2021 (O'Dea 2021). Through its functions, but mainly through applications – software installed on the device to perform various tasks – the smartphone illustrates the versatility and multiplicity of forms that experiences of nature mediated by new technologies can take. Thus, the smartphone enables both person-assisted and fully virtualized experiences. Here, we discuss the nature experiences in which the smartphone participates in a real experience and develop the other aspect, entirely digitized and no longer involving a direct relationship with a real environment, in the following section.

Thus, in the context of nature experiences where the person is physically present and in contact with the elements of nature, the technological mediation of the smartphone mainly involves providing information and knowledge about the surrounding natural environment. These experiences of nature, where we seek to identify, i.e. to put a name to the species we encounter, are very similar to naturalist experiences. In this context, we find naturalist guides transposed from the paper medium to the digital medium, such as the *Guide ornitho* or *the Audubon Bird Guide*. As well as being enriched, the digital medium allows access to tools, notably visual and audio, that the printed medium does not allow (Farnsworth et al. 2013). Applications to help identify the species we encounter are also among the resources taking part in the new experiences of nature mediated by the smartphone. Taking advantage of the development of identification algorithms and the advanced functionalities of new-generation smartphones, a wide variety of automatic species identification applications have emerged over the last 10 years. As with the naturalist guides mentioned above, the aim of these applications is to help identify an animal or plant encountered during a walk in a forest or garden. However, unlike an experience where you use a guide to identify the animal or plant yourself, these applications perform automatic identification based on algorithms and artificial intelligence. In fact, they play a more active role in the identification process than field guides: they analyze the user's observations, photographs and sound recordings, and propose one or more species names associated with a likelihood index. The prevalence and quality of these applications, as well as their use, are only increasing, coupled with the ever-growing number of smartphones in use. To address the current biodiversity crisis, the Intergovernmental Platform on Biodiversity and Ecosystem Services (IPBES)[3] has called in its latest report (IPBES 2019) for ways to get more people involved in preserving natural environments and biodiversity, which is known as environmental citizenship (Jørgensen and Jørgensen 2021). In particular,

3 Available at: https://ipbes.net/ [Accessed November 10, 2022].

this report highlights the importance of obtaining environmental knowledge from a wide range of educational sources and formal and informal experiences, at different scales from local to global. It thus highlights the fact that knowledge related to nature and biodiversity can be validly apprehended and transmitted as part of a bundle of learning experiences (Nightingale 2016), including among others experiences of an individual or collective nature in which technologies can play an important part. Through their success and popularization, species recognition apps are enabling a larger number of people to gain access to knowledge about nature and biodiversity in their everyday environment (Uzunboylu et al. 2009).

However, beyond the naturalist experiences lived in the context of our leisure activities, a large part of the naturalist observations are carried out within the framework of biodiversity monitoring programs and/or citizen science programs, including in particular projects involving species identification apps, such as Pl@ntNet for the identification of plants by image or BirdNET[4], which identifies birds using sound recordings. Traditionally, these researcher-led monitoring programs aimed at answering a scientific question relied on volunteers to collect observations in the field, i.e. species identifications using identification keys or field guides, or the execution of monitoring protocols, such as setting up and collecting data from sound recorders. For example, there are historical monitoring programs and annual events, such as the National Garden Bird Count by the French Museum of Natural History and the Ligue pour la protection des oiseaux (LPO, French League for the Protection of Birds) in France, the Christmas Bird Count by Audubon in America and the Big Garden Birdwatch by the Royal Society for the Protection of Birds (RSPB) in the UK, which collect tens of millions of bird sightings every year. While these naturalist experiences may seem a far cry from more contemplative or aimless experiences, such as forest or mountain walks, they are no less important in terms of what they can bring to participants in the form of experiences and memories created, environmental knowledge acquired and social links created within participant communities and with scientists. The importance of citizen science in terms of what it can bring to people's experiences of nature was highlighted during the Covid-19 crisis. Around the world, lockdowns limited the public's ability to contribute to data collection in the field (Corlett et al. 2020; Rose et al. 2020). However, there was a real awareness of the nature present in the direct vicinity of people's homes, which has been highlighted in the media. As a result, several citizen science programs that can be carried out from home have seen a significant increase in the number of observations (Peterson 2020). Similarly, online citizen science platforms, such as zooniverse.org, which presents dozens of projects and enables citizens to train in species identification and then participate in photo-based bird identification and counting programs, for example, have also seen an unprecedented increase in the number of participants (Wisconsin 2020). Over the past decade, the growth and success of social networks online and participatory science have

4 Available at: https://birdnet.cornell.edu/ [Accessed November 10, 2022].

fostered the emergence of large, structured communities of observers who participate in biodiversity monitoring and contribute data to online platforms such as eBird, iNaturalist and Pl@ntNet. These platforms facilitate the rapid sharing and exchange of information between participants, enabling them to submit and manage their observations using databases accessible worldwide, as well as identifying and validating other participants' data. All of these data are of great importance to scientists, who would be unable to collect such vast quantities of observations, identifications and records themselves. Their importance is such that the eBird and Artportalen (Swedish species observation system) platforms provide the two largest datasets for the Global Biodiversity Information Facility (GBIF)[5], an international network and data infrastructure. The GBIF is funded by the world's governments and aims to provide free access to data on all forms of life on Earth for everyone, everywhere. In total, more than 50% of the species occurrence records of the GBIF come from observations by volunteers in citizen science programs (Waller 2019).

10.4. Virtualized experiences of nature, from social networks to video games

Apart from nature experiences in which people are assisted by technology, there are also fully virtualized experiences, which can be experienced via smartphones, as well as via other digital media, such as tablets or computers. These experiences can include footage of real environments, as in nature documentaries or photographs of nature and animals, or fully digitized environments, such as in video games. They differ from previous experiences in that they no longer involve physical interaction with natural environments, and technological mediation is no longer an add-on to the experience, but the very framework in which the experience takes place. These experiences are also singular in that they are entirely scripted. With the exception of films like *The Velvet Queen* (Munier 2021), where the time spent on the lookout is part of the construction of the spectator's experience, in animal documentaries, we only see moments chosen from hours of recording by the film crew where the animals are visible. We do not spend hours on the lookout in the forest or mountains, waiting for the animals to arrive. In the same way, what we show on social networks, on Instagram, for example, whether nature-related or not, is subject to a selection and optimization process to get the best possible content: not everything is "Instagrammable". There are online guides that explain to photographers how and which photo to take, how to choose what to post and how to make a "cohesive" content flow when posting their photographs, in order to attract users to the platform. As a result, in many accounts, images of nature are taken and posted to fit the coherence of the feed, to correspond to a global trend and not to realistically depict the natural world. In terms of learning about environmental knowledge and

5 Available at: www.gbif.org/fr/ [Accessed November 10, 2022].

awakening to the climate and biodiversity crises, this scripting of real-life experiences, as well as a certain standardization of what is represented in them, could create a standardization of people's knowledge of nature and conservation issues. Ballouard et al. (2011) demonstrated this by asking French schoolchildren to identify a mixture of 37 different species, both local and exotic, and to name each species precisely. They showed that local species were less frequently identified compared to exotic and emblematic species, such as great apes or big cats, which are very often visible on social networks. This study highlights a disconnect between people and real, local biodiversity, and this disconnect is accentuated by modern vicarious experiences in which biodiversity is often limited to a small number of charismatic species. If we add this limitation of knowledge to the optimization of content detailed above, then this current trend could condition people to think that biodiversity is only made up of exotic, charismatic species from faraway places. The result would be a global ignorance of what local biodiversity is all about. What is more, if people's only contact with nature is through this medium, and new generations learn nothing about the species that they may encounter in their immediate, everyday environment, this could lead to a general indifference to the fate of this biodiversity. The global standardization of what we learn and know, of what we are aware of, could thus have an influence on what we are prepared to protect in the future (Heathcote 2021).

This phenomenon of scripting and optimization is all the stronger in virtual environments such as video games where all visible and audible elements, as well as those with which it is possible to interact virtually, are computer-modeled. While these experiences are similar to those described above, they differ from them in that they enable people to interact with, move around in and explore these digital environments via virtual avatars, like the characters played in video games. A good example of the positive impact of a virtual experience on environmental awareness is the study conducted by Crowley et al. (2021). In this study, the researchers looked at the educational potential of a big-budget video game purchased by millions of players, the action-adventure game *Red Dead Redemption 2* (*RDR2* hereafter). Their hypothesis was that, with its detailed simulation of late 19th-century North American ecosystems and the ability to roam freely in them, the game would offer players the chance to learn about real-world wildlife. They asked players who had spent time playing the game, and others who had not, to take part in a quiz designed to identify 15 real-world animal species that could be encountered in-game. Their results showed that *RDR2* players correctly identified more species than other players. Furthermore, *RDR2* players reported that, in addition to identifying species, they also learned about animal behavior and species interactions in-game. Here, the video game is a source of informal learning about the real biodiversity of North American ecosystems. The challenge, based on results like these, is to encourage other forms of informal learning in technology-mediated nature experiences. This could take the form, for example, of informative messages about the protection status of a species whose photo we see on Instagram, as is already the case if the image has been characterized as potentially unsuitable for a certain audience due to its violent nature, or informative messages about ecosystems encountered in video games taking place in natural environments that can be encountered in the real world. In 2012, French video game publisher Ankama took a step forward in this direction by introducing the notion of ecosystem management in its video game *Wakfu*:

> Kill too many animals without giving them time to reproduce, and they will disappear forever. Mow down too much wheat without replanting, and it will be your last harvest... You are free to protect or exploit natural species until they are totally extinct. Your world, your decisions. But it's also up to you to bear the consequences.

10.5. What can be done with these experiences?

In this chapter, we have addressed the broad spectrum of techno-mediated experiences, detailing several of them. As we have seen, while they all share a technological edge in their practices, they can also differ greatly from one another in terms of their relationship with nature, whether real or virtual, incarnate or not, and in what they can bring in terms of personal enrichment. In increasingly sedentary urban societies, where real nature experiences on a daily basis are becoming ever more difficult, nature experiences enabled by new technologies, natural environments encountered in documentaries, social networks and even the virtual worlds of video games can be, for hundreds of millions of people, the way to find the nature they do not encounter in their daily lives, and to escape the city. For example, when online gamers are asked why they play video games, one of the main reasons they give is to "escape from their daily lives" (Yee 2006). Moreover, when asked to name and describe the places they like most in the game they play, places with verdant, omnipresent and peaceful nature are the most cited by World of Warcraft players, and particularly by those who rarely frequent nature spaces and live in large conurbations (Truong et al. 2018). In a similar vein, Xu et al. (2021) showed that during the Covid-19 pandemic in the UK, watching nature videos on Facebook and social networks elicited positive emotions and could help people feel more relaxed and promote states of recovery from stressful situations and mental fatigue. Of course, in terms of embodiment, of physical interactions with nature, techno-mediated nature experiences are generally considered to be less beneficial than real nature (Mayer et al. 2009), and we are not proposing that virtual experiences replace real ones. At a time when the climate and biodiversity crises are increasingly visible in the media and the effects they have on our daily lives, it is important that both the companies behind these media and the communities who use them as a means of communication seize every available opportunity to raise awareness of these issues. In view of their omnipresence in the daily lives of an ever-increasing number of people, it is in everyone's interest to learn and understand what these techno-mediated experiences have to offer in terms of individual well-being, as well as in terms of education and pro-environmental commitment. However, it is also important to ask what the consequences would be for our societies if these techno-mediated experiences were to become the new benchmark for experiences of nature. The experience obtained through screens and virtual universes, however satisfying, is not as complete, rich or varied as a real, embodied experience of nature, in the sense that, compared to the latter, the quantity of sensory stimuli and information is much greater. For example, a video following a person walking in the forest may give us pleasure through the images, sounds and immersion it provides but it is a far cry from the real experience of walking in a forest, the accompanying smells of humus and undergrowth, the sensation of the humidity in the air, the wind, the heat and sunlight on our skin, and the texture of the substrate under our shoes: all the elements that make a direct experience one that anchors us in a natural environment. As techno-mediated experiences become ubiquitous, people's point of reference for assessing the state of preservation of a natural environment, as well as their awareness of environmental issues, and in particular new generations growing up in a connected world, may only be based on experiences lived online, on social networks, where algorithms are designed to show us things that match our tastes; experiences that are unilaterally positive, safe and sensorially less rich.

The main challenge ahead is to find ways of ensuring that these techno-mediated experiences do not become the norm. We need to look for the bridges between these techno-mediated experiences and real-life experiences, and use them to ensure that people continue or find the desire to step out of this mediation through technology to live direct, rich experiences of sensory contact outside the home. This will involve, for example, the creation of social links and communities, as in citizen science programs where participants share, help and encourage each other. It could also come from education programs teaching us how to deal with a techno-mediated life. Indeed, in societies where new technologies occupy more and more space, it is not just nature experiences that are impacted. Education in new technologies and the practices they imply is necessary on many levels, including virtual otherness and the real consequences of actions on social networks and the need to learn to recognize real and fake sources of information. Learning to identify what is real from what is scripted, so that we can live an optimal experience, should be part of this education.

10.6. References

Ballouard, J.-M., Brischoux, F., Bonnet, X. (2011). Children prioritize virtual exotic biodiversity over local biodiversity. *PLOS ONE*, 6(8), e23152. doi: 10.1371/journal.pone.0023152.

Bratman, G.N., Anderson, C.B., Berman, M.G., Cochran, B., de Vries, S., Flanders, J., Folke, C., Frumkin, H., Gross, J.J., Hartig, T. et al. (2019). Nature and mental health: An ecosystem service perspective. *Science Advances*, 5(7), eaax0903. doi: 10.1126/sciadv.aax0903.

Bull, M. and Howes, D. (2016). Editorial: The expanding field of sensory studies. *Senses and Society*, 11, 1–2.

Casey, E.S. (2009). *Getting Back into Place: Toward a Renewed Understanding of the Place-World*. Indiana University Press, Bloomington.

Clayton, S., Colléony, A., Conversy, P., Maclouf, E., Martin, L., Torres, A.-C., Truong, M.-X., & Prévot, A.-C. (2017). Transformation of experience: Toward a new relationship with nature. *Conservation Letters*, 10(5).

Crowley, E.J., Silk, M.J., Crowley, S.L. (2021). The educational value of virtual ecologies in Red Dead Redemption 2. *People and Nature*, 3(6), 1229–1243.

Farnsworth, E.J., Chu, M., Kress, W.J., Neill, A.K., Best, J.H., Pickering, J., Stevenson, R.D., Courtney, G.W., Vandyk, J.K., Ellison, A.M. (2013). Next-generation field guides. *Bioscience*, 63, 891–899.

Fulkerson, M. (2014). Rethinking the senses and their interactions: The case for sensory pluralism. *Frontiers in Psychology*, 5.

Heathcote, G. (2021). Animals of Instagram: Taxonomic bias in science communication online. *Journal of Science Communication*, 20, 1–19. doi: 10.22323/2.20040210.

Hughes, J., Rogerson, M., Barton, J., Bragg, R. (2019). Age and connection to nature: When is engagement critical? *Frontiers in Ecology and the Environment*, 17, 265–269.

Ingold, T. (2000). *The Perception of the Environment: Essays on Livelihood, Dwelling and Skill*. Routledge, London.

IPBES (2019). Global assessment report on biodiversity and ecosystem services of the Intergovernmental Science-Policy Platform on Biodiversity and Ecosystem Services. Report, Bonn.

Jørgensen, F.A. and Jørgensen, D. (2021). Citizen science for environmental citizenship. *The Society for Conservation Biology*, 35, 1344–1347.

Kellert, S.R. (2012). *Birthright: People and Nature in the Modern World*. Yale University Press, London.

Kothencz, G., Kolcsár, R., Cabrera-Barona, P., Szilassi, P. (2017). Urban green space perception and its contribution to well-being. *International Journal of Environmental Research and Public Health*, 14, 1–14.

Larson, L.R., Szczytko, R., Bowers, E.P., Stephens, L.E., Stevenson, K.T., Floyd, M.F. (2019). Outdoor time, screen time, and connection to nature: Troubling trends among rural youth? *Environment and Behavior*, 51(8), 966–991. doi: 10.1177/0013916518806686.

Loureiro, A., Veloso, S., Rebola, F., Olivos, P., Lima, M.L., Aragonés, J.I. (2013). Outdoor exercise and connectedness with nature : Relation to wellbeing. *International Conference on Environmental Psychology*.

Lumber, R., Richardson, M., Sheffield, D. (2017). Beyond knowing nature: Contact, emotion, compassion, meaning, and beauty are pathways to nature connection. *PLOS ONE*, 12(5), e0177186. doi: 10.1371/journal.pone.0177186.

Mayer, F.S., Frantz, C.M., Bruehlman-Senecal, E., Dolliver, K. (2009). Why is nature beneficial? The role of connectedness to nature. *Environmental Behaviour*, 41, 607–643.

Moreno, M., Reid Chassiakos, Y.L., & Cross, C. (2016). Media use in school-aged children and adolescents. *Pediatrics*, 138(5), e20162592. doi: 10.1542/peds.2016-2592.

Nightingale, A.J. (2016). Adaptive scholarship and situated knowledges? Hybrid methodologies and plural epistemologies in climate change adaptation research. *Area*, 48, 41–47.

O'Dea, S. (2021). Number of smartphone users from 2016 to 2021. *Statista* [Online]. Available at: https://www.statista.com/statistics/330695/number-of-smartphone-users-worldwide/ [Accessed 10 November 2022].

Peterson, C. (2020). Americans are observing nature during the pandemic, helping scientists with research. *National Geographic Magazine* [Online]. Available at: https://www.nationalgeographic.com/animals/article/citizen-science-increasing-pandemic-insects [Accessed 16 November 2022].

Pink, S. (2015). *Doing Sensory Ethnography*. Sage Publications, Thousand Oaks.

Pyle, R.M. (2011). *The Thunder Tree: Lessons from an Urban Wildland*. Oregon State University Press, Corvallis.

Reid Chassiakos, Y.L., Radesky, J., Christakis, D., Moreno, M.A., Cross, C. (2016). Children and adolescents and digital media. *Pediatrics*, 138(5), e20162593. doi: 10.1542/peds.2016-2593.

Rideout, V.J., Foehr, U.G., Roberts, D.F. (2010). Generation M2: Media in the lives of 8- to 18-year-olds. Report, Kaiser Family Foundation.

Soga, M. and Gaston, K.J. (2016). Extinction of experience: The loss of human-nature interactions. *Frontiers Ecology Environment*, 14, 94–101.

Stuster, J.W. (2000). Bold endeavors: Behavioral lessons from polar and space exploration. *Gravitational and Space Biology Bulletin*, 13, 49–57.

Thibaud, J.P. (2011). The sensory fabric of urban ambiances. *The Senses and Society*, 6, 203–215.

Truong, M.X. (2018). Construction et perception de la part olfactive de l'expérience de nature : complémentarité des relations cognitives, écologiques et sensorielles de la nature. PhD thesis, National Museum of Natural History, Paris.

Truong, M.-X.A. and Clayton, S. (2020). Technologically transformed experiences of nature: A challenge for environmental conservation? *Biological Conservation*, 244, 108532. doi: 10.1016/j.biocon.2020.108532.

Truong, M.X., Prévot, A.C., Clayton, S. (2018). Gamers like it green: The significance of vegetation in online gaming. *Ecopsychology*, 10, 1–13.

Ulset, V., Vitaro, F., Brendgen, M., Bekkhus, M., Borge, A.I.H. (2017). Time spent outdoors during preschool: Links with children's cognitive and behavioral development. *Journal of Environmental Psychology*, 52, 69–80.

Uzunboylu, H., Cavus, N., Ercag, E. (2009). Using mobile learning to increase environmental awareness. *Computers and Education*, 52, 381–389.

Wisconsin, D.N.R. (2020). The snapshot July 2020 [Online]. Available at: https://dnr.wisconsin.gov/topic/Research/projects/snapshot/articles/july2020.html#articleOne [Accessed 15 October 2021].

Xu, S., Murrell, G., Golding, S.E. et al. (2021). #Springwatch #WildMorningswithChris: Engaging with nature via social media and wellbeing during the COVID-19 lockdown. *Frontiers in Psychology*, 12, 42–59.

Yee, N. (2006). Motivations of play in online games. *Cyber Psychology Behavior*, 9, 772–775.

11

Belonging to the World to Think of the Link: The Relationship with the Natural Environment as a Crucible of Relatedness

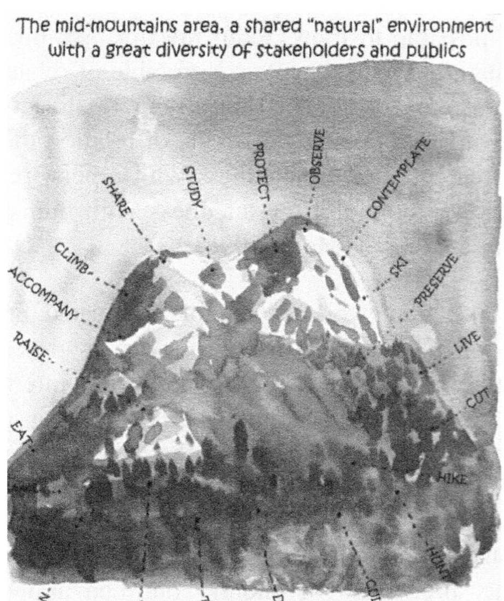

Figure 11.1. *Mid-mountain area, a shared "natural" environment. Source: Julie Polge (2021). For a color version of this figure, see www.iste.co.uk/kohlmann/linking.zip*

Chapter written by Amélie COULBAUT-LAZZARINI.

11.1. Introduction

To conclude this work, we propose to take a step aside and question the link to nature, beyond digital devices and links to the diverse data that new technologies enable us to take into account and analyze. While the previous chapter questioned the materiality and structure of human/environmental links in digital devices, the production of data on nature and the contribution of automatic tools (explainable artificial intelligence) to environmental understanding and engagement, we choose here to consider what makes it possible to think about the link. This position, rooted both philosophically and empirically, questions communication (particularly environmental communication) in its original sense of *communicare* ("to be in relation with", "to link").

With the idea of belonging to the world, this chapter reminds us that humanity cannot arrogate to itself the piloting of the Earth (Maris 2018), being only one living being among many others. From this, we think of the link becoming necessary to imagine and implement a diplomacy (Morizot 2017), i.e. a mode of relationship enabling everyone, human or not, to coexist and to co-evolve. In order to better define what makes it possible to think about the link, we propose to consider the relationship with the natural environment as a crucible of relatedness (De Bal 2003, 2009; Morin 2008; Morin and Wolton 2011). In our final section, we take a closer look at this concept, which articulates the levels of relation that Morin specifies as an act of relatedness that implies "relatedness with others, relatedness with one's own, relatedness with the community, relatedness with humanity and, ultimately, insertion into cosmic relatedness" (Morin 2008).

Positioned within the framework of complex, situated and engaged thinking (Coulbaut-Lazzarini and Couston 2021), this chapter describes the link as a relationship to the natural environment built around three interrelated axes or levels – both empirical and theoretical – constituting an exploration of relatedness. These axes articulate the relationship to the self, the relationship to others and the relationship to the world of the frequenters[1] of a French mid-mountain area.

We propose therefore to set out the ground and context of the empirical study, and then, through the three lines of enquiry outlined above, to show how the relationship with the natural environment can constitute a crucible for the development of relatedness, both as a theoretical notion and as a pragmatic reality.

1 Under this term, we include all of those who take part in various leisure activities, whether physical activities, nature walks or others, as well as professionals (in tourism, photography, etc.) working in the area, i.e. all humans moving around and likely to interact with the environment of the regional natural park (including herds and other animals).

11.1.1. *A foothold: the mid-mountain region*

Our analysis is based on a research-action project in environmental communication developed in the Bauges range[2]. This project anchors our research perspective in the mid-mountain region, a sensitive natural environment whose accessibility, thanks to its proximity to urban areas, has generated strong growth in affluence in recent years. In fact, the territorial scale of our experiments is centered on the regional natural park (RNP) of the Bauges range. More specifically, we focused our attention on the mid-mountain sites of the Savoie Grand Revard and Aillons-Margériaz domains, made particularly attractive by the recent context we discuss later. These areas, which are close to the major urban areas of Annecy, Chambéry and Aix-les-Bains, have seen a strong influx of new residents in recent years, and are seeing their visitor numbers multiply at the same time as the expansion of their tourism and leisure facilities within their perimeter.

11.1.2. *Context: transitions, end of lockdown and links to the environment*

Our thinking is set against a backdrop marked over the past decade, and even more so since 2019–2020, by cyclical factors accompanied by major trends.

Among the cyclical elements are the various lockdowns/lifting of restrictions that the world and France experienced, which have contributed to inflections, at least momentary, in ways of living and thinking[3]. The massive use of digital technology for work and leisure, and the increased sharing of images of wild animals, birdsong and skies free of industrial pollution via digital networks and the online press, have reinforced a "need for nature", particularly among city dwellers. This need, sometimes fueled by hybrid digital/physical activities adapted to lockdown situations[4], generated unprecedented flows to nearby natural areas during restriction-ending operations[5]. Over and above these short and significant periods, the restrictions on activities that accompanied them, and which sometimes lasted a long time, created conditions for the evolution of people's links and relationships with themselves, with others and with the world, which the framework of our research project enables us to examine.

---

2 The Communication et interactions humains-environnement dans les espaces naturels alpins de proximité (COMHUNENVI) project, cofinanced by the joint call for projects – Edition 2021: Zone Atelier Alpes – Fédération FREE-ALPES – Labex ITTEM.

3 See the numerous studies and press and research articles that have flourished on the subject, for example by Oger (2020), Parise (2020) and Statista (2021).

4 See, for example, Tela Botanica's Botany MOOC from April 2020.

5 See *Lettre ouverte au président de la République, au Premier ministre et au préfet*, December 13, 2020. Available at: www.facebook.com/michkrae/posts/10158066740307613 [Accessed January 21, 2021].

In particular, in the mid-mountain region, we have been able to observe the effects of the health-related shutdown of ski lifts in winter 2020–2021 on the activities and behaviors of humans and, in part, nonhumans.

However, the evolution of the relationship between humans and the rest of the living world is a part of major trends, such as the effects of climate change, which are increasingly documented (IPCC 2022), as well as a part of the dynamics of diversification of leisure practices (Jorand et al. 2009) and of the multiplication of stakeholders (Achin 2015; Perrin-Malterre 2016) and of a desire to reconnect with the world around them (Chanvallon and Héas 2011).

These elements generate a modification of relationships, of human/environmental links, of uses and representations of the natural environment. Here, we attempt to decipher these relationships, first through the question of the relationship to ourselves, then to others and finally to the world, composing the constituents of relatedness.

11.1.3. *Methods*

Our field study is based on a questionnaire survey[6] conducted in March–April 2021 on the Aillons-Margériaz and Savoie Grand Revard domains with a random sample of 500 respondents and on a summer version of the study in July–August 2021 in the Bauges range with a random sample of approximately 150 respondents. We also carried out participant observations in the spring and summer of 2021, with various stakeholders within the perimeter of the Bauges range regional national park. Finally, we carried out an analysis of some of the regional national park's communication documents, notably the visuals for its awareness-raising campaign deployed in summer 2021.

11.2. Activities, environment and relationship to self

11.2.1. *The natural environment as a medium for intrapersonal communication?*

At a first level, leisure activities in the natural environment reveal the self-relationship of participants through the study of their motivations: resourcing, overcoming, accomplishment (Queval 2004) and so on. We evoke the idea of intrapersonal communication, in order to understand the relationship with ourselves,

6 The winter questionnaire was largely based on the one developed by Léna Gruas as part of her research work (Gruas 2021), with the addition of a few specific questions relating to information and communication systems.

based on the notion of the affective body (Martin-Juchat 2008), which enables us to experience bodily affects and emotions.

Indeed, as we can see from the responses to our winter and summer questionnaires, physical activities in the natural environment largely reflect the affects and sensations of those who take part in mid-mountain leisure activities. In order to simplify reading, we have divided the responses to the question "what motivates you to take part in this activity?" into three separate figures (Figures 11.2–11.4), and grouped the modalities that make most sense together.

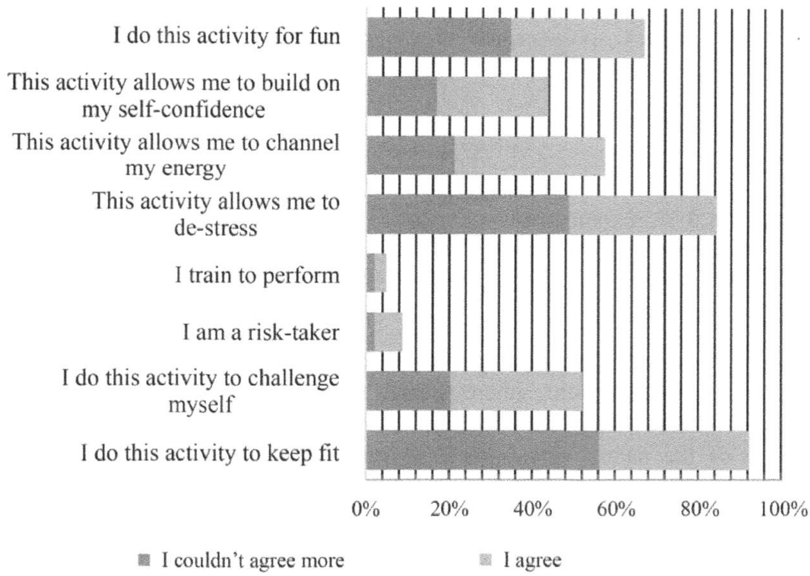

Figure 11.2. *Percentages of responses to certain modalities of the question: "What are the reasons that motivate you to practice this activity?", part 1. For a color version of this figure, see www.iste.co.uk/kohlmann/linking.zip*

If we focus solely on the modalities that concern the relationship with ourselves, we note a hedonistic aspect ("to have fun"), quite expected in leisure activities, but above all, the prevalence of the search for renewal ("to de-stress", mentioned by nearly 85% of respondents), self-control ("to channel my energy", mentioned by over 57% of respondents) and even self-assertion ("to build my self-confidence", mentioned by 44% of respondents). Above and beyond physical activity, our participants' responses show that it is a one-on-one experience with themselves (Figure 11.2). Activity is seen as a support, almost a pretext, for this self-talk.

It could no doubt be argued that practice alone is the issue here, but other modalities underline the link to the environment in which people evolve (Figure 11.3).

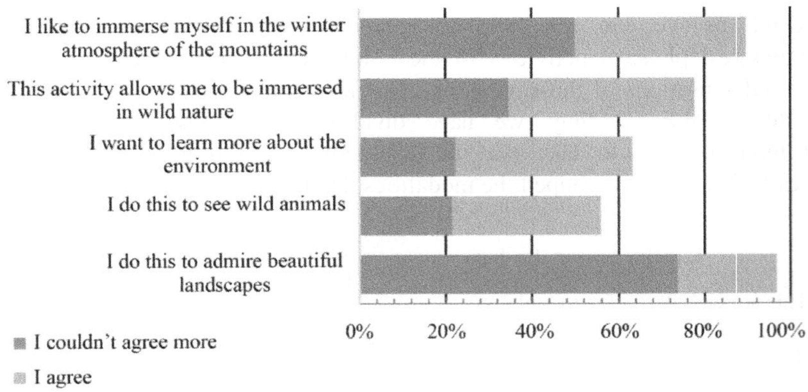

Figure 11.3. *Percentages of responses to certain categories of the question: "What are the reasons that motivate you to practice this activity?", part 2. For a color version of this figure, see www.iste.co.uk/kohlmann/linking.zip*

Thus, the beauty of the landscape was praised by 97% and 100% in summer, but above all, the mountain atmosphere (nearly 90% in winter, 96% in summer) and immersion in nature (nearly 78% in winter, 91% in summer) were cited, attesting to the importance of the natural environment in implementing the intrapersonal dialogue enabled by practice. To further test this hypothesis, we included in the summer version of our questionnaire the modality "to reconnect with the environment" (Figure 11.4). We note that this modality received 90% support, confirming the analysis of winter responses.

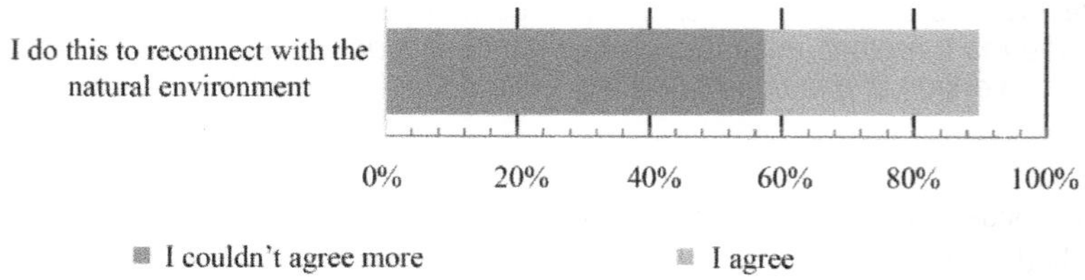

Figure 11.4. *Percentages of responses to certain modalities of the question: "What are the reasons that motivate you to practice this activity?", part 3. For a color version of this figure, see www.iste.co.uk/kohlmann/linking.zip*

While the responses obtained suggest the existence of intracorporeal communication experienced during mid-mountain activities, the rate of positive responses to modalities concerning landscapes, atmosphere or reconnection with the natural environment seems to reveal the importance of the environment in the possibility of expressing the relationship with ourselves. In other words, for our respondents, the mid-mountain natural environment is an ideal medium for intracorporeal communication.

11.2.2. *Physicality as a means of expressing a link*

The use of the body and perceptions through physical activities in the mountains appears to be a means of expressing a first form of connection, to ourselves and to the world, which passes through the spheres of emotions (Martin-Juchat 2008). These emotions are intimately linked to the way in which we view the mountain environment in which we engage in physical activity (Figure 11.5).

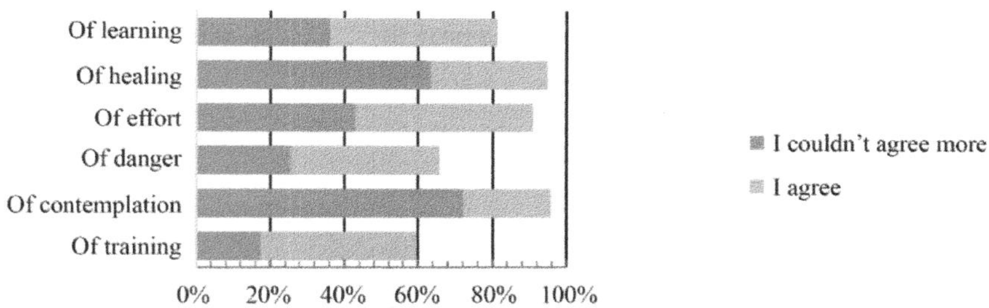

Figure 11.5. *Main response proportions to the multiple choice question: "Do you consider the mountain environment to be a place: ...". For a color version of this figure, see www.iste.co.uk/kohlmann/linking.zip*

Contemplation may score highest (over 95% in favor of the modality), but it does not overshadow the specific features of the environment, whose dangerous nature remains underlined (nearly 66% of responses). The healing mentioned above follows closely behind (94.7%), echoing the question of intrapersonal dialogue. However, the link to the environment is also expressed bodily through the notion of effort (mentioned by over 90%). More broadly, the question of learning (over 81% of responses) reveals another aspect of a link – to ourselves and to the environment – that is at once bodily, cognitive and global. Without denying the use of digital technology as a potential mediator of the body to the practice and the practice environment (notably via connected health applications, GPS tracks, etc.), we do not include it in the analysis, as our questions did not allow us to exploit this type of parameter. Only one question, on the preparation of the outing, integrated the digital dimension into the practice. However, only 1% of our respondents had downloaded GPX tracks.

While other works in ICS analyze the emotional manifestations of corporeality as a medium for media relations, we here understand the emotions arising from perceptions of the natural environment as a first level of connection, to ourselves (Ruiz 2000), which forms the basis for other forms of the link.

11.3. Collaboration and relationships with others

At a second level, the new collaborations that are being set up between human actors as part of research projects or for the development of communication devices make it possible to explore the relationship with others among those who frequent natural spaces. On the one hand, we focus our analysis on the relationship between practitioners and others, and, on the other hand, between the players involved in the search for a communication system to promote links with the mid-mountain environment (including the Bauges range regional natural park, the Office Français de la Biodiversité, breeders and various service providers, such as mid-mountain guides, etc.) (Figure 11.6).

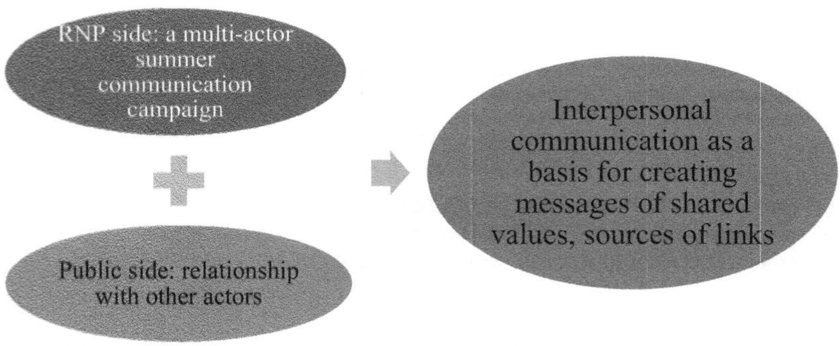

Figure 11.6. *Interrelationships and link building*

11.3.1. *Collaboration, interaction and sharing among leisure users*

The public who frequent the area are interested in interacting with other practitioners, as well as with people who are not present, with whom they would like to share their experiences. Contrary to certain hypotheses that led us to consider several mountain activity specialist sites in the response modalities, the majority of the experience-sharing was envisaged on generalist social networks. Many handwritten or spoken comments specify "in private mode" or "for my friends and family".

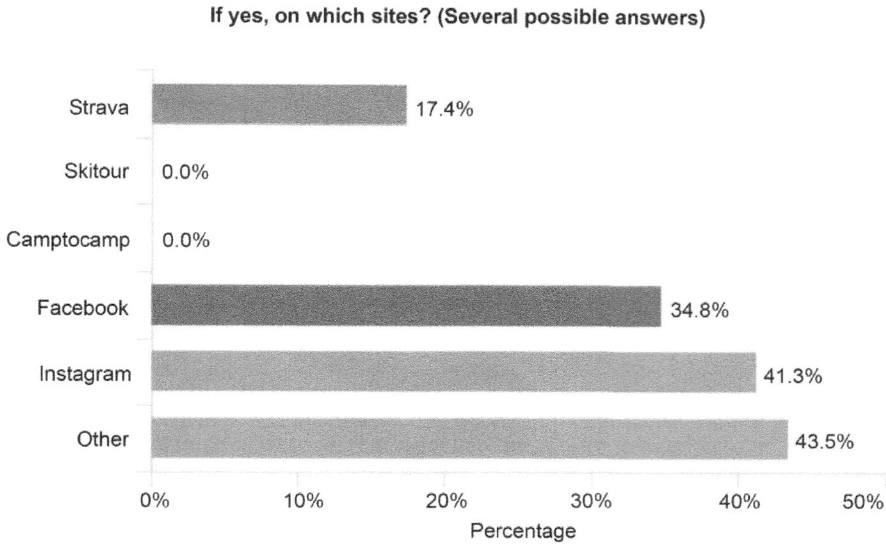

Figure 11.7. *Percentages of responses to the sub-question "If yes, on which sites?" proposed to respondents who said they would like to share their experience of the day during the winter survey. For a color version of this figure, see www.iste.co.uk/kohlmann/linking.zip*

Note that the "other" responses mainly mentioned family WhatsApp groups or SMS/MMS to friends and family. In the summer, WhatsApp, which was included in the response options, came out on top (31%, followed by Strava 8%, Facebook 7% and Instagram 5%).

More generally, our data show that in the winter, 87% of respondents usually took part in mid-mountain outings with others: 77% indicated that group outings were one of their motivating factors (Figure 11.7); 74% intended to share their experience after their outing.

In the summer, these figures rose to 89%. A total of 81% indicated that collective practice was one of their sources of motivation, and 54% shared their experiences on the Internet at the end of their practice (47% "with my family and/or my circle of friends", 7% "on an Internet site accessible to all"). In our population, sharing and collaboration seem to be restricted to circles of acquaintances and affective proximity. From physical practice to digital interactions, links are built or strengthened within preexisting social groups.

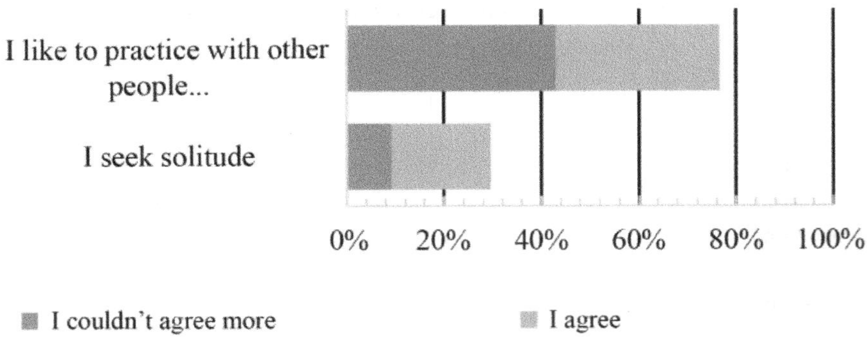

Figure 11.8. *Percentages of responses to certain modalities of the question: "What are the reasons that motivate you to practice this activity?", part 4. For a color version of this figure, see www.iste.co.uk/kohlmann/linking.zip*

As far as the players are concerned, the Bauges range regional natural park explicitly positions itself as a mediator[7], in the position seeking to bring out a shared vision and values, co-constructed with the other human players in the area, whose stakes are diverse and sometimes divergent. From tools to human devices, we now look at this co-construction. The implementation of the summer communication campaign created for summer 2021, which we present below, is a clear illustration of this.

11.3.2. *Territorial communication supported by the regional natural park: co-developed tools for a shared vision*

The co-development of tools, particularly communication tools, is an integral part of the way RNP actors think and act[8]. However, the communication campaign for summer 2021 took these practices a step further, by extending the pooling of stakeholders. Not only were the stakeholders from two RNPs mobilized[9], but they also integrated local workers into their approach, in particular mountain farmers, but also, for effective implementation, actors from the resorts.

7 See the park's website. Available at: www.parcdesbauges.com/fr.

8 See the regional national park charters. An example is available at: www.parcdesbauges.com/fr/revision-charte.html#.Y4SLf3bMKUl.

9 Bauges range and Chartreuse.

(A)

(B)

Figure 11.9. *Examples of posters for the regional natural park communication campaign, summer 2021*

For this season, they opted for a visual campaign centered on herds (Figure 11.9), placing domestic animals at the heart of the awareness campaign. While this choice has already been made in other RNPs, such as the Pilat, for example (Kohlmann 2017), it may nevertheless be questionable, as it does not correspond to the RNP's emblematic animals (the chamois and the black grouse) or to the wild imaginary often associated with these territories. However, it is clearly in line with the RNP's philosophy of strengthening relationships with others. It should be noted that these other people include both humans (leisure activities, farmers, etc.) and animals (herds, domestic animals accompanying hikers, as well as, indirectly, those living in the wild near the herds). In fact, with the sharp rise in visitor numbers following the lockdowns, the management of relations between visitors, herds and breeders crystallizes the question of the relationship with the land in the summer period. Whether it is a question of access to water (especially drinking troughs), to meadows, the management of fence gates, the presence of domestic dogs or interaction with patous, it is a question of relationships with others, which communication tools aim to harmonize.

The campaign features colorful, humorous images, with messages that are both explanatory and inciting, structured around recurring elements: the slogan "The mountain... worth respecting!" and a friendly "Welcome to our environment" sign remind frequenters that while they are free to belong to this territory and to use it within the limits of respect for others (human and nonhuman), it does not belong to them.

11.3.3. *Human territorial communication*

In addition to the visual communication tools disseminated in the field (in the form of posters, flyers, etc.) and on the park's digital platforms (website, social networks, etc.), the RNP's territorial environmental communication relies on human-based devices. This human communication relies as much on the people recruited by the RNP as on external players with whom the park collaborates.

The deployment of ecovolunteers in the region during the two main months of the summer season helps to convey the park's messages to visitors. These ecovolunteers are trained in raising awareness and mediation skills. The park's messages are also relayed by mid-mountain guides appointed by the resorts, who are also trained in a joint training session with the ecovolunteers.

In addition, the RNP welcomes and supports mediation and link-building initiatives undertaken by outside players. For 2021, a research-creation residency ("Chemins faisant"[10]) spent three weeks surveying the park's territory, offering workshops and other ways of connecting participants with their environment (weekend open-air dance workshops, choreographic walks, etc.). The park is also involved in a number of programs and other research-action projects[11] that contribute to this environmental communication in these mid-mountain regions.

These elements of communication weave links to others, as well as point to a third type of link, one that explores our relationship with the world.

11.4. Experiences of connection and relationships with the world

Finally, at a third level, the relationship with the world can be studied through the possibilities for integrating nonhuman actors into these systems. In particular, we analyze nature walks in which the natural environment comes into play as a stakeholder in environmental communication.

In connection with the territorial human communication exposed previously, we can evoke a first type of device, which we analyzed within the framework of our participating observations, proposed by the ecovolunteers to interested people who met at the Creusates peat-bog: the observation of the insects of the bog. Here, it is the insects, which, through observations and research into their molting, provide elements of understanding to visitors. The youngest immerse their hands in the pond to "feel like insects in the water" (child's speech, July 2021); the oldest scrutinize the molts like treasures, look for the plants they are attached to, touch, smell, listen, look and try to feel the living environment of small animals. The ultimate challenge of these communication and linking devices, which we can experience through these experiences of nature (Prévot 2020) is thinking–feeling with and thinking–feeling like (Coulbaut-Lazzarini and Couston 2021) the others that we have discovered and this world to which we all belong.

Over the course of our research project, we wanted to test the discourse on this relationship to the world as envisaged by the mountain's frequenters. We questioned their representations of the mid-mountain environment (Figure 11.10).

10 Available at: www.parcdesbauges.com/fr/actualite/chemins-a-ciel-ouvert-a-la-croisee-des-bauges-315.html#.Ys6PL2DP3IU.

11 Our COMHUNENVI project, as well as a LEADER program project.

If we consider that preservation corresponds to an issue with too many response biases (given that it risks being considered as the main "correct answer" expected) to be taken into account here, the other modalities cited by the greatest number of people remain interesting. Discovery was the top priority (if we consider the "strongly agree" responses), but understanding, loving and sharing this special environment were also widely emphasized. Indeed, not a single respondent rejected these assertions: 97% saw the mountain environment as a place to understand, almost 96% as a place to love and over 88% as a place to share, with the remaining few percent being neutral on these aspects.

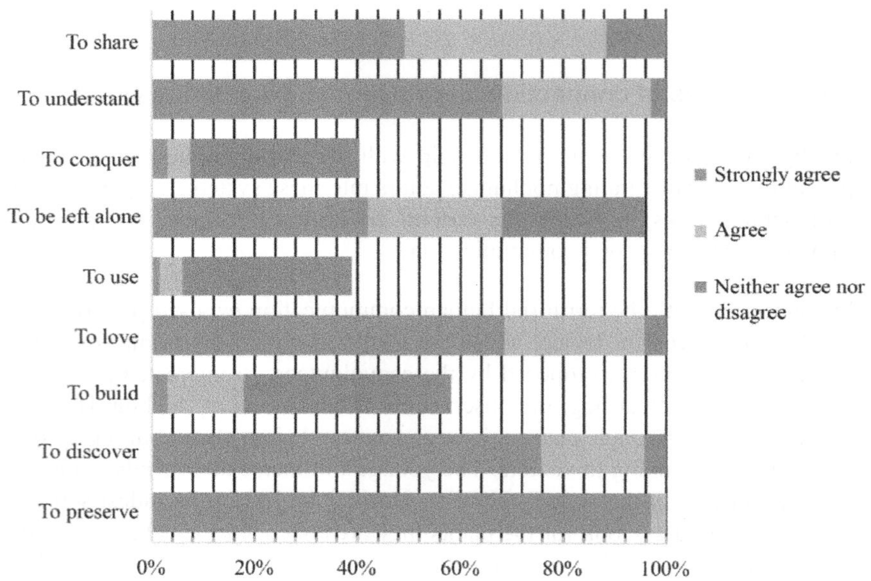

Figure 11.10. *Proportion of responses to the question: "in your opinion, the mountain environment is above all a place: ...". For a color version of this figure, see www.iste.co.uk/kohlmann/linking.zip*

These figures would represent an incredible human–environment harmony if they could be generalized to the general population. However, although limited to the small sample of visitors who agreed to answer our questionnaire (approximately 500 people in winter and 145 in summer), our analysis reveals a willingness to establish or maintain a human–environment bond in the natural areas of the Alps.

11.5. Relatedness, the link between links?

On a theoretical level, the three axes highlighted aim to formalize this link, through the concept of relatedness, as a triple relationship to ourselves, to others and to the world. The relationship with the natural environment is seen as a catalyst for understanding this triple relationship, each level of which is interdependent (Figure 11.11).

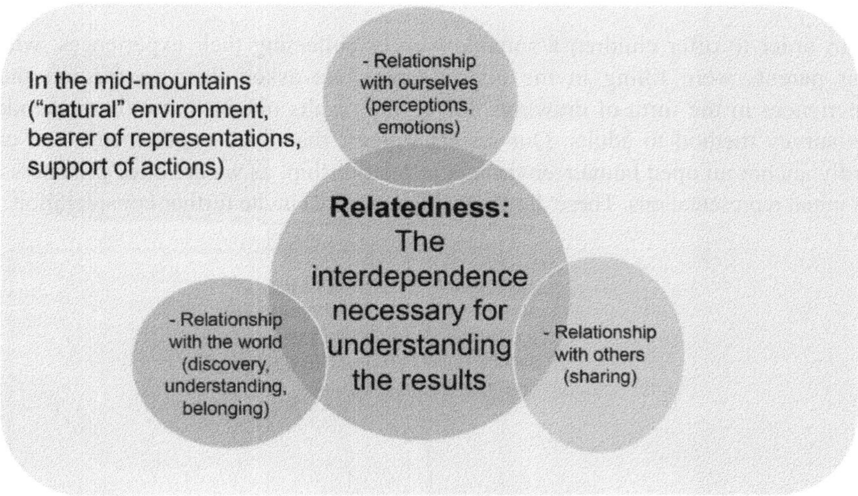

Figure 11.11. *Schematic diagram of the mid-mountain dependence relationship. For a color version of this figure, see www.iste.co.uk/kohlmann/linking.zip*

Indeed, as Haraway (2020) reminds us, links are only truly felt in experience, in the turmoil of the moment and the place experienced. The mid-mountain environment, as a support for a specific experiential time, enables embedded knowledge (Martin-Juchat 2002).

The synergy of three types of relationship to ourselves, to others and to the world, anchored in the mid-mountain environment, builds this connection. The relationship with ourselves is experienced in an intracorporeal and emotional dialogue; the relationship with others is perceived in the sharing of experiences situated in the mid-mountain environment; finally, the relationship with the world makes us feel that we belong by immersing ourselves in this environment, a milieu that encompasses and crosses these three levels.

However, when we tested ways of representing lived experience beyond the discursive aspects, our investigations suggested that one aspect was missing for the relatedness to be complete.

11.6. Openness: the missing link

11.6.1. *From bodies to thoughts*

In order to offer children a suitable way of collecting their experiences, while their parents were filling in the questionnaire, we asked them to recount their experiences in the form of drawings. Given the results obtained, we then extended this survey method to adults. Our results suggest that lived experience alone can hardly anchor an open human–environment relationship, as we are often prisoners of our initial representations. These drawings (Figure 11.12) invite further consideration.

Figure 11.12. *Drawings by children of mid-mountain areas, 2021*

11.6.2. *In search of imaginary worlds*

If the word clouds extracted from the questionnaires already suggested this, the drawings reveal a vision of the mid-mountains imbued with a wild and free character. There are no barriers or boundaries in the drawings, even though the survey sites are dotted with them. We can assume that the abstraction of the drawing erases the markers of compartmentalization. However, other elements were even more striking.

All of the children's drawings, obtained in midsummer in a mountainous region with gentle topography, were made up of faintly marked plateaus or peaks of depicted pointed summits with a corolla of snow. Adults were shown the same peaks, but with less snow. As the instructions were to represent the experience they had had on the day they were interviewed, the results suggest that the impact of the imaginary remains strong enough to withstand the test of the moment, as if body and mind had not lived through the same experience.

Thinking in terms of a link, of relatedness, would then require us to integrate a reconstruction of images that would enable us to perceive a belonging to the world. This would be an initial level of relatedness, included in the relationship to ourselves, even before intracorporeal dialogue, which would enable us to unify thoughts and perceptions. This idea may not seem very new, but it needs to be brought up to date in our contemporary societies forged on dualisms (Simondon 2005). As we observe the implementation of new social–environmental communication devices, notably by the RNP, based on narratives involving physical experimentation, we need to explore the narratives as a means of recreating the mind–body link.

11.7. References

Achin, C. (2015). La gouvernance de la diversification comme enjeu de l'adaptation des stations de moyenne montagne : l'analyse des stations de la Bresse, du Dévoluy et du Sancy. PhD thesis, Grenoble Alpes University, Grenoble.

Chanvallon, S. and Héas, S. (2011). Man and nature: Senses and sensitivities. *Natures Sciences Sociétés*, 19(4), 355–364.

Coulbaut-Lazzarini, A. and Couston, F. (2021). Manifeste pour penser la communication environnementale à la lumière des liens humains/non-humains. *Revue française des sciences de l'information et de la communication*, 21 [Online]. Available at: http://journals.openedition.org/rfsic/10021.

De Bal, M.B. (2003). Reliance, déliance, liance : émergence de trois notions sociologiques. *Sociétés*, 80(2), 99–131.

De Bal, M.B. (2009). Éthique de reliance, éthique de la reliance : une vision duelle illustrée par Edgar Morin et Michel Maffesoli. *Nouvelle revue de psychosociologie*, 8(2), 187–198.

GIEC (2022). *Climate Change 2022: Mitigation of Climate Change. Contribution of Working Group III to the Sixth Assessment Report of the Intergovernmental Panel on Climate Change*. Cambridge University Press, New York.

Gruas, L. (2021). Côtoyer les sommets, coexister avec l'animal sauvage. Contribution à la sociologie des pratiques sportives en milieu naturel. PhD thesis, University of Savoy Mont Blanc, Chambéry.

Haraway, D.J. (2020). *Vivre avec le trouble*. Les Éditions des mondes à faire, Vaulx-en-Velin.

Jorand, D., Mao, P., Biard, É., Obin, O., Suchet, A. (2009). La place des sports de nature dans les stratégies de diversification de l'offre en station de moyenne montagne. Discours et pratiques dans les Alpes françaises. Report.

Kohlmann, É. (2017). Gérer/aimer. Communication et nature dans le parc naturel régional du Pilat. *Questions de communication*, 32, 51–74.

Maris, V. (2018). *La part sauvage du monde*. Le Seuil, Paris.

Martin-Juchat, F. (2002). La notion d'intercorporéité dans les arts martiaux orientaux. In *Les médiations du corps*, Caune, J. and Dufrêne, B. (eds). Stendhal University, Grenoble, 192.

Martin-Juchat, F. (2008). Penser le corps affectif comme un média. *Corps*, 4(1), 85–92.

Morin, E. (2008). *La méthode*. Le Seuil, Paris.

Morin, E. and Wolton, D. (2011). Grand entretien. *La Revue Hermès*, 60, 241–254.

Morizot, B. (2017). Nouvelles alliances avec la terre. Une cohabitation diplomatique avec le vivant. *Tracés. Revue de Sciences humaines*, 33, 73–96.

Oger, A. (2020). Covid-19 : top 10 des changements dans nos modes de vie. *WE DEMAIN* [Online]. Available at: https://www.wedemain.fr/ralentir/https-www-wmaker-net-wedemain-covid-19-top-10-des-changements-dans-nos-modes-de-vie_a4714-html/ [Accessed 11 July 2022].

Parise, F. (2020). Le Confinement, Une Transition Vers de Nouveaux Modes de Vie ? *The Conversation* [Online]. Available at: http://theconversation.com/le-confinement-une-transition-vers-de-nouveaux-modes-de-vie-134616 [Accessed 11 July 2022].

Perrin-Malterre, C. (2016). Processus de diversification touristique autour des sports de nature dans une station de moyenne montagne. *Mondes du Tourisme*, 11 [Online]. Available at: http://journals.openedition.org/tourisme/1012.

Prévot, A.C. (2020). De nouvelles relations à la nature pour des changements transformatifs de nos modèles de société ? *Annales des Mines. Responsabilité et environnement*, 100(4), 23–27.

Queval, I. (2004). *S'accomplir ou se dépasser : Essai sur le sport contemporain*. Gallimard, Paris.

Ruiz, D.M. (2000). *Les quatre accords toltèques. La voie de la liberté personnelle*. Jouvence, Bernex-Geneva.

Simondon, G. (2005). *L'individuation à la lumière des notions de forme et d'information*. Million, Grenoble.

Statista (2021). Changement du mode de vie après le confinement en France 2020. *Statista* [Online]. Available at: https://fr.statista.com/statistiques/1111739/changement-habitudes-mentalite-confinement-france/ [Accessed 11 July 2022].

Conclusion

Digital, natural… and social

The aim of this book was to question the link to nature in the digital age. As presented in the introduction, the interest is twofold: firstly, to be able to enter into the details of the technological and social arrangements of the digital era that govern the choice of devices put in place; and secondly, to take advantage of the ambivalence of the term "link" between restraint and extension to reflect on our relationship to nature and to ourselves in this new context. However, can the latter really be described as "new"? In the first chapter, we were able to define four major periods and qualify them in terms of the evolution of devices, but ultimately, if digital technology amplifies the managerial dimension of our Western relationship with nature – materialized here by the structuring and the multiplication of biodiversity data – does it radically alter our relationship with it?

In the light of the various works presented in this book, this is by no means self-evident. In the first part of this book, it is not our relationship with nature that digital technology seems to be changing, but rather the forms of sociability proposed through these new devices, whether around herbarium collections, social networks or naturalist exchange platforms. Nature itself remains an object to be preserved, on which to project values. Thus, the digital devices constructed around nature seem to be able to inscribe themselves in the double historical movement: love and management of nature, a double movement that has existed in the West for several centuries, and is still reflected in our practices, representations and public policies. The quarrel between Muir and Pinchot at the end of the 19th century is emblematic of this tension between "the poet and the scientist" (Kohlmann 2017).

Conclusion written by Émilie KOHLMANN.

The changes brought about by digital technology seem to lie elsewhere, in the forms of social relations produced by these new devices, and this is clearly understood in the second part of this book. Far from being merely a technical presentation of how biodiversity data are processed by the various IT protocols, this second part never ceases to assert the place of stakeholders, partnerships and citizens in the debate. Sharing, mediation and communication can be seen behind technical choices.

The chapters in the final section can be understood in this context. The groups that form on mobile applications or on social networks do not necessarily correspond to the groups of amateur naturalists known until now. Their motivations and commitments are also evolving. Nature and the digital world can then become a pretext for reflection on the renewal of forms of conviviality (Illich 2014) and the role of online devices in its construction (Charvolin and Kohlmann 2022).

Beyond these aspects, digital technology, whether through its use in situ or its possibilities for remote immersion and knowledge of nature, could enable new players and new individualities to meet and build an imaginary, a common narrative concerning their natural environment. The observation of these new forms of involvement and socialization is not confined to the question of citizen participation in the production of naturalist knowledge (Heaton et al. 2018) or to a direct, standardized experience of nature. Indeed, the relationship with nature is not universally constructed through this filter, and other ontologies do exist (Descola 2005).

The digital, the link... and the liana

To continue with the reflections initiated by the various authors in this book, we propose to open a dialogue between the notion of "link" mobilized here and that of "liana" used by Touam Bona in his *Cosmopoétique du refuge*. The correspondence is easy to make, firstly at the etymological level – the two terms have the same origin in French (*lien, liana*) – and also at the semantic level, since the double movement of reliance and hindrance can be found in the word:

> Because they intertwine trees and weave canopies, lianas – like mycelium on another level – work to produce the tropical forest as a polyphonic body; but they can also become those "threads that trap the demon as in a spider's web" (Bona 2021, p. 46).

Having established these commonalities, what does the liana bring with it that the link does not? This passage through the figure of the liana serves to highlight a number of elements, of which we retain just two: the living and globalization.

First and foremost, the liana underlines the power of living things and their autonomy, their will outside any human will or fantasy of control. The liana is the proliferation of the living. It is the unexpectedness of twists and turns. It is also the embodiment of the link with other living elements, of biodiversity in its purest sense (Coppens 2010):

> [...] the liana has a formidable gift for interweaving, and is the voluble plant par excellence (a voluble plant is one that wraps itself around a support). Lacking a trunk (a self-supporting structure), its escape to the heavens is only possible because it leans on others, because it mingles with others, intertwining them [...] (Bona 2021, p. 57).

In this sense, thinking about the liana, even more than thinking about the link, forces us to reconsider our relationships with nature, the ones we choose to construct when we design our mobile observation applications or when we play online in a virtual universe. Is nature merely an object? Do we recognize its own power and will? Are we putting Aldo Leopold's *Land Ethic* (2013) into practice? Or, on the contrary, are we caught up in a surge of data production that increasingly reifies nature?

As a second step, the liana suggests breaking out of modern thinking and its dualisms (Latour 2010), and opening up to non-naturalistic cultures (Descola 2005). If we are to move away from a vision of nature as passive and to be preserved as a virgin, anthropology may be an interesting avenue to follow. Nature is not just fragile and to be preserved or benevolent and to be venerated (Gaia). She lives, she gives, she takes (Caillé et al. 2013), she is also danger and war:

> More often than not, we only talk about the use of plants in terms of "benevolence" and "care". [...] Yet even today, many indigenous peoples in struggle, many communities in dissidence, cultivate an offensive use of the plants that surround them and the territories they inhabit (Bona 2021, p. 63).

In this context, we feel that it is necessary to reflect on digital technology. Its recurrent use and presentation as a means of reducing the environmental impact of human activities[1] also allows us to question the uniformalization effect of the theme of biodiversity on a global scale through the creation of portals such as the *India*

1 The question of the relationship between digital technology and the environment, when criticized, is often tacked onto that of digital pollution or digital sobriety (Ferreboeuf 2019).

Biodiversity Portal[2] or the *Gabon Biodiversity Portal*[3]. Is the Western representation of nature in the process of supplanting locally constructed relationships to nature?

Digital technology allows us to question the power relations underlying our relationship with nature in a new way, the "victorious" representations as well as those that are disappearing, and the depoliticization of these issues (Comby 2019). It is a form of inscription. "Power stands behind editorial forms" (Souchier et al. 2019, p. 159). Looking at different biodiversity monitoring websites, conflicts appear smoothed and visions uniform; yet when conducting field studies, "indigenous peoples, NGOs, developers, when sharing the same place, have radically different practices and visions of nature" (Roué 2003, p. 597). What application will enable us to "think like a reindeer" (Roturier and Roué 2015, p. 104) and propose a relationship with nature that is sensory, non-accountable and relational? The question remains open. To answer it, we need to maintain a multidisciplinary approach and an openness to international research.

References

Bona, D.T. (2021). *Sagesse des lianes : cosmopoétique du refuge, 1*. Post-éditions, Paris.

Caillé, A., Chanial, P., Flipo, F. (2013). Présentation. Que donne la nature ? : l'écologie par le don. *MAUSS*.

Charvolin, F. and Kohlmann, É. (2022). Les relations numériques à la nature : une socialbilité à repenser. *Natures Sciences Sociétés* [Online]. Available at: https://doi.org/10.1051/nss/2022028 [Accessed 10 November 2022].

Comby, J.B. (ed.) (2019). Retour sur la dépolitisation des enjeux écologiques. *Manuel indocile de sciences sociales*. La Découverte, Paris, 470–480.

Coppens, Y. (2010). *Biodiversités : nouveaux regards sur le vivant*. Le Cherche midi, Paris.

Descola, P. (2005). *Par-delà nature et culture*. Gallimard, Paris.

Ferreboeuf, H. (2019). Pour une sobriété numérique. *Futuribles*, 429(2), 15–31.

Heaton, L.D., Millerand, F., Dias da Silva, P., Proulx, S. (2018). *La reconfiguration du travail scientifique en biodiversité : pratiques amateurs et technologies numériques*. Les Presses de l'Université de Montréal, Montreal.

Illich, I. (2014). *La convivialité*. Éditions Points, Paris.

Kohlmann, É. (2017). Gérer/aimer : communication et nature dans le parc naturel régional du Pilat. *Questions de communication*, 32(2), 51–74.

2 Available at: https://indiabiodiversity.org/ [Accessed on September 12, 2022].

3 Available at: https://gabonbiota.org/portal/ [Accessed on September12, 2022].

Latour, B. (2010). *Nous n'avons jamais été modernes : essai d'anthropologie symétrique*. La Découverte, Paris.

Leopold, A. (2013). *A Sand County Almanac and Other Writings on Ecology and Conservation*. Library of America, New York.

Roturier, S. and Roué, M. (2015). Le Pâturage, C'est toute une science ! *Techniques et Culture. Revue semestrielle d'anthropologie des techniques*, 92–109.

Roué, M. (2003). ONG, peuples autochtones et savoirs locaux : enjeux de pouvoir dans le champ de la biodiversité. *Revue internationale des sciences sociales*, 178(4), 597–600.

Souchier, E., Candel, É., Gomez-Mejia, G., Jeanne-Perrier, V. (2019). *Le numérique comme écriture : théories et méthodes d'analyse*. Armand Colin, Malakoff.

List of Authors

Camille BERNARD
LIG
Grenoble Alpes University
France

Pierre BONNET
AMAP
Cirad
Montpellier
France

Ikram CHRAIBI KAADOUD
Lab-STICC
IMT Atlantique
Brest
France

Lisa CHUPIN
DICEN-IdF
University of Paris
France

Amélie COULBAUT-LAZZARINI
GRESEC
Grenoble Alpes University
France

Catherine DE LAVERGNE
LERASS-CERIC
Paul Valéry University Montpellier 3
France

Catherine GAUTHIER
GRESEC
Grenoble Alpes University
France

Marie-Caroline HEÏD
LLERASS-CERIC
Paul Valéry University Montpellier 3
France

Alexis JOLY
LIRMM
INRIA Montpellier
France

Émilie KOHLMANN
GRESEC
Grenoble Alpes University
France

François MUNOZ
LIPhy
Grenoble Alpes University
France

Daniel THONON
LPO AuRA
Lyon
France

Minh-Xuan TRUONG
SLU
Uppsala
Sweden

Index

E, F

G, I

K, L

M, N

O, P

R, S

T, U, V, W

Other titles from

iSTE

in

Science, Society and New Technologies

2023

APCHAIN Thomas
Favela Tours: Building Otherness in the Favelas of Rio de Janeiro
(Tourism and Mobility Systems Set – Volume 6)

CARDON Alain, EL HAMI Abdelkhalak
Fundamental Generation Systems: Computer Science and Artificial Consciousness, the Informational Field of Generation of the Universe, the Sixth Sense of Living Beings
(Digital Sciences Set – Volume 4)

CURULLI Irene G., IKIZ KAYA Deniz, KHAEFI Arghavan
Heritage Education for Climate Action
(Research in Architectural Education Set – Volume 2)

ELAMÉ Esoh
The Sustainable City in Africa Facing the Challenge of Liquid Sanitation
(Territory Development Set – Volume 2)

JURCZENKO Emmanuel
Climate Investing: New Strategies and Implementation Challenges

LYUBAREVA Inna, WALDECK Roger
Diversity of Methodological Approaches in Social Sciences: Example of the Analysis of Media and Online Information
(Modeling Methodologies in Social Sciences Set – Volume 3)

PARET Dominique, CRÉGO Pierre, SOLÈRE Pauline
Smart Patches: Biosensors, Graphene and Intra-Body Communications

VENTRE Daniel, GUILLOT Philippe
Electronic Communication Interception Technologies and Issues of Power

VENTRE Daniel, LOISEAU Hugo
Cybercrime during the SARS-CoV-2 Pandemic (2019-2022): Evolutions, Adaptations, Consequences
(Cybersecurity Set – Volume 3)

2022

AIT HADDOU Hassan, TOUBANOS Dimitri, VILLIEN Philippe
Ecological Transition in Education and Research

CARDON Alain
Information Organization of The Universe and Living Things: Generation of Space, Quantum and Molecular Elements, Coactive Generation of Living Organisms and Multiagent Model
(Digital Science Set – Volume 3)

CAULI Marie, FAVIER Laurence, JEANNAS Jean-Yves
Digital Dictionary

DAVERNE-BAILLY Carole, WITTORSKI Richard
Research Methodology in Education and Training: Postures, Practices and Forms
(Education Set – Volume 12)

ELAMÉ Esoh
Sustainable Intercultural Urbanism at the Service of the African City of Tomorrow
(Territory Development Set – Volume 1)

FLEURET Sébastien
A Back and Forth Between Tourism and Health: From Medical Tourism to Global Health
(Tourism and Mobility Systems Set – Volume 5)

KAMPELIS Nikos, KOLOKOTSA Denia
Smart Zero-energy Buildings and Communities for Smart Grids
(Engineering, Energy and Architecture Set – Volume 9)

2021

BARDIOT Clarisse
Performing Arts and Digital Humanities: From Traces to Data
(Traces Set – Volume 5)

BENSRHAIR Abdelaziz, BAPIN Thierry
From AI to Autonomous and Connected Vehicles: Advanced Driver-Assistance Systems (ADAS)
(Digital Science Set – Volume 2)

BÉRANGER Jérôme
Societal Responsibility of Artificial Intelligence: Towards an Ethical and Eco-responsible AI
Technological Prospects and Social Applications Set – Volume 4)

CORDELIER Benoit, GALIBERT Oliver
Digital Health Communications
Technological Prospective and Social Applications Set – Volume 5)

DOUAY Nicolas, MINJA Michael
Urban Planning for Transitions

GALINON-MÉLÉNEC Béatrice
The Trace Odyssey 1: A Journey Beyond Appearances
(Traces Set – Volume 4)

HENRY Antoine
Platform and Collective Intelligence: Digital Ecosystem of Organizations

KOLOKOTSA Denia, KAMPELIS Nikos
Smart Buildings, Smart Communities and Demand Response
(Engineering, Energy and Architecture Set – Volume 8)

LE LAY Stéphane, SAVIGNAC Emmanuelle, LÉNEL Pierre, FRANCES Jean
The Gamification of Society
(Research, Innovative Theories and Methods in SSH Set – Volume 2)

RADI Bouchaïb, EL HAMI Abdelkhalak
Optimizations and Programming: Linear, Non-linear, Dynamic, Stochastic and Applications with Matlab
(Digital Science Set – Volume 1)

2020

ALAKTIF Jamila, CALLENS Stéphane
Migration and Climate Change: From the Emergence of Human Cultures to Contemporary Management in Organizations

BARNOUIN Jacques
The World's Construction Mechanism: Trajectories, Imbalances and the Future of Societies
(Interdisciplinarity between Biological Sciences and Social Sciences Set – Volume 4)

ÇAĞLAR Nur, CURULLI Irene G., SIPAHIOĞLU Işıl Ruhi, MAVROMATIDIS Lazaros
Thresholds in Architectural Education
(Engineering, Energy and Architecture Set – Volume 7)

DUBOIS Michel J.F.
Humans in the Making: In the Beginning was Technique
(Social Interdisciplinarity Set – Volume 4)

ETCHEVERRIA Olivier
The Restaurant, A Geographical Approach: From Invention to Gourmet Tourist Destinations
(Tourism and Mobility Systems Set – Volume 3)

GREFE Gwenaëlle, PEYRAT-GUILLARD Dominique
Shapes of Tourism Employment: HRM in the Worlds of Hotels and Air Transport
(Tourism and Mobility Systems Set – Volume 4)

JEANNERET Yves
The Trace Factory
(Traces Set – Volume 3)

KATSAFADOS Petros, MAVROMATIDIS Elias, SPYROU Christos
Numerical Weather Prediction and Data Assimilation
(Engineering, Energy and Architecture Set – Volume 6)

MARTI Caroline
Cultural Mediations of Brands: Unadvertization and Quest for Authority
(Communication Approaches to Commercial Mediation Set – Volume 1)

MAVROMATIDIS Lazaros E.
Climatic Heterotopias as Spaces of Inclusion: Sew Up the Urban Fabric
(Research in Architectural Education Set – Volume 1)

MOURATIDOU Eleni
Re-presentation Policies of the Fashion Industry: Discourse, Apparatus and Power
(Communication Approaches to Commercial Mediation Set – Volume 2)

SCHMITT Daniel, THÉBAULT Marine, BURCZYKOWSKI Ludovic
Image Beyond the Screen: Projection Mapping

VIOLIER Philippe, with the collaboration of TAUNAY Benjamin
The Tourist Places of the World
(Tourism and Mobility Systems Set – Volume 2)

2019

BRIANÇON Muriel
The Meaning of Otherness in Education: Stakes, Forms, Process, Thoughts and Transfers
(Education Set – Volume 3)

DESCHAMPS Jacqueline
Mediation: A Concept for Information and Communication Sciences
(Concepts to Conceive 21st Century Society Set – Volume 1)

DOUSSET Laurent, PARK Sejin, GUILLE-ESCURET Georges
Kinship, Ecology and History: Renewal of Conjunctures
(Interdisciplinarity between Biological Sciences and Social Sciences Set – Volume 3)

DUPONT Olivier
Power
(Concepts to Conceive 21st Century Society Set – Volume 2)

FERRARATO Coline
Prospective Philosophy of Software: A Simondonian Study

GUAAYBESS Tourya
The Media in Arab Countries: From Development Theories to Cooperation Policies

HAGÈGE Hélène
Education for Responsibility
(Education Set – Volume 4)

LARDELLIER Pascal
The Ritual Institution of Society
(Traces Set – Volume 2)

LARROCHE Valérie
The Dispositif
(Concepts to Conceive 21st Century Society Set – Volume 3)

LATERRASSE Jean
Transport and Town Planning: The City in Search of Sustainable Development

LELEU-MERVIEL Sylvie, SCHMITT Daniel, USEILLE Philippe
From UXD to LivXD: Living eXperience Design

LENOIR Virgil Cristian
Ethically Structured Processes
(Innovation and Responsibility Set – Volume 4)

LOPEZ Fanny, PELLEGRINO Margot, COUTARD Olivier
Local Energy Autonomy: Spaces, Scales, Politics
(Urban Engineering Set – Volume 1)

METZGER Jean-Paul
Discourse: A Concept for Information and Communication Sciences
(Concepts to Conceive 21st Century Society Set – Volume 4)

MICHA Irini, VAIOU Dina
Alternative Takes to the City
(Engineering, Energy and Architecture Set – Volume 5)

PÉLISSIER Chrysta
Learner Support in Online Learning Environments

PIETTE Albert
Theoretical Anthropology or How to Observe a Human Being
(Research, Innovative Theories and Methods in SSH Set – Volume 1)

PIRIOU Jérôme
The Tourist Region: A Co-Construction of Tourism Stakeholders
(Tourism and Mobility Systems Set – Volume 1)

PUMAIN Denise
Geographical Modeling: Cities and Territories
(Modeling Methodologies in Social Sciences Set – Volume 2)

WALDECK Roger
Methods and Interdisciplinarity
(Modeling Methodologies in Social Sciences Set – Volume 1)

2018

BARTHES Angela, CHAMPOLLION Pierre, ALPE Yves
Evolutions of the Complex Relationship Between Education and Territories
(Education Set – Volume 1)

BÉRANGER Jérôme
The Algorithmic Code of Ethics: Ethics at the Bedside of the Digital Revolution
(Technological Prospects and Social Applications Set – Volume 2)

DUGUÉ Bernard
Time, Emergences and Communications
(Engineering, Energy and Architecture Set – Volume 4)

GEORGANTOPOULOU Christina G., GEORGANTOPOULOS George A.
Fluid Mechanics in Channel, Pipe and Aerodynamic Design Geometries 1
(Engineering, Energy and Architecture Set – Volume 2)

GEORGANTOPOULOU Christina G., GEORGANTOPOULOS George A.
Fluid Mechanics in Channel, Pipe and Aerodynamic Design Geometries 2
(Engineering, Energy and Architecture Set – Volume 3)

GUILLE-ESCURET Georges
Social Structures and Natural Systems: Is a Scientific Assemblage Workable?
(Social Interdisciplinarity Set – Volume 2)

LARINI Michel, BARTHES Angela
Quantitative and Statistical Data in Education: From Data Collection to Data Processing
(Education Set – Volume 2)

LELEU-MERVIEL Sylvie
Informational Tracking
(Traces Set – Volume 1)

SALGUES Bruno
Society 5.0: Industry of the Future, Technologies, Methods and Tools
(Technological Prospects and Social Applications Set – Volume 1)

TRESTINI Marc
Modeling of Next Generation Digital Learning Environments: Complex Systems Theory

2017

ANICHINI Giulia, CARRARO Flavia, GESLIN Philippe, GUILLE-ESCURET Georges
Technicity vs Scientificity – Complementarities and Rivalries (Interdisciplinarity between Biological Sciences and Social Sciences Set – Volume 2)

DUGUÉ Bernard
Information and the World Stage – From Philosophy to Science, the World of Forms and Communications (Engineering, Energy and Architecture Set – Volume 1)

GESLIN Philippe
Inside Anthropotechnology – User and Culture Centered Experience (Social Interdisciplinarity Set – Volume 1)

GORIA Stéphane
Methods and Tools for Creative Competitive Intelligence

KEMBELLEC Gérald, BROUDOUS Evelyne
Reading and Writing Knowledge in Scientific Communities: Digital Humanities and Knowledge Construction

MAESSCHALCK Marc
Reflexive Governance for Research and Innovative Knowledge (Responsible Research and Innovation Set - Volume 6)

PARK Sejin, GUILLE-ESCURET Georges
Sociobiology vs Socioecology: Consequences of an Unraveling Debate (Interdisciplinarity between Biological Sciences and Social Sciences Set – Volume 1)

PELLÉ Sophie
Business, Innovation and Responsibility (Responsible Research and Innovation Set – Volume 7)

2016

ANDRÉ Michel, SAMARAS Zissis
Energy and Environment
(Research for Innovative Transports Set – Volume 1)

BLANQUART Corinne, CLAUSEN Uwe, JACOB Bernard
Towards Innovative Freight and Logistics
(Research for Innovative Transports Set – Volume 2)

BRONNER Gérald
Belief and Misbelief Asymmetry on the Internet

COHEN Simon, YANNIS George
Traffic Management
(Research for Innovative Transports Set – Volume 3)

EL FALLAH SEGHROUCHNI Amal, ISHIKAWA Fuyuki, HÉRAULT Laurent, TOKUDA Hideyuki
Enablers for Smart Cities

GIANNI Robert
Responsibility and Freedom
(Responsible Research and Innovation Set – Volume 2)

GRUNWALD Armin
The Hermeneutic Side of Responsible Research and Innovation
(Responsible Research and Innovation Set – Volume 5)

LAGRAÑA Fernando
E-mail and Behavioral Changes: Uses and Misuses of Electronic Communications

LENOIR Virgil Cristian
Ethical Efficiency: Responsibility and Contingency
(Responsible Research and Innovation Set – Volume 1)

MAESSCHALCK Marc
Reflexive Governance for Research and Innovative Knowledge
(Responsible Research and Innovation Set – Volume 6)

PELLÉ Sophie, REBER Bernard
From Ethical Review to Responsible Research and Innovation
(Responsible Research and Innovation Set – Volume 3)

REBER Bernard
Precautionary Principle, Pluralism and Deliberation: Sciences and Ethics
(Responsible Research and Innovation Set – Volume 4)

TORRENTI Jean-Michel, LA TORRE Francesca
Materials and Infrastructures 1
(Research for Innovative Transports Set – Volume 5A

TORRENTI Jean-Michel, LA TORRE Francesca
Materials and Infrastructures 2
(Research for Innovative Transports Set – Volume 5B)

VENTRE Daniel
Information Warfare – 2nd edition

YANNIS George, COHEN Simon
Traffic Safety
(Research for Innovative Transports Set – Volume 4)

Printed and bound by CPI Group (UK) Ltd, Croydon, CR0 4YY
28/07/2026
14931341-0005